THE FIRST

THE FEW

THE FORGOTTEN

ROCKFORD

PRESENTED BY

ROCKFORD HISTORICAL
SOCIETY

PUBLIC

FOR

WOMEN'S HISTORY MONTH

LIBRARY

THE FIRST

THE FEW

THE FORGOTTEN

Navy and Marine Corps Women in World War I

Jean Ebbert and Marie-Beth Hall

NAVAL INSTITUTE PRESS

ANNAPOLIS, MARYLAND

Naval Institute Press
291 Wood Road
Annapolis, MD 21402

Library of Congress Cataloging-in-Publication Data
Ebbert, Jean.
The first, the few, the forgotten : Navy and Marine Corps women in World War I / Jean
Ebbert and Marie-Beth Hall.
p. cm.
Includes bibliographical references and index.
ISBN 1-55750-203-X (alk. paper)
1. World War, 1914–1918—Women—United States. 2. United States. Navy—Women—
History—20th century. 3. United States. Marine Corps—Women—History—20th century.
I. Hall, Marie-Beth. II. Title.
D639.W7 E23 2002
940.4'0092'273—dc21

2001044714

Printed in the United States of America on acid-free paper ⊗
09 08 07 06 05 04 03 02   9 8 7 6 5 4 3 2
First printing

To those intrepid trailblazers, the first enlisted women.

They proved it could be done.

CONTENTS

PREFACE

ON 21 MARCH 1917, on the eve of America's entry into World War I, Secretary of the Navy Josephus Daniels overturned centuries of tradition by inviting women to enlist in the service. Eventually, almost twelve thousand women enlisted in the U.S. Navy, another 305 in the Marine Corps. Women were already in the service as nurses in the Army Nurse Corps, established in 1901, and the Navy Nurse Corps, established in 1908. Those women were not enlisted, nor were they commissioned, although they were generally treated as officers.

The women of our story were enlisted just as men were, doing many of the same jobs, receiving the same pay, subject to the same military regulations, wearing similar uniforms, and required to meet the same standards of performance, and they earned veterans' benefits. Yet naval historians have overlooked these women. In fact, a reader can peruse book after book on U.S. naval history and find little or no mention of *any* military women's contribution.

We first became aware of the story of the navy and marine women of World War I as we began research for our earlier book, *Crossed Currents: Navy Women in a Century of Change,* first published in 1993 and now in its third edition. The story of the World War I navy women became the first chapter.

We had unearthed more material than could fit in a single chapter, and in 1995 we began further research. This book is the result, our salute to those few doughty women willing to answer a most unconventional call to the colors during a war, who were then all but forgotten.

The historical significance of these first, few, and all-but-forgotten women is twofold. First, the U.S. Navy and Marine Corps found that they could absorb women quickly and effectively with no loss of discipline or public respect. The residue of that finding was a lingering confidence that women could be safely employed in an emergency, and it undergirded to some degree the establishment of the services' respective women's reserves ("WAVES" and "Women Marines") in 1942 and 1943. Second, throughout their lives, the World War I women expressed their pride in having served and their gratitude for what their service had provided them. They were active citizens of their nation, loyal veterans of the U.S. Navy and Marine Corps, and ardent members of the American Legion. Their most poignant contributions were, of course, the patriotic sons and daughters they raised, many of whom have followed in their footsteps.

ACKNOWLEDGMENTS

MANY, MANY PEOPLE in addition to those named here helped with our long research for this book, which stretched from 1982 to 1999. Throughout, Dr. Harold Langley of the Smithsonian Institution has robustly encouraged us by pointing us toward sources and reviewing drafts of our texts. He and Dr. Margaret Vining, also of the Smithsonian, helped us gain financial assistance from the National Yeoman F fund.

Drs. Dean Allard, Martha Crawley, and Regina Akers of the Naval Historical Center and Mrs. Lena Kaljot of the USMC Historical Center greatly facilitated our searches, as did Ms. Becky Livingston of the National Archives, Dr. Judith Bellafaire and Ms. Britta Granrud of the Women in Military Service for America (WIMSA) Foundation archives, and Dr. Evelyn Cherpak, curator of the Naval History Collection of the Naval War College. We thank the Women Marines Association and its members for sending us back issues of its newsletter, 'Nouncements. We are also particularly indebted to Capt. John V. Hall, USN (Ret.), for critical review and discussion, and to Capt. Leigh Ebbert, USN (Ret.), for his support and professional advice.

Two sources of information merit special attention: Eunice Dessez and Joy Bright Hancock. Both had been yeomen (F), and both are now deceased. In 1955, Dessez wrote *The First Enlisted Women,* the only published book-length treatment of the yeomen (F). She also collected and compiled a vast amount of information from more than five thousand women veterans like herself. Those papers were rejected by the Library of Congress, then languished in an attic, and eventually became available to researchers via the Naval Historical Center. Dessez's book and her papers recount details and reflect attitudes reported nowhere else. Hancock's memoir, *Lady in the Navy,* published in 1972, is uniquely valuable because of its author's monumental career with the Navy Department, extending from 1917 to 1953, culminating in her position as the first assistant to the chief of naval personnel for women.

Finally, we are indebted to the women themselves for their own efforts to preserve their history. The *Note Book,* published quarterly from 1928 through 1985 by their postwar organization, the National Yeomen F (NYF), recounts their stories in their own words. We trust that this book, too, faithfully carries forward their memory.

THE FIRST

THE FEW

THE FORGOTTEN

ONE

Breaking with Tradition

Gee, I wish I were a man. I'd join the Navy.
Navy recruiting poster, World War I

RADIO STATIONS ALL ACROSS the country and in U.S. possessions startled listeners with the announcement, on 21 March 1917, that the U.S. Navy was now enrolling women. True, in 1908 the navy had established a nurse corps, which by 1917 included more than 460 women. The nurses were neither enlisted in the navy nor did they hold commissions as officers; they served with the navy rather than in it. In the public's perception—and in the navy's, too—the nurses' role overshadowed their gender. They were trained professionals with a noble and compassionate mission, not a military or naval one, even though their job was to keep men healthy enough to conduct a war. But the navy's 21 March announcement heralded something quite new and different: Women would be enrolled and sworn into service just as men were. Navy Secretary Josephus Daniels took this radical step because he saw that the navy needed them. Fortunately, he faced no legal barrier to enrolling them, because the very idea of women in either the army or the navy was so astounding, so nearly inconceivable, that no law against it existed.

Help Wanted

For nearly three years Americans had watched Great Britain, France and, until 1917, Russia at war with Germany and Austria. Most had hoped that this country could stay neutral. A strong pacifist movement had developed in the century's first decade, as part of a larger move toward progressive reforms; many women held strongly pacifist views. By late 1915 and early 1916, the possibility of going to war against Germany began to take shape. When Germany announced in January 1917 that its submarines would blockade Britain and destroy any ships that challenged the blockade, President Woodrow Wilson saw little choice but to break off diplomatic relations. Nonetheless, he promised not to make war against Germany so long as her submarines did not actually attack American shipping. But by mid-March German submarines were attacking American ships just off the U.S. East Coast. Neutrality was no longer possible.

When the nation formally entered the war in April 1917, the federal government recognized that women's labor was needed. Women sold war bonds and conserved food, knitted garments, and provided toiletry kits to servicemen. Many took the place of men leaving their jobs to enlist. To increase food production, the Woman's Land Army was created in December 1917; in its first year fifteen thousand women joined. When the military publicized its need for nurses, about one-fifth of the nation's nurses volunteered.

Requirements for civilian workers in government also grew. The proportion of women in civil service doubled, from between 5 and 10 percent before 1917 to 20 percent during the war. Male lawyers resigned from public commissions, boards, and committees directly concerned with home-front war efforts, leaving women lawyers to fill the vacancies. Forced to fill gaps left by departing doctors, hospitals and schools began to open their doors to women; women physicians were admitted to the U.S. Public Health Service. Finally, women entered factories, aircraft plants, and shipyards to operate machinery in jobs until then assumed to be beyond their capabilities.[1] Thus the news that the navy would enroll women came as a surprise, to some even as a mild shock, but outrage and protest were absent.

The Navy's Need to Enlist Women

Secretary of the Navy Josephus Daniels faced innumerable problems as the navy began to mobilize. One of the most urgent was the shortage of men for the rapidly increasing number of warships, which more than tripled between January and December of 1917, from three hundred to a thousand. This large new fleet needed the several thousand male yeomen (the navy's term for clerks) then stationed ashore. Daniels could not rely on the civil service to replace the shore-based yeomen, because its employment processes were so ponderous: It took six months to hire anyone. Besides, no funds existed to pay more civilians. Moreover, when an earlier secretary of the navy had attempted to create a corps of civilian women for routine clerical work, he discovered that "some measure of more or less unreasonable prejudice seems to exist on the part of some officers." The navy needed clerks who were actually navy members, subject to rules and discipline, whom it could move and employ however it saw fit.[2] Fortunately for Daniels and the U.S. Navy, the remedy was at hand, lying unsuspected in the language of the Naval Act of 1916.

The act created a naval reserve force. Eligibility for the force's first three components was restricted to former members of either the navy or the merchant marine or crew members of ships registered to be taken over by the navy in the event of war, all of whom were men. But the fourth component, namely the Naval Coast Defense Reserve Force, was open to "all persons who may be capable of performing special useful service for coastal defense."[3] Members of Congress apparently found it unthinkable that women might try to join the Naval Reserve. Daniels, however, found the idea eminently thinkable. His wife was active in the suffragist movement, and he was probably aware that Great Britain had already established a women's program for its own navy, titled the Women's Royal Naval Service and popularly known as the WRENS.

On 7 March 1917, the Bureau of Navigation (the Navy Department office having cognizance over personnel) asked the navy's judge advocate general whether women could be enrolled in the Naval Coast Defense Reserve Force. Someone—possibly Daniels—already had a broader vision than most as to what women could do for the navy, for the bureau's inquiry noted that women could be "utilized as radio operators, stenographers, nurses, messengers, chauffeurs, etc. and in many other capacities in the industrial line."[4]

Individual navy members had also considered the possibility. For example, Lt. Walter Decker, recruiting officer for the Second Naval District, headquartered in Newport, Rhode Island, had asked the Navy Department for information about enrolling women. Also, Lt. Cdr. Frederick Payne, recruiting officer for the Fourth Naval District, headquartered in Philadelphia, was discussing with his superior officer the idea of enlisting just one woman, which would dramatize the navy's need and thereby spur male recruiting. There was so much talk about the navy enlisting women that the man in charge of personnel at the Washington Navy Yard prepared to enroll his niece as the first navy woman other than a nurse.[5]

Regardless of where and with whom it originated, the idea of enlisting women would probably have languished had not Secretary Daniels immediately endorsed it. In mid-March he announced, "After careful reading of [the Naval Reserve Act] . . . nothing can be found which would prohibit the enrollment of women. On the contrary, it is believed that their enrollment was contemplated." Thus the navy now had a new and previously untapped source of "persons . . . capable of performing special useful service." No evidence of the navy's considering women for reserve membership appears in its official records or in those of the congressional hearings. Lengthy testimony had focused on the numbers of reservists needed, but gender was never mentioned.[6]

On 19 March the bureau sent a letter to the commandants of all naval districts, that is, the regional directors of its shore establishment, authorizing them to enroll women in the Naval Coast Defense Reserve Force as "yeomen, electricians (radio), or in such other ratings as the commandant may consider essential to the district organization." The letter echoed Daniels's assertions that the legislation did not prohibit the enrollment of women and that women's eligibility had indeed been discussed.[7] The commandants were not ready for what followed. Their recruiting offices' capacities were already strained in trying to accommodate an influx of men eager to serve, and now here were throngs of women as well. About *their* enrollment the beleaguered recruiters had received little or no guidance, and one can easily imagine that some of them thought that letting these eager young women put on navy uniforms and help out was no bad idea. Only several days later did the bureau send enough guidance to allow them to handle the flood of women applicants.

Lieutenant Commander Payne, however, was primed and ready to act. On 21 March 1917, he enrolled Loretta Perfectus Walsh, who is recognized as the navy's first enlisted woman. As he had pondered and discussed the idea over the preceding weeks, Payne had realized that it would succeed only if he could find the right woman. He found her almost immediately, for she was already working next door in his wife's office. Two years earlier the recently formed Navy League had designated Mrs. Payne to organize its Philadelphia women's committee to provide knitted garments and comfort kits for sailors. Demands on her office multiplied rapidly, and soon she needed an assistant. She asked the nearby Lackawanna Business College to recommend someone, explaining that she could offer only a very small salary because of the many demands on the Navy League's resources. Whoever took the job would have to consider that forgoing a larger salary was her contribution to the war effort. The college recommended Loretta Walsh, who had just completed her course, wanted to work for preparedness, and would accept any salary offered in order to do so.

Walsh came from a family of achievers: Two of her brothers and one of her uncles were physicians, another uncle was a county superintendent of schools, and one of her aunts had run a business while rearing a family of ten children. Not only was she patriotic, she was also intelligent, diligent, and highly personable. When Payne asked if she would be willing to enlist and explained all that it might entail, she agreed enthusiastically. Payne promptly called the press and told them to come to the Naval Home the next morning to witness the historic event. (The Naval Home, a residence for needy retired enlisted men, was at that time located on the grounds of the naval hospital in Philadelphia.) They came, and by the next day newspapers across the nation had the story. The *New York Times* put it on page two.[8]

As the word began to spread that the U.S. Navy was indeed accepting women for duties other than nursing, many questions arose. Members of Congress and private individuals bombarded the Navy Department with questions about how and where to enlist and about the women's employment in general. The department told one and all that women were being enrolled in order to free men needed at sea, and applicants should go to the nearest naval district headquarters.[9] Thus the navy widely disseminated its rationale—wartime need —for this radical innovation and, at the same time, kept the numerous and often exasperating mundane problems of enrolling the women localized in recruiting stations throughout the land.

Navy Recruiting

Different naval districts faced different needs and opportunities. Some districts were headquartered in or near large cities and included one or more naval facilities, for example, the First Naval District (Boston), Third (New York), Fifth (Norfolk), and Ninth (Great Lakes). Employees of the naval facilities and families of navy men made up significant portions of these districts' populations; their interest in the navy all but guaranteed an enthusiastic and sometimes overwhelming response to the call for women. In these districts and others like them, the response was so great that many women in effect never left the recruiting station where they had enrolled; they were set to work immediately helping out the recruiters who had just sworn them in.

These districts also had widely ranging needs; as the *Newport (R.I.) Daily News* reminded its readers, the navy had no intention of sending women to sea, but local women could be sent anyplace within the Second Naval District. Most of them would be assigned to the training station in Newport. Too, such districts had resources unlikely to be found in more sparsely populated areas. In Springfield, Massachusetts, for example, city officials wrote to the secretary of the navy that an entire class of young women studying wireless telegraphy wanted to know if the government could use their services. The Bureau of Navigation suggested they get in touch with naval district commandants and helpfully—perhaps hopefully—provided a list of same.[10]

Recruiters in less populous districts faced different challenges. In districts encompassing the far western states, where most residents had little or no familiarity with the navy, only a relative handful of women ever knocked on recruiters' doors. Those who did might be assigned to recruiting teams that traveled to remote areas, or they might be sent to the district's headquarters.

Or, if they could not be employed within the district and were willing to be sent outside it, they might be sent anywhere.

The navy in some instances asked private firms to help find women to fill critical roles. For example, its supply base in South Brooklyn, New York, asked the Globe Wernicke Company to recommend someone to set up a filing system. The company suggested Gertrude Murray, one of its employees, who joined the navy on 18 April 1917. In Norfolk, the admiral commanding the naval base asked the local telephone company to recommend the best person to operate the base's first switchboard.[11]

The Navy Department in Washington, D.C., had acute needs for women with special skills. The Bureau of Supplies and Accounts, for example, issued an urgent call for four women qualified as card-punchers. Conversely, it could also use women with little more to commend them than vigorous good health and patriotic fervor. One office particularly sought such women as messengers, for it had found that women who had office experience or business education were not satisfied with messenger tasks. Couriers in Washington, however, needed some measure of initiative, discretion, and common sense, for their work might take them anywhere in the city, even to the White House.[12]

As the war went on and the yeomen (F) proved how useful they could be, the navy intensified their recruitment. For example, in August 1918 it took out a full-page advertisement for women in the *Washington Star*.[13]

One young woman not only contributed to the recruiting efforts of 1917, she became a famous icon of the navy itself. The well-known poster artist, Howard Chandler Christy, was at the navy recruiting office in Los Angeles on the day that Bernice Tongate enrolled. He suggested that one of the recruiters lend her a navy white hat, a jumper (the familiar V-necked tunic with the wide square collar), and a neckerchief to wear while he sketched her. To the finished drawing someone added the words, "Gee, I wish I were a man. I'd join the Navy." Soon all over the country there appeared posters showing her winsome smile, with her tousled curls under the white hat perched on the back of her head. Tongate served on active duty for three years and became a chief yeoman. Later she told an interviewer that she wished the artist had put "that cap on my head in a different manner. That certainly was not regulation!"[14]

Testing Skills

The navy's procedures to determine the applicants' skills varied according to where and when the recruiting took place. In the first few weeks, some recruiters were quite unprepared for the numbers of women who crowded their facilities. Most quickly rallied, however, and soon were putting their applicants through rigorous examinations to identify the most skillful among them. Some recruiters were also able to call upon help from private sources. At Boston, more than five thousand women applied between March 1917 and November 1918, the vast majority of them seeking to become yeomen. The first applicants for the yeoman rating were tested at the navy yard for their abilities in

> shorthand, typewriting, plain copying, letter writing, and spelling. Over five thousand were examined, and of this number 1,192 were enrolled. Most of the girls enrolled had at least a high school education and several years' experience in business. About three thousand of these applicants were examined at the Clark Shorthand Institute, which kindly offered the use of its equipment to the government without expense. Quite a number were examined at the High School of Commerce and at McDonald's Commercial School, . . . also . . . without charge.[15]

The Bureau of Medicine and Surgery evidently believed that it had a far better understanding of how to fill its personnel needs than did the Bureau of Navigation. Rather than requesting enlisted women to fill its empty billets, it much preferred to identify one or more qualified civilian women and then ask permission to enroll them. However, it firmly opposed enrolling women physicians. That opposition had been tested as early as 1915, when a female physician had inquired about enrolling. After outlining her impressive credentials, she added that three American female physicians were serving in France, two as commissioned officers with the French army, and the third as the director of a military hospital. These circumstances, she wrote, "encourage me to think that a trained woman" who could meet the qualifying requirements "might be acceptable for similar work in this country. I would like to be on the reserve list in the event that need should arise for my services." The navy's surgeon general replied promptly: "This Bureau is not prepared to recommend that women physicians be appointed in the Medical Reserve Corps of the navy."[16]

The navy's opposition to enrolling female physicians was reasonably founded, given that most men would have been painfully embarrassed to be examined or treated by one of them at that time. Once this nation entered the war, so many male physicians left their regular practices for military service that the small number of women practicing medicine were needed to fill the home-front vacancies. Nor did the bureau approve of enrolling women to replace male hospital corpsmen in their "strictly professional duties," but it did favor enrolling them to replace male corpsmen "on shore duty, whose duties are strictly clerical in nature."[17]

Physical Examinations

A major hurdle for some of the recruiting offices was the physical examination required for each recruit. Lieutenant Commander Payne in Philadelphia solved this problem before he enrolled Loretta Walsh: He simply asked for a navy nurse assigned to the adjacent Naval Home to assist a navy doctor in conduct-ing the exam. In late March recruiters received official instructions regarding physical examinations for women. Female applicants could be rejected for the same conditions that would exclude men, such as weakness, defective vision, speech impediment, heart or lung disease, or possessing fewer than twenty teeth. The instructions included a table of physical proportions for height and weight that was to be regarded as a standard rather than an absolute guide. Women should be between sixty and seventy inches tall and weigh between 112 and 150 pounds. Variations in height (one inch) or weight (seventeen pounds) were allowed for desirable applicants in good health. Moreover, "marked dis-proportion of weight over height" was no reason to reject an applicant unless she was positively obese. Recruiters were advised to conduct examinations as Payne had, in a navy hospital with a navy nurse in attendance. If that were not practical, then examiners had to be sure to "use tact and avoid offense" but be thorough nonetheless. The applicant was to wear a light, loose gown for the examination, and "corsets should invariably be removed."[18]

Out at the Pearl Harbor Navy Yard in the Territory of Hawaii, in April 1917, the first woman to enlist had to be sent back to her home while workers built a dressing room for women's examinations.[19] In Chicago, however, a corner merely curtained off from the rest of the male-populated recruiting station served as the women's physical examining facility.

Even that was better than what some women encountered at the naval hospital in Washington, D.C. One former yeoman (F), Helen Butler, wrote that there, after disrobing, she "joined a long line of stripped females, holding bath towels around their middles . . . in that open hallway, waiting to be scrutinized by one weary, over-aged M.D. responsible for examining that long line. He weighed us, measured us, listened to our hearts, and passed us along at furious speed." The woman next to her, reduced to tears, said, "You act like you don't mind having no clothes on!" Trying to reassure her, Butler replied, "Oh, after the first couple of times you get used to this sort of thing." The woman found little reassurance in that answer and subsequently steered clear of Butler whenever they happened to meet.[20]

Some recruiters, lacking the resources of a navy hospital or a navy nurse and evidently unqualified to accept or reject applicants for medical reasons, did so anyway. In Huntington, West Virginia, for example, the young navy man giving preliminary and very rudimentary physicals to the women applicants turned down Mary Price, saying she had swollen tonsils. Unwilling to give up, a few days later she traveled to Parkersburg, along with those women who had passed the preliminary. The assisting navy nurse, not knowing that Price had been rejected, sent her into the navy physician. He said her tonsils were just fine and passed her.[21]

Bypassing Black Women

Eventually more than 11,880 women found the navy's invitation to apply for enlistment exhilarating and irresistible; the greatest number in service at any one time, on 1 December 1918, was 11,275, or roughly 2 percent of the navy's active-duty strength. The largest numbers of women came from the populous eastern states: New York, 2,324; District of Columbia, 1,874; Massachusetts, 1,324; Virginia, 1,071; and Pennsylvania, 1,067. From the remaining states, the numbers ranged from one (New Mexico) to 557 (California) (see appendix B). The U.S. territories—Hawaii, Guam, Puerto Rico, and the Panama Canal Zone

—contributed a total of 63 women. Even two British subjects enlisted: One had been living in Canada, the other in the United States.[22]

However, of the 11,880 enlisted women, only fourteen are known to have been black.

It was not that black American women lacked patriotism. They had offered their services just as freely and eagerly as other women. They knitted and sewed for black soldiers and helped their families. They raised funds for government-issued bonds and for the Red Cross. Short-handed war industries agreed to hire black women, although they paid them less than white women. Many worked in menial jobs, but they also operated elevators and telephone switchboards, drove motor trucks and signaled trains. The problem lay not with them but instead with racist attitudes that pervaded American society. The navy, which had once been relatively open to enlisting black men, had begun to accept them only as messmen (servants to officers) and coal shovelers; even at the height of the war they composed only about 1 percent of the navy's total force.[23]

No matter how much the navy might need women, Secretary Daniels had no intention of enlisting black women. That may have owed something to his southern origins, but it certainly owed much to the Wilson administration's overall aversion to serving black people's interests. Congress and army officers had loudly protested efforts to afford black soldiers even a few of the privileges, comforts, and opportunities allowed to white soldiers. The Army Nurse Corps eventually accepted eighteen black nurses but confined them to duty in the United States and to nursing only black men.[24] The Navy Nurse Corps had no black women.

Black women who applied to enlist in the navy, like a young woman in Boston who wanted to serve as a messman, were turned away. Daniels received at least two complaints about this discrimination. In August 1918 an officer of the National Association for the Advancement of Colored People (NAACP) wrote him about "two cultivated young colored women, graduates of the high and normal schools" who had tried to enlist and been "plainly told that no colored people would be accepted." Yet here before him, the writer said, was also a copy of the *Washington Star* in which the navy was advertising for "women without previous clerical or office experience . . . to enlist as clerks and messengers." If these positions were open to white women only, he added, that should be plainly stated "and thus save self-respecting, well-intentioned colored people from needless humiliation."

The next month a Norfolk man wrote to Daniels that the Norfolk Navy Yard had been calling for women to enlist for the last three months; many women had responded and been accepted, but "colored women" were rejected. He asked, "Does this discrimination against any qualified citizen have the approbation of the government, or is it local prejudices of which the government knows nothing?"[25] The navy secretary's diaries and letter files contain no replies to these writers, although he was a prolific correspondent. What could he have said? The rejection the black women experienced spoke for itself.

How then did fourteen—and maybe more—black women enlist in the navy? The only account of these women's services is a sixty-year-old book, long out of print, which credits their enrollment to John T. Risher, a black civilian who was chief of the muster roll section in the Navy Department.[26] Authorized to hire his own staff, he decided to make use of the "abilities and talents of the colored youth of this country . . . [M]ore than a dozen young colored women have been engaged in the capacity of yeowomen in this muster roll section." Fourteen women are named. The first enrolled was Armelda Greene of Mississippi, followed by Pocahantas A. Jackson, Catherine Finch, Sarah E. Howard, Anna G. Smallwood, Carroll E. Washington, Josie Bomar Washington, and Inez R. McIntosh, all of Mississippi; Fannie Foote and Maud C. Williams of Texas; Ruth A. Wellborn and Olga F. Jones of Washington, D.C.; and Sarah Davis of Maryland. Risher also managed to hire, or cause to be enrolled, several black men as yeomen.

Navy muster rolls of the period show that Greene enlisted on 12 August 1918, and the rest followed in September and October. All were originally designated as "Landsmen for Yeoman," that is, as apprentice yeomen. When they were discharged in September 1919, all had been rated as yeomen third class, except Greene, who had been promoted to yeoman second class. Evidently the women did their work well, and a white chief yeoman (F) is quoted as admiring their "tidiness and appropriate demeanor both on and off duty which the girls of the white race would do well to emulate."[27]

It is not known how John Risher managed to enroll these women in the navy, in the heart of a segregated Navy Department in the heart of a segregated city. It is known, however, that among their descendants are several prominent African Americans, including journalist Courtland Milloy and the late Secretary of Commerce Ron Brown. Little else has been recorded about them. One investigator found that their families "seem never to have regarded the women's service as noteworthy," although Brown was once quoted as saying that he had "always wondered how his grandmother came to be buried in Arlington Cemetery."[28]

A Few Good Women

By the summer of 1918, the carnage on the European battlefields forced the Marine Corps to follow the lead of Navy Secretary Daniels. Ever since the United States had entered the war, the Marine Corps had been short of clerks in its permanent offices, particularly at headquarters in Washington, D.C. So great was the demand that men were rushed through their clerical training, and many had little notion of how to perform their duties. Yet these same marines struggling with the paperwork here at home were ready for battle and were desperately needed overseas. Would the navy's solution suit the Marine Corps? Could the women of the business world help the USMC?

Gen. George Barnett, commandant of the Marine Corps, surveyed the Washington offices, asking if they could use female help. They certainly could, they answered, and right now. Those responding to Barnett's inquiries said that about 40 percent of the work done at headquarters could be done by women— although it might take two or three times as many women to accomplish the work. Furthermore, it would be best to enroll them "gradually" so that they could be trained by the clerks they were relieving. On 2 August 1918, Barnett asked Daniels for authority to "enroll women in the Marine Corps Reserve for clerical duty in Washington and at other Marine Corps offices in the United States where their services might be utilized to replace men who might be qualified for active field service." Daniels granted the authority promptly, and the public received the announcement on 12 August.[29]

What the marines needed most were stenographers, bookkeepers, accountants, and typists, but recruiters were also to consider any woman with considerable experience in office work and evidence of exceptional ability.[30] At other Marine Corps offices, women were also sought who could replace the recruiters themselves.

The first enlisted woman marine was Opha Mae Johnson. She was already working at headquarters, in the civil service, and was enrolled on 13 August. The advice to enroll the women gradually was swept away by the crowds of women who swamped USMC recruiting offices. The Marine Corps had very clear ideas as to the women it wanted—nothing but the best (a few good women, one might say)—and it quickly provided guidance to its recruiters. Each applicant had to be at least eighteen years old, although an exceptionally qualified woman a few months younger might be considered; she had to be of excellent character, neat appearance, and proven ability and experience. Each was to furnish three letters of recommendation, and, if possible, was to be interviewed by the head of the office where she was to be assigned; some highly promising applicants were even sent to Washington for the interview.

Marines met head-on the challenge of how to pick out its few good women from among the many. The officer in charge of Marine Corps Recruiting, Col. Albert McLemore, himself led the screening of the two thousand women who applied in New York City. One of those women later told an interviewer,

> Male noncommissioned officers went up and down the line asking questions about experience, family responsibilities, etc., and by the process of elimination got the line down to a few hundred. Applicants were interviewed by one officer and finally given a stenographic test. Colonel McLemore conducted the shorthand test and dictated so fast, that one after another left the room. Those who remained were taken, one-by-one, into Colonel McLemore's office and told to read back their notes. . . . If the colonel was satisfied with our reading, we were required to type our notes and timed for speed and accuracy. More and more applicants dropped by the wayside, until only five of us were left. We were told to report back the next day for a physical examination.[31]

Marine recruiters benefited from the navy's experience with administering physical exams. The marine recruiter in Washington even got advance warning that he could expect an influx of women applicants in the next six weeks and that the navy's recruiting office would perform the physical examinations, following the guidelines already in use for female navy applicants. He then needed only to complete the enrollments and send the applicants to USMC Headquarters.[32] Presumably, marine recruiters outside Washington could also seek cooperation from their local navy counterparts.

By 1 September 1918, thirty-one women had successfully applied and were on active duty. Two and one-half months later, on 11 November when the armistice was signed, 277 were on duty, and a total of 305 had served at some time.

Colonel McLemore advised all enlisted women that they could be summarily dismissed if they failed to maintain the high standards of the Marine Corps. To those women to whom he personally administered the enlistment oath, he added that he "wanted it distinctly understood that there was to be no flirtatious philandering with the enlisted men at headquarters on the part of the female reservists."[33] No record has been found as to whether he warned the enlisted men at headquarters against flirtatious philandering with the female reservists.

Enrolling women in the U.S. Navy and Marine Corps as an emergency measure in wartime was a good idea whose time had come. The Department of the Navy soon found its shore establishment brimming with efficient, hardworking women who rapidly learned to handle its clerical work—and eventually much more. The navy could send the men whom they replaced to ships, while the male marines were freed to fight in France.

TWO

Joining the Navy

There I was, a little 18-year-old girl being shipped clear across the
continent . . . for wartime duty in our nation's Capitol . . . among the first
women to be enlisted in the NAVY, the wonderful, salty old U.S. Navy.

Frances Bishop Boyd, former yeoman (F)

WHO WERE THESE THOUSANDS of women so eager to go where no women
had ever gone before? They were as widely varied in their backgrounds, skills,
experiences, and motivations as the young men joining the navy. They ranged
from experienced business administrators to women having no business skills
whatever; some were in their late teens, others were nearing middle age; some
had wealthy parents and advanced educations, others had neither families nor
schooling. The motives of nearly all included patriotism, frequently combined
with some wish for adventure and for wider opportunities.

Eager Enlistees

The most striking fact about the first women other than nurses to join the
U.S. Navy is that they themselves thought it was an altogether splendid idea.

Women eager to answer the call to colors besieged recruiting offices and became indignant when they were turned away because many recruiters were not prepared to enroll them. In Pittsburgh, during the twenty-four-hour period ending on 24 March 1917, no men applied to enlist but eight women did. By the end of March—still one week before the United States entered the war—one hundred women had joined the navy. On the day the nation declared war against Germany, more women from all across the country hastened to enlist, including at least two women from the Territory of Hawaii. By late May a total of 725 women had signed on. The brisk pace never let up. When the navy's cable censor office in New York announced in July that it needed more people, a hundred more women applied than could be accepted; the office placed their names on file for future reference. One year later, women were still enthusiastically signing on; they stopped only when the navy announced in late 1918 that it would accept no more.[1]

These first enlisted women in the U.S. Navy and Marine Corps came from varied backgrounds, with a wide range of skills. Many had high levels of abilities honed by work experience. These included women already at work in business, holding responsible jobs as executive secretaries, supervisors, and administrators. Many had been trained at business colleges in stenography, typing, and management of records. A few, such as telephone operators, telegraphers, and draftsmen, had quite specialized skills, and the navy actually sought them out.

A few women were graduates of four-year colleges and universities; had they been men, they would have qualified for commissioned rank. Several bacteriologists, including Dr. Estella Warner, a graduate of the University of Oregon, were enrolled in Seattle to work in laboratories and to train nurses. Three others served at the naval hospital in Portsmouth, New Hampshire. Chief Yeoman Marion Towne was a lawyer who had been the first woman to serve in the Oregon state legislature. In contrast, many of the younger women had little training or work experience and could offer the navy only their willingness to work and learn.[2]

Women already working for the government often were especially skilled but could join the navy only if they obtained releases from their civil service jobs; their superiors had to be able to replace them. By February 1918, the shortage of civil servants was so great that Secretary Daniels issued a direct order forbidding their enrollment.[3]

Various motives inspired these young women to answer the call to serve. The dominant force was patriotism. As one woman later wrote to a friend, "We had the idea that every time we hit a letter on the typewriter we were driving another nail in the Kaiser's coffin."[4] Often entwined with patriotism were the bonds of kinship. Many of the women anxious to enlist had fathers, brothers, even husbands who were already serving or about to serve or, in a few poignant cases, already casualties. A Baltimore woman who had married a navy man in June 1917 was widowed five months later when his ship was torpedoed. She promptly enlisted, citing her pride in the navy and adding, "It's all right to knit, and I do knit, but if we women are going to do our bit in this war many of us must put on the uniform and get busy."[5]

The desire to serve caused some women to lie about their age, still others to defer college. Some women in relatively high-paying jobs left them to accept the navy's lower salary, while other women were quick to appreciate how well navy pay compared with that of other occupations they could realistically hope to enter.[5] One recalled, "I said, 'Myrtle, we don't have any experience, and the navy could be nice! They'll pay us pretty good and they might send us anywhere, even to Paris!'"[6]

Many young women were eager for adventure—or at least something less humdrum than the other destinies they saw awaiting them; if the adventure happened to help the war effort, so much the better. Unlike their brothers who joined the navy, they might not see the world, but they might see more of their own country, a possibility that often pleased them much more than it pleased their families. Some joined almost willy-nilly, because a friend did, or someone suggested it to them.[7] A reporter working for her father, editor of the Miami *Herald,* described her enlistment as "a bit of an accident":

> The Navy had sent a ship from Key West to Miami to enlist men and women into the Naval Reserve. I was supposed to do a story for the *Herald* on the first woman to enlist in the state of Florida. We'd been told that the wife of the plumber . . . across the street from the newspaper was going to sign up.
>
> I arrived at the ship and the next thing I knew I was sticking up my hand, swearing to protect and defend the United States of America from all enemies whatsoever. I guess they talked me into it. I called my father at the paper and said, "Look, I got the story on the first woman to enlist. It turned out to be me." He said, "I admire your patriotism but it leaves us a little short-handed."[8]

Others were more intentional, traveling long distances to enroll and volunteering to go wherever they might be sent. For some, the heart of the adventure was being among the very first and the very few women to become enlisted, uniformed members of the armed forces. A few signed on as part of entire units joining the reserve forces.[9]

Whatever their motives, these women displayed a lot of mettle. Some faced severe parental disapproval, even wrath. One woman recalled that her mother "broke into tears and insisted I just could not do that," while another woman, on learning that her daughter had joined the navy, "got quite hysterical and said over and over, 'You can't go—you can't go.'" Another mother seemed to think her daughter had entered life-long servitude: "Oh sister, can you ever get *out?*"[10] In another family, it was the father who objected. "My mother was shocked but my father blew his top" and threatened to try to nullify his daughter's enlistment contract. In contrast, some parents encouraged their daughters to enroll, seeing opportunity for them as well as fulfilling a patriotic obligation. Even when one navy man objected strongly to his sister's enrollment and tried to tell their parents that "women in the navy weren't up to par morally," her parents didn't object.

Some parents had a change of heart: "My parents were devastated when I joined the navy—mostly surprised, I think. However, when I came home at Christmas on leave, I saw they'd put an American flag in the window to show how proud they were of me." Several sets of sisters enrolled together; at least two underage girls enlisted, one of them with her mother.[11]

Reporting for Duty

Often the new recruit's first experience as an enlisted woman was to travel, under navy orders, by train and/or steamboat, to her new duty station. Most women reporting from West Virginia, for example, were ordered to one of the numerous naval facilities in and around Norfolk. Over a hundred of them eventually enlisted, most from Huntington, Parkersburg, or Clarksburg. They would leave their home state on an evening train, arriving at Washington the next morning at eight o'clock. Twelve hours later they would embark on the overnight steamer to Norfolk.[12] Others made even longer journeys. One who came from the West Coast probably spoke for many as she described how the journey affected her: "I remember it well. It was the first time I had ever been any further east of the Mississippi than Chicago. All afternoon we had been traveling through old towns; towns and places that had been nothing but printed words in our history books suddenly became alive and real."[13]

For a few women, just getting onto a train was problematic. Five women who enlisted in Houston were housed dismally in a barracks for two weeks until they could be shipped to Washington. "They put us in one big room which had only one bed. Three of us slept in it, one at the foot, and one in a cot."[14]

Living Quarters

Some women were able to live at home or with family friends, mollifying those parents who were uneasy about their daughters' enrolling. Even so, for other women, it was a long commute to work. Joy Bright, for example, from Holly Beach, New Jersey, lived with family friends in Philadelphia and served at the New York Shipbuilding Corporation in Camden. Each day she took a ferry across the Delaware River and then a twenty-minute train ride. She later wrote, "Ferry and trains were so jam-packed with shipyard workers that it was not unusual to ride straddling the couplings."[15] When Mary Price arrived in Portsmouth, Virginia, to serve at the navy yard there, she and three friends rented rooms nearby. When she was later transferred to the naval station across the Elizabeth River in Norfolk, the crew of a small navy vessel took her to work and back on board each day. Rosella Hallisey commuted on a similar craft from Boston Harbor to Commonwealth Pier. Similarly, many of the women who served at the navy base in Algiers, Louisiana, on the west bank of the Mississippi, lived in New Orleans and crossed the river each day on a navy tugboat.

Most of the women serving at Pearl Harbor in Hawaii lived in Honolulu, some at home and some at the YWCA. Most of them commuted each day on the only railroad on the island, whose engine and coaches were toy-sized compared with those on the mainland. A navy yard craft, the *Navajo,* made the same trip, and a few women much preferred that voyage to the jolting train ride. Perhaps the most unusual commute was that of Marie Forde, who served at the Commonwealth Pier in Boston. At one point, her entire office was temporarily moved to a marine depot in Hingham, Massachusetts, about twenty-five miles south of Boston, but somewhat less by water. Most of the affected navy women simply commuted every day via the New York–New Haven rail line. When the railroad company went on strike, Marie and several others went back and forth on a navy submarine. "I think the government had to settle that strike very quickly . . . it couldn't have lasted very long. But while it did, the navy had to get us where they needed us."[16]

Only rarely was the navy able to provide quarters for the navy women serving at duty stations too far distant for them to live at home. Finding adequate housing was often a major hurdle, especially for girls and young women who had neither the experience nor guidance to help them in their first encounters with a large city, many of them away from their families for the first time. Some arrived in Washington, D.C., with little besides the clothes they were wearing, for uniformed recruiters had told them they would receive a hundred-dollar clothing allowance when they arrived.[17]

In Norfolk and Washington, and probably in other cities with large navy populations, naval authorities prevailed upon citizens to offer rooms for rent. One woman from North Carolina, upon arriving in Washington, D.C., went first to the YWCA, but it was filled. She then turned to the list of people who had agreed to rent rooms and "just missed getting into the home of Secretary . . . Daniels, who was from down home," but found a place at the home of another cabinet member. She moved out quickly when she realized he "had been married three times and had children from all three marriages under this one roof." Finally she settled into another home that offered her kitchen privileges, "which was fine, as food was expensive and eateries were always filled."[18]

Some women innocently leased rooms from landlords who gouged them. Mabel Vanderploeg, for example, joined two other yeomen (F) in renting a room for ten dollars each a month. When a fourth joined them, the landlady raised the rent to thirty-five dollars, the amount she paid for the entire house, as the women later discovered. Under the circumstances, having to heat water and carry it upstairs to bathe was the last straw, and they soon happily took up the offer of a kind neighbor to use *her* facilities, marching down the street every Saturday with towels over their arms. Other women met kinder landlords who became guides, good friends, and confidantes, establishing friendships that lasted well beyond wartime. For a fortunate few, strength lay in numbers. One group of seven women, all graduates of Vassar who had enrolled together, rented an entire house in Washington and hired a maid.[19]

The housing problem for women working in Washington became so acute that by the summer of 1918 the Navy Department was surveying its female employees and yeomen (F) to see how many would want to live in one of the three dormitories that it had hired a private corporation to build in the city with government funds. Each dormitory would house approximately twelve hundred women, have its own cafeteria and auditorium, and be supervised by a matron. The residents would pay a nominal sum to live in rooms nine by thirteen feet, with tiled showers.[20] The war ended before these plans could be completed.

In a few instances, the navy did provide quarters. One former yeoman (F) sent to Washington from her home in Chicago recalled that the navy had leased some apartments "with just the barest essentials" and assigned two women to each. The women who served at the Mare Island Shipyard near San Francisco lived in a former marine barracks, newly refurbished for their use. One of the women who lived there for seventeen months recalled it as being comfortable and pleasant but not without certain hallmarks of navy life. "Every morning the chief master at arms would come to the building but not enter it, then bang a stick against one of its corners, shouting 'Rise and shine! Rise and shine!' He made quite a racket." Each morning the women commuted to their jobs on a two-car train dubbed the "Powder Puff Special." At Newport, Rhode Island, members of the YWCA's housing committee viewed the navy housing as unsatisfactory for yeomen (F) and asked navy officials if they were planning to improve it. Secretary Daniels wrote to the committee chairman that the navy did not require the yeomen (F) to live in the housing but instead gave them a subsistence allowance to cover their room and board. That was the best solution in everyone's interest, Daniels said, so the navy had no plans to fix the housing at that time.[21]

Reactions to the Women

Public reaction to the yeomen (F) varied. The *Washington Post* and other papers received many letters on the topic. One retired colonel, who must be given credit for accurate foresight, expostulated, "First the women wanted to vote. Then Alice Roosevelt started them smoking cigarettes! Now they're talking about being soldiers! Next thing we know they'll be cutting off their hair and wearing pants!"[22]

The *Newport (R.I.) Daily News* offered a more judicious view in an editorial in May 1917: "Every woman who may be called upon to do the work of a man will not be worth so much as the man whose place she will take, but . . . it is quite possible that in some cases the substitute will develop enough capacity to make her more valuable than the man she succeeds . . . [the question] is not really one of sex, but of ability and value."[23]

Reaction within the navy was more uniform and generally positive. Most of the men with whom the yeomen (F) worked were intent on getting the war won, and since the women were efficiently helping to achieve that goal, the men regarded them and their work at least neutrally if not downright favorably. Estelle Richardson, one of the first women to enroll, reported that her boss, a retired navy captain recalled to active duty, "thought we were men." In a time when society admired and mostly conformed to courteous and restrained behavior between men and women, the hardworking men and women wearing uniforms of the same service found little difficulty in working together smoothly toward the common goal. Some supervisors and commanding officers even made sure to include the women in the social life of the unit in which they worked.[24]

A few women had special protection, due to their family connections. Helen Douglas's father, for example, was working in the Brooklyn Navy Yard as a construction supervisor when she and her sister enlisted. She later reported, "The men didn't mind me and my sister being in the navy. They were always polite. It may have helped that they knew my father wouldn't allow any funny business. But I don't remember any of the other girls saying anything bad. Everyone was just trying to do the job."[25]

Comparable circumstances facilitated welcomes for some other women. Lucy and Sidney Burleson, for example, daughters of the U.S. Postmaster General, both college graduates and both working for admirals, were not apt to be greeted with anything but abundant courtesy. Joy Bright had the good fortune to be introduced by a family friend to a navy captain who guided her through the enrollment process.[26]

The *Newport Recruit,* newspaper of the Newport Training Station, reflected navy men's generally good-natured view of the women. Its first reference to their advent appeared in the April 1917 issue, calling it "The Invasion of the Sailorettes" and suggesting that the women might well offer serious competition for good assignments. A year later the paper devoted several pages to a full-length article on the women, noting that the station was proud of them "because of their strict attention to duty and the efficient manner in which they have adapted themselves to the service." Carefully detailed and admiring, the article featured several attractive photographs of groups of yeomen (F) at work and at leisure on the station. It concluded with a laudatory poem, one verse of which was

> I've been in frigid Greenland and in sunny Tennessee,
> I've been in noisy London and in wicked, gay Paree,
> I've seen the Latin Quarter, with its models, wines, and tights,
> I've hobnobbed oft with Broadway stars who outshone Broadway lights;
> But North or South or East or West, the girls that I have met
> Could never hold a candle to a Newport yeomanette.

Finally, the December 1918 issue had a page of sketches showing how a woman might respond in certain situations: getting her hair cut (scowl), seeing a mouse (dropping her rifle), seated at her desk (her wastebasket is adorned with a large ribbon bow). The general tone was teasing, but clearly affectionate.[27]

Not all was sweetness and light. In the September 1918 issue of *Our Navy,* R. C. Shepherd editorialized that women should not have the same rating badge as male yeomen because they could not do the work at sea and thus "cheapen[ed] the badge." Capt. J. L. Taussig of the Bureau of Navigation rebutted sharply:

> There are more [male] Yeomen doing shore duty than in any other rating and many of these Yeomen have never been to sea and it is beginning to look that even in spite of all our efforts we are not going to be able to get them to sea. In view of this I see no reason why the Yeomen should consider that their ratings have been cheapened by the Yeowomen wearing the same badge.[28]

Evidently some navy men did not think that going to sea and perhaps getting shot at was as desirable as staying ashore, which might account, at least in part, for the disdain, offensive remarks, and downright meanness that some women met. One former yeoman (F) recalled indignantly, "The man I was supposed to relieve so he could go to sea didn't go to sea at all! Instead, they sent him to college and made him an officer. He boasted about that." In one particularly offensive situation, when a yeoman (F) second class objected to working overtime for her boss's girlfriend, he responded by threatening to give her a dishonorable discharge. More common were hostile remarks, like that of one man who declared he was "not goin' to work alongside no woman" and hoped that being ordered to China might save him from that fearful prospect.[29]

Marines

The motivation of women aspiring to join the Marine Corps was much the same as that of the navy women. The pay was better than that offered by most civilian employers. Also, of course, the spirit of adventure ran as strong in young women as it did in young men. But patriotism topped the list.

Perhaps the highest degree of patriotism was that shown by Private Ingrid Jonassen, who was surprised when she received her first paycheck. She had enlisted expecting no monetary compensation whatever, only room and board while she was on duty.[30] For some women with husbands, sweethearts, or brothers already at war, the desire to serve the country often was one and the same as the desire to support their loved ones. Some women were motivated by the Marine Corps's reputation as an elite branch of service—they wanted to be marines because they wanted to be marines. That evidently was Jane Van Edsingna's point of view. "To a nineteen-year-old girl swinging from a subway strap, it was the turning point of her life. Her eyes caught the words of an ad in a newspaper: 'For the first time in its history the United States Marine Corps is enlisting women. . . .' The next morning she didn't go to work. . . . She headed for a downtown Manhattan recruiting office. A few weeks later she was in Washington." [31]

As with the navy, sister joined sister, even though underage, in enlisting.

Edith Macias was only seventeen when she signed on with her older sister, Sarah. "She'd been telling her bosses and the D. Appleton Publishing Company she was nineteen, so, she thought, why not the Marine Corps too?" A few reversed the process. Daisy Lingle, then a thirty-six-year-old Washington, D.C., housewife, wasn't above telling a similar lie. The USMC said that thirty-five was the maximum age, so Mrs. Lingle simply said she was thirty-three. "I don't know why I joined. I just got it in my heart to join."[32]

Others left high-paying work in order to enroll. A woman who wrote Hollywood screen plays enrolled under her pen name, Lela Leibrand. Equally determined was the plucky young lady who, although a speed stenographer, failed the stiff typing test that would qualify her for entry. She returned the next day to try again. The officer in charge recognized her, then "got up and leaned over the desk and shook my hand and said, 'That's the spirit that will lick the Germans, I will allow you to take the test again!'" This time she passed and soon was on her way to Washington. In contrast, Olive May Bond, a native Washingtonian who was the first woman to operate an Addressograph™ machine, had no trouble demonstrating her value as a clerical worker.[33]

By mid-September more than thirty women had signed up with the Marine Corps. Several were stationed in recruiting offices across the country, and others were sent to whatever marine facilities could employ them. Approximately half of the 305 who eventually were enrolled worked at the USMC headquarters in Washington.[34]

Although Opha Mae Johnson, the first woman to enroll, was able easily to slip out of her civil service job at Marine Corps headquarters, female civil servants employed in other government agencies had a harder time. In the competition between the armed services and the civil service, the former held all the cards: the appeal to patriotism, adventure, sometimes better wages, and the determination of the women intent upon enrolling. One Department of Agriculture employee, when told she could not join the Marine Corps, said she would simply resign from civil service, work somewhere else briefly, then enroll. The recruiter told her (with some reluctance, she thought) that she would be accepted if she "got a release." Her resignation constituted her release and she was soon sworn into the marines. Another woman, a stenographer and secretary for the War Industries Board, got her release by agreeing to train some new employees for her fast-growing department.[35]

Finding housing in Washington was just as hard for the women marines as for the yeomen (F), perhaps harder, for by 1918 nearly all of the city's available housing was filled. The Navy Department did what it could. It leased the Hotel Vendôme, at the corner of Third and Pennsylvania Avenues, in which to lodge some of the women marines. Then Mrs. John D. Rockefeller, member of the War Council and "an enthusiastic advocate of women in the military," discovered that the Georgetown Preparatory School in Rockville, Maryland, had buildings so new they had not yet opened. She prevailed upon the school to lease them to the government for the duration. Seventy lucky women—roughly half of those serving at Marine Corps headquarters—were able to live there, one of them reporting it as "a beautiful place with private rooms, and excellent food prepared by a former tearoom owner." Residents commuted downtown by trolley, as did many others living in the suburbs of Maryland and Virginia.[36]

The women enlistees entered their new work with little fuss or commotion. For many, the smoothness of their entry owed far more to their own mettle than to any assistance from the navy. Some who had never before left home unchaperoned traveled alone considerable distances to strange cities where, more often than not, they had to find their own lodgings, then commute to work via public transportation. The women were proud of their contribution to the war effort, and most relished the opportunities to grow and learn.

THREE

Uniforms

'Til it wilted I wore it, I'll always adore it, my real U.S. Navy blue gown.

Former yeoman (F) Virginia Carrigan, adapting
lyrics of a popular World War I song

ARMED FORCES TAKE UNIFORMS SERIOUSLY. Among other functions, uniforms immediately identify those who wear them, they promote recruitment, and they project a favorable image to the taxpaying public. Both the U.S. Navy and the Marine Corps had good reason to provide their women with tasteful uniforms as soon as possible. However, the uniform designers did not foresee the clothing needs of women who ended up in nonclerical jobs. Fortunately, local commanders allowed appropriate variations. Also, demand sometimes outran supplies, so that months went by before all the women were fully uniformed. In the interim, confusion arose about what the women could or should wear and who was to pay for their uniforms.

Creating the Uniform

As soon as Loretta Walsh agreed to enroll in the Naval Reserve, Lieutenant Commander Payne, recruiting officer at the Naval Home in Philadelphia, notified the press that a very newsworthy event would take place at the Home the following morning, 21 March 1917. He had already arranged for Walsh's physical examination and now needed only to come up with a uniform. Together with his wife and her sister, he devised an outfit that suited the occasion perfectly. Walsh greeted the press wearing the cap and jacket of a navy chief petty officer. Her hat was much like those worn by commissioned officers: an unstiffened white crown rising from the black band encircling her head, with a stiff black bill straight over her forehead. On the band, centered over the forehead, was the chiefs' insignia, an anchor with a rope twisted around its shank. Her jacket was made of dark blue serge, double-breasted, with brass buttons and a belt that was sewn across the back. Under the jacket Walsh wore a white shirtwaist with a black four-in-hand tie. Her skirt was dark blue, ending just above the ankle, revealing black hose and shoes. She looked unmistakably *navy* and unmistakably feminine. Some subsequent photos showed her carrying a pistol, and one cartoonist portrayed her wearing a saber. Payne later claimed, proudly and accurately, that the official uniform eventually prescribed by the navy for the yeomen (F) closely resembled the one Walsh wore as she took her enlistment oath.[1]

Half a continent away, Beulah Worrell of Minneapolis knew nothing of Walsh's enrollment but heard from a neighboring navy recruiter that the navy might enroll women. On 6 April 1917, the day the United States entered the war, he told her it was now official. She signed up immediately and, like Walsh, was enrolled as a chief yeoman. She, too, took her inspiration from the male uniform but modeled hers after her son's. Not yet a chief, he wore the familiar blue serge tunic worn by generations of sailors, with the V-neck opening into the wide square collar, edged with three rows of thin white braid. Under the collar was tied a black silk neckerchief. Worrell took the tunic and neckerchief just as they were, then converted the bell-bottom trousers into a skirt. She also modified the regulation flat "pancake" hat, keeping the band around the forehead but replacing the flat crown with a fuller one made of black velvet.[2]

Perhaps spurred by cartoonists' images of pistol and saber, which assuredly had no place in its plans for the women, the navy promulgated a description of a uniform for "women enrolled in the Naval Reserve Force" on 17 April, less than a month after Walsh had enrolled. It appeared first as a memorandum, and then as "Change # II" it was inserted into the current *Uniform Regulations*. The memorandum described only a "coat" (jacket) and skirt. The coat was like that worn by male chief petty officers, except that it was single-breasted, and the skirt's hem was to come four inches above the anklebone. These items were to be of plain navy serge or white drill cloth. Women were not required to wear them, but they were to wear an official pin, the Naval Reserve Force Device, when on active duty. If they did wear a uniform, they were to wear only what was specified.[3] A later description was published as "Change in Uniform Regulations, No. 15." It specified the coat and skirt in greater detail and added descriptions of shirtwaist, neckerchief, hat, hose, shoes, and gloves.

Credit for the design is given to Rear Adm. Ashley Robertson, and its approval to Secretary Daniels, after "a number of persons expressed their ideas on the subject." Daniels later took full credit: "The picture of you girls in your uniforms has proved what a good designer I am. . . . Some people thought they ought to wear something like pants. Some had different ideas. . . . Another problem was the length of the skirts. . . . Should we have a long skirt that would sweep the decks, or should we have them . . . above the knees?" After seeking "the wise counsel of the women . . . we decided on about eight inches from the ground."[4]

The results were a slightly shaped jacket that covered the hips, with a rolling collar and four buttons. On each hip was a patch pocket, and a two-inch plait ran vertically, front and back, from each shoulder to the hem. A belt ran under these plaits, in a manner known as "Norfolk style." Rating badges identical to those of male sailors were worn in the same place, that is, on the jacket's left sleeve, midway between elbow and shoulder. Matching skirts also had two patch pockets at hip level and were to be "made full at the bottom and to fit the figure over the hips." Under the coat was a tailored shirtwaist, plain and long-sleeved, buttoned down the front, worn with a black tie. Regular navy neckerchiefs were tied under the shirt's collar when it was unbuttoned. Plain high-topped or low-cut shoes of black leather, white canvas, or buckskin were worn with plain black or white hose. Hats were to be "straight-brimmed sailors, of navy-blue felt or white rough straw," the brims about three inches wide and the crowns about four inches high. White cotton gloves completed the outfit.[5]

Getting Squared Away

In June of 1917 the navy asked clothing manufacturers to bid for contracts so that it could order a thousand each of blue serge suits, blue felt hats, and white straw hats, and two thousand white drill suits. Suppliers were to have the uniforms ready one week after receiving the contracts. Even after manufacturers had begun to supply the uniforms, demand often outran supply; some women had to wait weeks or months before receiving them. As a result, many women bought patterns created by civilian firms, then made the uniforms themselves or turned the job over to seamstresses. In New York, two hundred women who had been wearing arm brassards indicating their rank organized themselves to adopt a uniform. One woman, well-meaning but uninformed, made her own dress, of which she was very proud, then sewed on a chief petty officer's insignia just for decoration. This so offended her chief petty officer that he "proceeded to rip it off."[6]

The question of standardizing the uniforms soon became entangled with the question of how to pay for them and generated thick files of correspondence. Each naval district handled the matter in its own way, and much depended on how well the local paymasters were informed. Both the Thirteenth Naval District in Seattle and the First Naval District in Boston inquired whether it was legal to pay the women a uniform gratuity, since the uniform was not mandatory. The Bureau of Supplies and Accounts, the navy's judge advocate general, and Secretary Daniels all offered opinions, and eventually the comptroller of the United States Treasury handed down a ruling. On 24 May he noted that the Reserve Act of 1916 did not provide "specifically for *outfits* of *clothing*, but for a *gratuity* for uniforms" (original emphasis). He continued:

> While it is understood to be the practice to furnish enlisted men of the Naval Reserve Force entitled to a gratuity with clothing in kind because the Navy Department has such clothing in stock yet I know of no legal reason why another method of furnishing this gratuity might not be adopted when more convenient for the Navy Department. . . . [W]omen enrolled as yeomen may be paid in cash the uniform gratuity authorized in the act.[7]

Navy paymasters were accustomed to the long-standing practice of issuing a complete set of uniforms—a "full seabag"—to each incoming sailor, then each month thereafter giving him a small sum of money specifically to keep the seabag replenished and in good repair. But the women's circumstances were different, and it took some time to adjust and treat their uniforming equitably with the men's. For example, in June 1917 a woman stationed at Key West wrote to the auditor of the Navy Department that she had reported for duty on 16 April, when "uniforms, as were practicable for women, were issued me. . . . In the absence of specific regulations . . . all women enrolled as yeomen on duty in this station are wearing uniforms consisting of white skirts, navy blouses, caps., etc." Yet the paymaster there had received an order that no uniforms were to be issued to women and therefore docked her pay for those items, and he did not acknowledge the uniform gratuity the Naval Reserve Act of 1916 provided to all reservists upon enrolling. In light of the comptroller's ruling, the woman's pay was restored, but the episode highlighted the rampant confusion.[8]

In September the surgeon general urged the Bureau of Navigation to require that the women wear the uniform. It could then be manufactured in large quantities, thereby saving a significant amount of money. Moreover, he added, the Reserve pin worn by women not in uniform was too small to be noticed by anyone unfamiliar with its design, so that it was difficult to distinguish the women from "members of the general public." But a full year passed before the navy made the specified uniform mandatory.[9]

The challenge to prescribe, procure, and distribute a standardized uniform was compounded by the fact that each naval district was free to administer the uniform regulations as best suited its climate and work requirements. In the Territory of Hawaii, for example, yeomen (F) wore their summer whites year round; eleven of them posed in their whites for a photograph taken at Pearl Harbor on 11 November 1918, celebrating the end of the war. But two yeomen (F) who worked with highly classified material at the Cable and Postal Censor's Office were directed *not* to wear their uniforms at all, so as to conceal their connection to the navy.[10]

Hats were the most widely varying uniform component. Photographs show some women in a beret or tam-o'-shanter evidently adapted, like Beulah Worrell's, from the regulation banded flat hat, while others appear in a close-fitting cloche. Some women found that the brimmed hats flew off too easily in a strong breeze and adopted a fore-and-aft or "overseas" cap. One was photographed wearing the round, white "Dixie cup" hat traditional for navy sailors. Even where all of the women were wearing the brimmed hats, variations appear. Some of the winter brimmed hats were obviously of a thicker felt, perhaps even closely sheared beaver. The summer brimmed hats also varied somewhat, some being made of smooth straw while others appear to have a rougher texture.

The navy did not prescribe hair length for women, and some followed the newest style, a short bob popularized by dancer Irene Castle. Accustomed to seeing grown women wearing their hair long and pinned up, some navy officers found the short hair too radical. Jessie Arnold's commanding officer, upon viewing her new cut, told her "he was going to kick me out of the navy. So I said, 'Oh, I see you measure my brains by the length of my hair.' He said, 'That is all.' Later most all the girls cut their hair."[11]

A woman's job assignment sometimes required uniform innovations. Mary Price, for example, was assigned to a supply warehouse, filling ships' orders for small parts and hardware. "The parts were kept in big metal bins stacked all the way up to the ceiling. We'd climb up those straight metal ladders and put the items the ships had ordered into big baskets." For their working uniforms, she and the three other women doing the same job substituted overalls for their long skirts. The women in Key West were not the only ones issued men's tunics and neckerchiefs. Navy women assembling primers at a munitions factory in Bloomfield, New Jersey, were photographed wearing those items over dark pleated skirts. Too, personal and unofficial variations appeared, such as regulation uniforms embellished with lace collars. The Baker twins, who joined a Coast Guard unit, outfitted themselves in dark dresses with cummerbunds and shawl collars (see photo). By spring of 1918 supply channels had smoothed considerably. Many stations could issue a uniform to a woman as soon as she reported for duty; if not, she could order her uniforms from a navy clothing depot, just as male chief petty officers could.[12]

The obvious shortfall in the prescribed uniform was that it included no garments for outdoor wear. All through the winter of 1917–18, except for the relatively small number stationed in very mild climates, the women wore their own overcoats. In September 1918 a cape was prescribed, then an overcoat and a heavier shirtwaist for winter, and finally gray suede gloves.

Women at the Boston Navy Yard who had faced the previous winter with no uniform outerwear had found their own ways of keeping warm. Some had worn fur neckpieces over their jackets; some put on spats over their shoes; some kept their hands warm in muffs, while others had invested in fur coats.

After the navy prescribed capes and overcoats, they asked permission to continue wearing their own outer clothing, rather than spending forty dollars for the cape or fifty dollars for the overcoat. Their commanding officer endorsed their request, saying that asking them to buy the new uniform items was a lot to ask of women who had "already strained their financial resources by buying Liberty Bonds." However, the next higher authority, the commandant of the First Naval District, disagreed. He said that the women should not wear furs or fur coats over their uniforms as it was "undemocratic." Moreover, they could afford to buy winter uniforms, for "the pay of yeowomen is far beyond, probably double, the scale of wages for the same services in civil life." This must have stung the petitioning women, in view of the fact that women enrolling after 1 July 1918 were given a clothing gratuity of one hundred dollars, a substantial increase over the sixty dollars given to those who had enrolled earlier.[13]

The end of the war precipitated a final flurry of uniform variants. The first official change, an economy measure, was suggested by Rear Admiral McGowan only three days after the armistice was signed on 11 November 1918. Apparently supplies of uniforms were running short, and he saw little point in ordering more, because, "By the time the items are supplied, it's likely many of our women will have been disenrolled." Yet, a full month after the armistice, the Navy Department ordered that all female reservists still on duty were to have identification tags made "as required by General Order No. 294." Like the men in the Reserve Forces, women being released from active duty were required to keep their uniforms and outfit on hand and in good condition; they could wear them for up to three months following their release, but no longer.[14]

Pride in service and uniform led some of the female yeomen astray. As soldiers returned home from overseas wearing gold chevrons for foreign service, some navy women in Washington, D.C., were quick to add silver chevrons to *their* sleeves. Their commanding officer told them to remove same "*immediately*" (boldfaced in original). Some women's fondness for insignia, whether authorized or not, evidently died hard. Soon after the previous injunction was issued, a similar one appeared, this one evoked by the women's discovery of the navy "E" (for excellence), traditionally awarded by the navy to ships and other units whose crews had distinguished themselves in gunnery. The women wearing the E's were directed to "remove them at once."

Pride and Presentation

A few navy women disliked their uniforms. Many years later, one of them recalled hers as unflattering and poorly fitted, decidedly a comedown from her usual civilian attire, and we may suppose that some other women shared her opinion. Some complained that the whites were hard to launder and the felt hats drooped in the rain.[15] But far more approved of their uniform and wore it proudly. A group of yeomen (F) on duty in Washington, D.C., who spent long hours in drill after work, specifically to march in parades, took particular pride in their appearance. The navy and the women themselves called this group "the Battalion." After the war one chronicler wrote of them,

> This Battalion was a great inspiration to the girls who had worked so hard for the proper and universal wearing of the uniform. These women wore their uniforms with the greatest reverence and pride. . . . [To them] this uniform was and is a sacred trust. . . . A complete uniform was donated by a member of the Battalion, Mrs. Amy Hammond, to the New National Museum, where it was exhibited among the other uniforms of the Great World War.[16]

Onlookers were often impressed as well. More than fifty years later, the father of author Ebbert vividly remembered seeing them as a seventeen-year-old working near the navy offices in lower Manhattan: "The navy girls looked very snappy indeed."

The Navy Nurse Corps offered the sincerest compliment of all: imitation. The nurses had begun the war with no outdoor uniform, but by 1918 the navy authorized for them a uniform like that of the yeoman (F), except that the jacket was double-breasted and the hat more like the sailor's flat pancake. The nurse's cape was her great uniform distinction; it was lined in scarlet, à la the American Red Cross, and had a Nurse Corps device (gold acorn and oak leaf superimposed on a gold anchor, with letters "N.N.C.") on its collar.[17]

Pride in the uniform and some understanding of its historical significance extended throughout the yeomen (F)'s lifetimes and often passed on to their descendants. At a luncheon reunion in New York in 1951, "Shipmate Greta Bedell did a quick change at her table and blossomed forth in . . . uniform, complete with hat and cape. . . . many a shipmate wiped away a tear as she beheld it. . . . the pride in our service . . . symbolized by that uniform!" In 1976, the sister of former Yeoman (F) Pauline Greaves donated her complete uniform (along with several papers and photos, and five dollars to have the uniform pressed) to the museum in Jacksonville, Oregon, where Greaves had graduated from high school. Estelle Richardson Ruby's pride in her uniform radiated throughout her life. In 1982, not long before she died, she showed a visitor her carefully preserved uniform cape, lifting its weight easily over her now frail and bowed shoulders, adjusting the collar around her neck, then standing erect with lifted chin.[18] Her gestures expressed what another put into words:

> My dear old uniform of blue, I'll hate to lay you by
> And merely be a citizen when the blue-clad boys march by. . . .
> For you won me a place in the ranks of men; a chance to do my bit
> And now to go back and be "merely a girl," I hate to think of it.[19]

Former Yeoman (F) Virginia Carrigan undoubtedly expressed the sentiments of many when she modified the lyrics of a popular World War I song, "Alice Blue Gown":

> I once had a gown, it . . . was real Navy blue
> With stripes and an anchor and braid here and there,
> When I had it on, I walked on the air.
> 'Til it wilted I wore it,
> I'll always adore it,
> My real U.S. Navy blue gown.[20]

Marine Green

If the yeomen (F)'s uniform was a success, that of the women marines was a triumph. The Marine Corps had several advantages in this endeavor. First, it could benefit from the navy's pioneering efforts in design and procurement. Second, it had to deal with far fewer women—the navy had about forty times as many—and except for a small group serving at recruiting stations across the country, the marines were all located in one place, and they all did the same kind of work. Thus only two versions of the uniform were needed: winter and summer. Compliance with regulations could be enforced far more easily. With these two advantages, plus its fierce competitive spirit, the USMC achieved stunning results.

The USMC began by following the navy experience of adapting the existing male uniform and tailoring it to the female figure, but each uniform was made to order, so they fit far better than did most of the navy women's uniforms. The women marines' shirts, ties, and cloth chevrons indicating rank were identical to the men's, and no variations were allowed. Moreover, their footgear did not vary as the navy women's did. The women marines all wore high-top shoes in winter and low-cut oxfords in summer, which permitted uniformity in hemlines. The winter shoes were particularly stylish, with pointed toes and curved heels. That, plus the crisp forest green of the winter uniform, made it the women's favorite, especially for photographs.

Because they could not carry umbrellas, on rainy days the women could wear a brimmed hat much like that worn to this day by marine drill instructors. Otherwise they wore standard fore-and-aft caps of green wool for winter and khaki for summer. Like the men, they wore the marine insignia—eagle, globe, and anchor—pinned to their hats. They did not have the choice of overcoat or cape for winter outerwear: a dashing overcoat with a deep, turned-over collar was *it*.[21] Nor were they ever allowed to remove their ties and open their shirt collars as male marines were sometimes permitted to do. Like umbrellas, purses were banned; doing without a purse challenged the women's ingenuity. One of them explained: "The coat or blouse had a large pocket on each side which extended across the front. These commodious cavities were handy, but putting too many things in them created bulges which was strictly against regulations. To avoid this I kept a comb and brush in my desk, tucked my handkerchief inside a sleeve, and carried a small change purse so as to appear trim and neat. There was no need for a wallet."[22]

Trim and neat they certainly were. The expressions with which so many marine women gaze out from the old photographs suggest that they were fully aware of that felicity. Moreover, they had distinct ideas on how to enhance it. Both of their favorite enhancements were unauthorized. The first was to add the Sam Browne belt, that quintessential military accessory. Attached to the waist belt, at the back of the right hip, a second leather strap rises to the right shoulder, then slants across the chest to the front of the left hip, where it rejoins the belt. Pulled taut over an already close-fitting jacket, a Sam Browne belt accentuates a trim waist and well-formed torso, be the wearer a man or a woman. Despite repeated warnings from on high, many of the women appear not to have stopped wearing the belts; they only became more discreet, saving them for off-duty hours.

One anecdote suggests why compliance was not easily enforced. Cpl. Elizabeth Shoemaker was sternly admonished by the major for whom she worked never to wear the belt again. Not long afterward, notice came down that all officers were to wear Sam Browne belts in the great victory parade led by General Pershing, scheduled for the next day. "A mad scramble in the Washington stores to buy belts followed . . . and the stores were quickly sold out. The major who had been so cross at his secretary could not find a single belt in the whole city. . . . An hour before the parade he rang for her and asked if he might borrow hers, he even sent her home in an official car to get it."[23]

Some of the women marines also took to carrying swagger sticks. These slender batons, about twenty inches long, have long been a distinctive part of marine officers' garb (although carried only on certain dress occasions since World War II). Headquarters thundered to the women that they must not carry the swagger sticks, but those pronouncements were taken about as seriously as those about the belts.

One wonders what headquarters would have said had it known at the time what one woman marine wore while waiting for her regulation uniform. Out in Indianapolis, Lucy Ervin donned a bright blue, high-collared marine dress tunic, with a "web belt complete with red and gold stripes and a campaign hat." All this she wore above a black velvet skirt. Following her discharge, headquarters did find out about it, for she wrote and told them. The Quartermaster of the Corps promptly sent her the material and emblems for a winter uniform.[24]

Fortunately, the designs of both the navy and marine women's uniforms were conservative but smart interpretations of the men's uniforms. Their wearers generally thought highly of them, and so did the public. Although their creative accessorizing provoked stern reprimands from higher authority—and authority always won—the skirmishes showed that the women's high degree of independence had in no way been squelched.

Outfitting more than twelve thousand women in smart and distinctive uniforms garnered valuable publicity for the services. For the women, their uniforms were a source of pride and identity throughout their lives.

FOUR

Pulling Their Oar

My job was payroll and accounting. It wasn't glamorous, but it
was important. It was amazing how many little items that went
into a ship had to be accounted for on the books.

Helen Douglas Coutts Saul, former yeoman (F)

THE NAVY WOMEN OF World War I are known collectively as the "Yeomen
(F)" because most of them held clerical and administrative jobs, although the
navy rated at least five women with special previous training as "electricians,
radio." In the years since 1917–19, as women have moved into every job field in
the navy, including fields long considered nontraditional for women, "clerical
and administrative" suggests something far less bold, less skilled, and less
weighty than was actually true of the duties of many navy women and a few
women marines. The responsibilities that some of these women carried have
been consistently undervalued, if not altogether overlooked. Moreover, numerous yeomen (F) and a few women marines did anything *but* clerical work; they
drove trucks, broke codes, operated switchboards, and made munitions. Whatever their assignment, navy and marine women worked long hours, many of
them six days a week every week, and some worked night shifts.

When they enrolled, hardly any of them knew what jobs they would end up doing. But then, neither did the U.S. Navy or Marine Corps.

Clerks

By the end of 1917, thousands of yeomen (F) were replacing men in every naval district, including Guam, Puerto Rico, the Canal Zone, and Hawaii. A few even served in Europe. Typing from eight to five, six days a week and making at least six copies of everything was how many of them spent the war, keeping the Navy Department from drowning in its own paperwork.

Modern readers accustomed to the speed and convenience of word processors may not appreciate the labor and frustration experienced by even skilled typists handling the manual typewriters of the time. An efficient typist needed well-trained fingers to ensure a strong, accurate, and speedy touch. Shifting a lever to start the next line, moving to the next page, changing margins, and many other routine tasks now done either automatically or with one or two light keyboard strokes were done by hand, over and over again. Any typing error required erasure or possibly redoing the entire page. To make copies, the typist alternated a sheet of carbon paper with a sheet of flimsy paper for each copy required. Thus six copies required the original sheet plus five sheets of carbon paper interleaved with five "flimsies." A minimum of twenty-five words per minute, error-free, was considered entry-level typing. Experts could type two or even three times that fast. Eventually, everything that was typed had to be addressed, sent, and filed.

Even for the expert typists and stenographers and for women accustomed to office routines, transferring their skills to navy offices was a substantial challenge. A major part of that challenge was simply learning the navy's language: "muster," "drill," "temporary duty"—what did these mean? "Operations" evidently had nothing to do with surgery, and why was there such a huge difference between an "officer-in-charge" and a "commanding officer"? Why did a yeoman first class wear *three* chevrons on his sleeve while a yeoman third class wore *one*? How come the Marine Corps named its most junior officers second lieutenants while the navy called theirs ensigns? Why did you eat in a "mess"? Et cetera, et cetera. But all those naval terms, plus their uniforms, assured the women that they were truly in the service, truly doing men's jobs so that men could go to sea, and for some women the sea was very close. Indra Sayre, writing home to West Virginia from her job at the Norfolk Navy Yard, reported: "There was so much 'red tape' to go through and so much to learn about the work. . . . My work is the sub-chaser supply department. . . . From . . . my desk I can see battle ships, transports. and many sub-chasers coming and going all the time. . . . It makes you feel proud."[1]

The Bureau of Supplies and Accounts employed about twelve hundred reservists. At its headquarters in Washington, 134 yeomen (F) handled a wide range of assignments, from payrolls to transportation. Some of these enlisted women's responsibilities were awesome even by today's standards; they extended far beyond those ordinarily connoted by "clerk." In the Naval Communications Division, Yeomen Second Class Lucy and Sidney Burleson, daughters of the U.S. Postmaster and graduates of George Washington University, both worked in the bureau; Sidney, who had also completed a business course, was McGowan's personal secretary. Yeoman (F) Lorena Boswell was his administrative officer. Elsewhere in the bureau, twenty-two-year-old Anna Hayden, employed as a draftsman in civilian life, was the executive clerk of contract priorities. Two naval officers, one of them a son of the secretary of commerce, were her assistants. Yeoman (F) Laila Anders assisted the officer in charge of clothing, overseeing manufacturers' production of clothing for a quarter of a million enlisted men. Yeoman (F) Eleanor Griffith, an auditor in the disbursing division, routinely signed four-million-dollar vouchers, while another yeoman (F) was given authority to assign to railroad officials the priorities by which they were to ship navy supplies.[2]

Chief Yeoman Sue Dorsey was proposed for an officer's commission for the very good reason that she was doing an officer's work, and her boss, Rear Adm. Samuel McGowan, the navy's paymaster, recognized it, calling her "the most valuable woman in the government." She evaluated the performances of the navy's fifteen hundred pay officers and could assign them to various posts. The war ended before McGowan's proposal could be acted upon, but it remains a notable measure of value of yeomen (F) service. Three other women in the Navy Department—Yeomen Third Class Frances Burkhalter, Helen Hurley, and Maude Howell—were recommended to take the examination for promotion to the rank of ensign.[3]

Disbursing and payroll work occupied many of the women reservists, both in the Navy Department in Washington and out on the waterfronts. For example, Yeoman Third Class Ardelle Humphrey handled the invoices for ship repairs submitted by contractors, then passed them to her boss, the solicitor of the navy, who in turn checked them before forwarding them for payment. Yeoman Katie Greene was assigned to the payroll office in Algiers, Louisiana, which had been staffed completely by males. By war's end, only the payroll officer and one chief were men; the remaining sixty-three on the staff were yeomen (F). They handled the pay not only for all naval facilities in New Orleans but also for any navy ships coming into port there. The women often worked late into the night while waiting for a submarine to cruise upriver for supplies and its crew's wages. They were accustomed to working three and four nights a week, and three Sundays a month would not have been unusual for those in payroll work.[4]

Numbers of yeomen (F) clerks worked for the Bureau of Medicine and Surgery in Washington and at naval hospitals throughout the navy; they often witnessed heart-wrenching scenes. Cecelia Corcoran, stationed at the naval hospital in Algiers, Louisiana, recalled "how close to home the war was when the battleships came in with sailors and marines wounded in action or suffering from influenza, during the epidemic, which raged aboard ship." Another served at the naval hospital in Brooklyn and, like most of the yeomen (F), stayed on active duty until mid-1919. She wrote to a fellow veteran, "Although the war officially ended . . . in November 1918 our work was just beginning . . . and the sad sight of so many wounded men is still with me. I used to bring them to my home and go out on dates with them to help them adjust to a new life, perhaps without limbs or disfigured in some other way."

Other women helped procure enormous amounts of medical supplies and then forward them to their destinations. Helene Johnson worked at the Naval Medical Supply Depot at the navy yard in Mare Island, a huge facility employing thousands of men and women working night and day to supply destroyers, submarines, and battleships with appropriate medicines and other medical materials. "I typed and typed and TYPED requisitions. We worked long, long days, Saturdays, too."[5]

In numerous other offices yeomen (F) also handled large responsibilities, keeping the paperwork flowing. Chief Yeoman Helen O'Neill, for example, joined two male chiefs in checking all correspondence originating in the Navy Department's Division of Enlisted Personnel; she was responsible for training and supervising junior yeomen, some of whom were men.[6]

Messengers and Couriers

Yeomen (F) often served as messengers and couriers. Some recall being chosen for these assignments because, as one put it, "some guy said I was small and fast," while others had little or no secretarial skills or experience. One navy office requested low-ranking yeomen (F) for messenger service, suggesting that women of "robust constitution and limited education would probably produce the best results," whereas women with office experience or business education were dissatisfied with such an assignment. Some simply delivered messages and papers from one office or building to another, but others had more exciting destinations, such as the White House. One yeoman (F) managed to sit in the president's chair and years later entertained her grandchildren by telling them how she put her "feet on the rungs."

Another messenger working in communications at the Naval Overseas Transportation Service in New York was among the first in the United States to hear that the armistice had been signed. "On November 11, the officer on duty was taking down a message then coming in over the wire and motioned me to look at the paper. . . . [It] said the Armistice had been signed that morning. I read it and went back to my office." Later when the good news was officially announced, she was able to tell her commanding officer that she already knew.

Joy Bright started her navy career as a messenger at the naval shipyard in Camden, New Jersey, where she carried plans and papers between offices and ships. Later she was transferred to Cape May, where she was the personnel officer's yeoman; her main duties were maintaining the records of those assigned to the station, and she also served as the court stenographer for courts-martial.[7]

Naval Intelligence

The yeomen (F) who worked in naval intelligence, processing fingerprints, breaking codes, and censoring cables, handled extremely sensitive and important material. Some may have known as much about the course of the war as many of the men who far outranked them. Two women came to the navy already trained as wireless operators, and the navy enrolled them as electricians first class. When one of them, Marion Taylor, died in 1968 at the age of 86, her obituary noted that she was "the only woman in the Navy who knew all the movements of all the allied ships in the Atlantic . . . and she kept that secret, even from her husband, until the Navy released this information publicly in 1936. . . . [She] worked in the Shipping Board Office in Washington . . . where in a steel vault, behind a locked door, she received reports of all the allied ships, transmitted on a hidden telegraph system."[8]

Yeoman (F) First Class Lillian Budd was one of four people at the navy's communications center in Washington, D.C., who monitored message traffic from all the ships and shore stations between Washington and London. In a small cubicle they took messages in shorthand, transcribed them, and delivered them personally to President Wilson or to Secretary of the Navy Daniels or to Assistant Secretary Franklin D. Roosevelt. Working in six-hour shifts, they listened around the clock. Often the messages were difficult to hear, because of atmospheric conditions or rudimentary equipment. Audiotaping did not yet exist, so the listener had to catch the message accurately the first time or it might be lost beyond recall. Her immediate supervisor explained:

"You will receive S.O.S. calls, perhaps from sinking ships. You will receive word of the sighting of submarines so a warning may be broadcast. In short, UPON THE ACCURACY of your notes will depend the saving or LOSS OF LIVES." He added solicitously, "Do you think you can do it?"

. . . I said, "Yes, sir." But for the first time in my shorthand life I had qualms. Could I? I *had* to.

The most difficult job was the sinking of the U.S.S. *San Diego* after [it was] torpedoed. . . . After [I'd taken] shorthand for 36 hours, the Commander . . . asked me if . . . I could read the whole report to Mr. Daniels and his staff so he could select portions telling of the dead in order to notify next of kin before the newspapers reported news about the tragedy.

I read it aloud to Secretary of the Navy Daniels . . . and a whole staff of Admirals with gold braid up to their elbows, and when I was finished, Mr. Daniels shook my hand. With tears in his eyes, he said to me, "We are sorry this had to be done, but we are glad that we had YOU to do it for us." And . . . he paid me a rare compliment: "You know there is not a one of us here in this room who could have done what you have done."[9]

Nearly fifty yeomen (F) worked in the Naval Intelligence Office in New York, which dealt with cases of actual or suspected espionage and monitored the establishments known to be favorite sailors' hangouts, where alcohol was apt to loosen otherwise discreet tongues.[10]

Sometimes decoding involved unusual challenges. In the Office of the Chief of Naval Operations, eighteen-year-old Della White met such a challenge. She was one of three petty officers whose job was to help guide and protect convoys of army troop transports by keeping in constant touch with the two flagships leading the convoys, USS *Brooklyn* and USS *Pennsylvania*. Late one afternoon the chief petty officer took an incoming telephone call. Hearing only incomprehensible shouting, he silently shook his head and passed the phone to the first class, who after a moment shook his head and passed the phone to Yeoman (F) Second Class White. She immediately interrupted the caller and said, slowly and loudly: "Wait . . . a . . . minute!" Silence at the other end, so she continued in the same calm, slow voice, "I suggest you sit down, take a deep breath, count to ten, and then talk. I can then take your message." As the now intelligible words came, she took them in shorthand, then asked, "Signature?" The caller barked, "Benson!" Recognizing its urgency for the convoy, White immediately coded the message, sent it off, then sat down and leaned back with a mighty sigh. "By tomorrow I may be fired," she announced. "I just bawled out our boss, Admiral Benson."[11]

Telephone Operators

The navy's and the army's rapidly expanding need for wartime telephone operators led many yeomen (F) into this critical work within days after the nation entered the war. Until that time, switchboards had been operated almost exclusively by enlisted men. Mrs. Velma Hall had been chosen as the best person to operate the Norfolk Navy Base's first switchboard. She enlisted in 1917 and was promoted to chief in 1918. Transferred to the navy yard's switchboard at Portsmouth, Virginia, she reorganized the department and improved its service. About the same time, the Navy Department in Washington assigned a yeoman (F) to its two-position, one-person switchboard, the first woman to hold the job. She, too, was promoted to chief in 1918.

At the end of the war, fourteen yeomen (F) operated the Coaster's Harbor

Island Telephone Exchange at the Training Station in Newport, Rhode Island, which consisted of thirteen lines to the city and two hundred extensions.[12] One former yeoman (F) later described early reactions to the female operators: "Naval officers returning from sea duty received the shock of their lives when they picked up a telephone and heard a friendly female voice say, 'Good morning.' . . . The speed, alacrity and superior performance with which the calls were handled established women as permanent operators in the naval telephone system."[13] Telephone operators had to possess not only speed, dexterity, quick wits, and resourcefulness but also unquestioned discretion and loyalty. The files of the Office of Naval Intelligence tell of one yeoman (F) whose job as the switchboard supervisor for a headquarters of the Second Naval District in New London, Connecticut, was considered highly sensitive. Her misfortune was that her German-born father, who also lived in New London, then a small town, often loudly and publicly proclaimed his sympathies with his native land. The women working at the navy switchboard complained bitterly about him and refused to work for her, to the extent that her commanding officer finally had no choice but to recommend her release from the navy, even though her own loyalty and performance were beyond reproach.[14]

New Frontiers

The navy's manpower crisis propelled some yeomen (F) into jobs generally considered unsuitable for women to do, if not impossible. At munitions factories in Newport, Rhode Island, and Bloomfield, New Jersey, navy and civilian women assembled and filled torpedo primers. At first some of their supervisors judged them as "more timid and less aggressive than male workers" but admitted that they "took up the work rapidly." By the end of the war, their productivity surpassed all expectations. Secretary Daniels reported that, prior to the women's employment, 175 men were producing five thousand primers a week, but in July 1918, 340 women made fifty-five thousand a week. The work was arduous and called for deftness and a willingness to get dirty. One woman with grimy hands told a visitor she'd always wanted enough money to buy fine clothes. Now for the first time she was earning enough money to do that, "and here I am dressed in overalls!"[15]

In Norfolk, Virginia, a notice appeared in the local newspaper that women were wanted to drive light trucks at the Norfolk Naval Base—surprising, since most women did not even drive cars in 1918. This assignment involved delivering stores to the dozens of ships berthed there.[16] One driver later told a reporter that the stores could range from

> ... a box of pins to a huge anchor which had to be loaded by crane. Naturally, this work was often attended by great difficulties, especially in stormy winter weather. Many times I have had to help load [the] truck with my own hands, to say nothing of helping to dig it out of the mud when it was stuck with a couple of tons of brick or anchor aboard. From the first trip at 7 o'clock ... until the whistle blew at 5 o'clock, it was a constant rush, not even taking time for lunch. ... [I]t was my policy to "vamp" the ship's cook, and many a nice fat sandwich or steaming cup of coffee, caught on the fly, was my reward when making the rounds ... on a cold, lunchless day.
>
> One day I was horrified to find that in boarding a certain ship the only gangway was a huge rope, with a small line for a hand rail, stretched from the deck of one big ship to the one I had to board. A group of officers was standing on the quarterdeck politely waiting to see a woman lose her nerve. I determined, for the sake of all women in the service, that they should be disappointed, so casting one despairing look at the black water way down between the two hulls, I sauntered airily at that blessed rope as though my hair was not standing on end and my knees knocking with fright.[17]

Navy officials so admired the drivers' work that they again advertised in local papers, inviting more women to enlist specifically to drive trucks. "The girls who enlisted ... said that they were not actuated by selfish motives. They simply wanted to show that they can handle a motor car or motor truck [as well as] any chauffeur who ever shifted a gear." At the Norfolk Navy Yard, four yeomen (F) worked at the supply warehouse, filling ships' orders for small parts and hardware.[18]

Yeomen (F) also recruited for the navy, many of them very successfully. Loretta Walsh, for example, thanks in part to the extensive publicity given her enrollment and thanks even more to her own effervescent charm, was a particularly effective recruiter, credited with spurring enlistments of both men and women. Yeoman (F) Irma Alloway is reported to have enrolled more than seventeen hundred men in New York. Another woman in New York was credited with recruiting more than ten thousand men for the army and navy; the American Patriotic Society awarded her a gold medal.[19]

Recruiting stations sometimes were located in undesirable city neighborhoods, exposing the women to some risk when they had to work late. A senior recruiting officer praised highly the courage of Chief Yeoman (F) Margaret Thomas. Often she had to work past midnight at the recruiting office, then pass through an unsavory section of the city. "She would then strap a revolver on under her cloak and go home alone through this thug-infested section, refusing to accept an escort, as they were too much needed to carry on the work, which sometimes ran all through the night. . . . [I]t would take the highest kind of courage for a man to do this. . . . We were always ready for an emergency call to the police until we received her call back that she had arrived in safety."[20]

While Chief Yeoman (F) Loretta Walsh had set the style for recruiting, many more Philadelphia women followed her into this work. One night the recruiting officer at Philadelphia got "a hurry call . . . from Cape May and Wildwood, New Jersey, that they must have some assistance for recruiting as the men were not enlisting in the necessary numbers to [man] the sub-chasers that were needed for . . . patrol." He hastily rounded up another officer and two newly enlisted women, then set out on a drive at speeds that were as high as eighty miles per hour. The officers coached the women on how to address—evidently very effectively—the audience waiting for them in a local theater. "They made such an appeal that they filled the recruiting station that night and for days following. . . . [W]hen they got through telling those men that *they* had enlisted . . . they convinced every able bodied man that he was needed." Other women traveled all over their large assigned areas, recruiting in the wide open spaces of Oregon and Washington.[21]

At the Thirteenth Naval District's headquarters in Seattle, Washington, recruiters also looked outside traditional fields to find as many women as possible with whom it could replace men. The commandant's medical aide reported to the Bureau of Medicine and Surgery that they now had on board a "capable and practical pharmacist," whom they had rated a yeoman second class, and also desired to enroll Dr. Estella Warner (the bacteriologist mentioned in chapter 2) to take over the district's bacteriological laboratory. "Eventually these young women will have to qualify for promotion and confirmation," wrote the aide, "but in view of their particular training it will be necessary to waive a part of the examination, namely, stenography and typing."[22]

By spring of 1918, the Navy's Bureau of Construction and Repairs urgently needed women reservists to keep up with its ever-swelling needs for camouflage and drafting. It asked permission to enroll ten yeomen (F), all of them rated as first, second, or third class. A Washington, D.C., newspaper featured an article about this bureau, including a picture of a yeoman (F) cutting out on a jigsaw parts of model vessels that were used to study convoy movements.[23]

The Naval Act of 1916 provided that in time of war some components of the Lighthouse Service (at that time under the Department of Commerce) would be transferred to the navy. When the navy actually took over many of the lighthouses and lightships, it enrolled their keepers, including some women. In addition, at some lighthouses then being used as naval guard stations, yeomen (F) were assigned to take over clerical duties; sometimes the woman assigned was the only woman there. Not all of the navy women assigned were clerks. For example, Rose Lowther and Mary Wakefield were both enrolled as ship's cook fourth class to provide meals for the naval lookouts at, respectively, a lighthouse in Provincetown, Massachusetts, and at the Goat Island Lighthouse in Cape Porpoise, Maine.

Women in the U.S. Coast Guard

Not every woman who served along the nation's coastlines was officially enrolled in the Naval Reserve. Women in the Lighthouse Service for generations had gained respect for their skill and bravery. Lighthouse keeping was often a family affair; mothers, daughters, and sisters frequently joined their menfolk in keeping the lamps operating and rescuing unfortunate seamen. Thus, many women who spent the war literally watching the coastlines had been bred to their lonely tasks at remote headlands and promontories.

One prominent example was the lighthouse at Robbins Reef, one mile off Staten Island at the mouth of New York's great harbor. It was so dismal that many male keepers turned down the post after Jake Walker died in 1886. Kate

Walker, his widow, carried on so competently that President Benjamin Harrison appointed her head keeper in 1890. Her home was a forty-six-foot iron tower with five round rooms arranged one above the other, its front steps consisting only of the ladder that led to the water. There she raised her two children, rowing them back and forth to school on Staten Island. She slept little, especially in winter, for fear of letting the light go out. Keeping the light was a very strenuous matter. The wicks of the huge, oil-burning lamps had to be kept trimmed, and the machines that pumped oil to the lamps had to be rewound every five hours.

> I never really lose myself but keep my mind always on the light and the people out there who must have it. If I doze for a second, I always hear cries. They are the cries of little children who are being shipwrecked because I let the light go out.

When America entered the war in 1917, Walker was almost seventy and had spent half her life on Robbins Reef. She served throughout the war, retiring in 1919 to a farm on Staten Island.[24] In 1921, the secretary of commerce wrote to the secretary of the navy requesting that members of the Lighthouse Service who had served at least six months during wartime be awarded the Victory Medal. The medal was awarded to at least three women in addition to Walker.[25]

Genevieve and Dorothy Baker, nineteen-year-old twins from Brooklyn, New York, were the first uniformed women in the Coast Guard. Their two brothers were already serving as soldiers in France, and the twins, accomplished bookkeepers, had become yeomen (F). When the Coast Guard came under the navy's jurisdiction, they transferred. The Coast Guard's records of World War I mention yeomen (F) hardly at all, but it nonetheless reports that a "handful" served at Coast Guard headquarters in Washington, D.C.[26]

Overseas

More than forty yeomen (F) served outside the continental United States. The single largest group consisted of over thirty who served in the Territory of Hawaii. Most were already residents there, including several Chinese and native Hawaiian women. Some worked at the naval station at Pearl Harbor, others at the cable censor's office or the Fourteenth Naval District headquarters in Honolulu. Nearly all of them were designated as yeomen, but two are listed as electricians. At Pearl Harbor, where crews of German ships had chosen to sink their own vessels rather than surrendering them to the U.S. Navy, Virginia Sanborn was entrusted with typing and forwarding the translated secret records and other data that navy divers had salvaged.[27]

Officials in the Fourteenth Naval District evidently had no qualms about transferring women, for one woman who enlisted there did some notable traveling, courtesy of the U.S. Navy. Mabel Johnson enlisted in April 1917 and in June was transferred to Guam, where she was the only yeoman (F). While she was there, she later reported, crew members from a German ship that had approached the naval station came ashore and raided its storehouse. They escaped notice because all the navy personnel were on the other side of the island for target practice. In October she was transferred to the submarine base in San Pedro, California, was discharged there, and returned to her home in Hawaii.[28]

One woman is known to have served briefly in Puerto Rico and the Virgin Islands. Honora Kenney Henry was enrolled as a chief yeoman in April 1918 in New York and then served at the navy yard in Washington, D.C. A few months later she was ordered to San Juan and from there to St. Thomas, returning to Washington in mid-December. This chronology suggests, first, that she had considerable ability and experience to have been rated as a chief upon enlistment and, second, was sent to help out with some difficulty or shortage arising at these Caribbean facilities.

Almost twelve hundred miles to the southwest lies what was called the Panama Canal Zone, where six yeomen (F) are known to have served. Five of them enlisted there, four of whom remained after being released from active duty. They may be presumed to have been Canal Zone residents. The sixth woman enlisted in New Orleans, served in the Zone, then returned to New Orleans upon discharge.[29]

These women, transferring from one location to another, must have made these journeys by ship, most likely a navy vessel. Although the war of 1914–18 centered in the European theater, it was also fought elsewhere, for example, by

German raiders in the Pacific. Once the United States entered the war, any of its ships could become enemy targets, especially on the high seas, including the Caribbean.

The yeomen (F) who served in France and England of course faced the same hazards as they embarked on navy transports to cross the North Atlantic in 1917 and 1918. Those known to have returned to the United States did so after the armistice. Six women are known to have served in London or at one of several sites in France.

Chief Yeomen Winifred Gibbon of New York, a private secretary, and Edith Barron of Philadelphia, a dietitian, were the first enlisted women to serve in France. When the United States entered the war, each was working for a surgeon. Both surgeons joined a reserve medical unit being organized in Philadelphia, and their entire staffs enlisted with them. Civilians and American Red Cross chapters in both cities, as well as in Baltimore and Washington, D.C., contributed equipment and supplies. The units sailed for France in the summer of 1917 aboard USS *Henderson*. They arrived in September and were assigned to different base hospitals, Gibbon to Paris and Barron to Brest. Both were subsequently promoted to chief and returned to the United States on board USS *Agamemnon* within weeks after the armistice.[30]

The navy's base hospital enterprise was large and far-flung, stretching from the British Isles across France and down to Corfu and Genoa. It eventually included almost thirty-five hundred beds in France and Britain alone, plus temporary accommodations for another four hundred. As the tides of casualties ebbed and flowed, recovered or died or were returned home, the numbers of beds in various subsidiary hospitals shrank or expanded. The base hospital at Brest was the flagship of the system, with an average patient load of four hundred. When the flu struck in 1918, that number doubled (see chapter 8).

Brest was where the bulk of American troops disembarked and from which thousands of wounded were sent home. It distributed medical and surgical stores throughout the system and treated the sick and wounded from navy ships in the North Atlantic, the Bay of Biscay, and the English Channel, in addition to the survivors of attacks on merchant shipping. When Barron's unit arrived in Brest, they began to convert a partly unoccupied Carmelite nunnery, several centuries old, into a staff quarters and a hospital. The remaining sisters resisted being ousted, but "yielded after a nine-day legal squabble"; unit members cleaned up "in twelve hours its centuries of filth."[31]

Mary Buchanan Davis enlisted as a chief yeoman in April 1918 in Paris and served at the U.S. Naval Headquarters there, at the time the only yeoman (F) present. In September she was transferred to London, where she was discharged in December. That same month, Yeoman (F) Second Class Fern Oliver, who enlisted in July 1918 in Philadelphia, was transferred to Paris from London.[32]

Pauline Bourneuf enlisted in Boston and was sent to serve at a navy base hospital in France. She spoke fluent French and had a reputation for good judgment and tact. Her linguistic ability very likely accounts for her being assigned to the group of telephone operators under the supervision of the U.S. Army's Signal Corps. Popularly known as the "Hello Girls," these 233 women were selected because they spoke French.[33]

The names of five other yeomen (F) who are said to have served in Europe have been reported: Helen Cope in Naval Hospital 11, first in Scotland, then France; Glenn Clairmonte Gerbaulet, Paris and Brest; Ethel Gulling, "somewhere in France"; Florence Hooe, naval attaché's office in Paris; Margaret Mullady, naval attaché's office in London. However, the wartime muster rolls of those places, which are incomplete, do not show these names (see note 27).

Women Marines

Most of the women marines served at Marine Corps headquarters in Washington as clerks, typists, and stenographers, but not all of them had routine jobs. Several handled all the correspondence associated with casualties. At age eighteen, Violet Van Wagner was transferring "the details of injury or death onto the men's military records," then composing letters for the commandant's signature. Pearl Chandley recalled, "It was not a fun job. We instinctively developed a flair for words in such cases, and shared with the loved ones their grief, and also the pride of sacrifices made for our country." Jane Van Edsingna took over a desk in the medals and decorations branch, where she often stayed late into the evening on behalf of men who were receiving the Medal of Honor, waiting for long-distance calls to go through, arranging transportation and hotel reservations for the men and their families, and coordinating plans for the award ceremonies with the White House. One woman was assigned to the motor transport pool.[34]

At least two women were assigned to public relations. Private Martha Wilchinski was a writer and publicist. In one series of many photographs taken aboard the USS *Arizona,* berthed at the North River pier in New York City, she is shown saluting one of the ship's officers and going through various daily routines, such as drill, with male marines stationed aboard. The other publicist was Lela Leibrand, a former writer of screenplays, who claimed she had been transferred to the public relations department because she was such an inept clerk (perhaps purposefully so).

It soon became evident that Private Leibrand, like Wilchinski, knew how to garner publicity for the corps. She persuaded two aviators at the Quantico Marine Base to take her up in a marine hydroplane and then wrote an enraptured account of the experience. She also had her picture taken, belted into a leather coat, standing on the wing of the plane after her flight. Leibrand was more than a daredevil. Her experience in the film industry led to her editing marine training films. Her toughest assignment was editing film sent from the European front. Working under armed guards at the Smithsonian Institution, sometimes for eighteen to twenty hours at a time, she developed, dried, and edited "the bloodiest footage in the world."[35]

Other women served throughout the country as Marine Corps recruiters. Cpl. Florence Levi, for example, was the first woman marine in the West, enrolling at San Francisco in September 1918. She traveled extensively, recruiting in both Missoula, Montana, and Spokane, Washington. In Indianapolis, the Marine Corps enrolled Minnie Arthur as a sergeant and flew her from city to city all over the state to recruit. She was the first woman in Indiana to fly.[36] Another recruiter, Elizabeth Bertram, already knew how to shoot a rifle when she enrolled in the marines. When she learned that qualifying on the rifle range would raise her pay, she asked for a tryout. Highly skeptical, her major grudgingly allowed her to demonstrate her ability at a local police range. On a cold, rainy, windy day, with kibitzers snickering in the background, she

> did all right on the standing positions, fairly well on kneeling and sitting, and managed a few good shots prone; but every time I tried rapid fire the result was a disaster. I stuck it out for the full course but my shoulder was pounded into jelly ... my hair was stringing down from under my dripping

cap, my clothes were plastered with mud and even my face was dirty. The major sent me home in a closed car without comment. The next day, with . . . bruises spreading over my shoulder, arm and even on my chest, I was summoned to The Presence. "You seem to have qualified unofficially . . . and will be included in the next class at the official range. . . . In the meantime you may wear this," and he pinned his own engraved marksman medal on my blouse. I intended to execute a smart salute; but when I tried to raise my right arm I involuntarily yelled "Ouch!" instead, and ran to my desk in an agony of fear and shame. . . . Major Guggenheim, the strict disciplinarian, he of the hair-trigger temper and the blistering vocabulary, shot one glance at the astonished and apprehensive faces around him, and saved the day with a burst of hearty laughter.[37]

Even the statuesque actress Lillian Russell was called into service. At a theater one night, she was made an honorary sergeant to publicize recruiting. Maj. Ruth Cheney Streeter, director of the USMC Women's Reserve in World War II, later wrote that Russell "really packed them in."[38]

While originally enlisted to replace men performing clerical duties, many yeomen (F) were immediately placed in various kinds of nonclerical assignments that neither they nor the services had ever envisioned as being done by women. But the navy needed to have the jobs done, needed to have them done right, and needed them to be done right away.

Like the U.S. Navy, the Marine Corps originally envisioned its enlisted women only as clerks, and a far larger percentage of marine women did work in offices. But it, too, assigned a few women with special abilities to certain important tasks.

FIVE

Navy and Marine Corps Policies for Women

Cannot deal with women as with men.

Josephus Daniels in his diary, 1917

WHEN DANIELS DECIDED TO ENROLL women, navy officials had no time to think about what, if any, special policies and regulations that decision might require. The U.S. Navy's only policy toward women applicants was to follow normal procedures as closely as possible and get the women on the job *now*. Moreover, nearly everyone believed that the war would be over in six months, maybe sooner. If a woman met the normal navy standards for health, character, and ability to perform a job, sign her up. Whether she was single or divorced or married or had children or any other dependents was her business, not the navy's. Why waste time figuring out policies that would not be needed, answering questions that would never be asked?

Nonetheless, official responses to the women enlistees—policy, if you will —appeared very quickly.

Administrative Policies

The navy's first corporate contact with individual women occurred during the enrollment process. Since each naval district had considerable autonomy, each met the oncoming wave of women as best it could, ad hoc, with resulting variations that the navy could not tolerate for long. Immediately obvious, for example, was the question of uniforms. Other things were simply assumed. For example, the navy could not let its physicians examine prospective yeomen (F) without providing some guidance, as noted in chapter 1. Six months passed, and the war was not yet won; then more months went by, with more women serving. As experience grew, questions arose that had to be settled at some higher level than the local unit. Hence, policy accrued.

Assignments

The navy never had any intention of assigning women to ships—although many women yearned to serve at sea. But early on, some administrative confusion arose. Former Yeoman (F) Binnie Avalon, for example, later told how she had reported, as ordered, to a ship, bringing with her a complete set of uniforms. She ascribed the mistake to someone assuming from her first name that she was a man. The orders were quickly changed but not because she objected; rather, she wrote, "Almost took an act of Congress to keep me from going on that boat." The same thing happened to Joy Bright and probably to others.

The heart of the problem was that the navy had never before needed to signify on its rolls that some yeomen were women. Subsequently, navy rolls showed women yeomen as "Yeomen (F)." This nomenclature led to a new confusion: If spoken quickly or indistinctly, it was often heard as "Yeomanette," which seemed appropriate to some and was used by those who knew neither the proper term nor its origin. Secretary Daniels was outspoken: "I never did like this 'ette' business . . . if a woman does a job she ought to have the name of the job, so we put in parentheses (F)."[1] Immediately the navy changed its ways, and thereafter all women yeomen were identified as yeomen (F) (except for the very few rated as electricians).

The paymaster of the navy, Rear Adm. Samuel McGowan, also minced no words: "They must not be called yeowomen or yeomanettes. These women are as much a part of the Navy as the men who have enlisted. They do the same work and receive the same pay as men of the same rating. They are yeomen and have done yeoman service in the immensely increased work imposed upon the Navy by the war."[2]

It seems fitting that it was the paymaster who emphasized another assumption, one not commonly held at the time, namely, that women doing the same work as men and holding the same positions would receive the same pay.

When the pay director of the First Naval District (headquartered in Boston) learned of the enrollment of Rose Lowther as a cook, he objected to paying her as a navy member. He said he didn't see why the legislation covered women cooks "any more than it would a woman bandmaster or blacksmith." Secretary Daniels found that argument of no relevance and replied that Lowther was legally enrolled in the Naval Reserve and should get "the same pay and allowances as provided for that rating under exactly the same conditions as women enrolled . . . as yeomen."[3]

Marriage, Children, and Dependents

On the subject of a woman's domestic arrangements, the navy decided to have no policy. It did not exclude women with young children, as it did later (1942–74), nor did it help them with any arrangements for child care, as it does currently. If a woman had to leave her husband or ask others to look after her children while she was serving elsewhere, that was her business. The result was a number of yeomen (F) and women marines who left children in the care of others. When Elizabeth Bacon Heterick, for example, left home each morning for her duties at the Navy Department, neighbors and another son, an adult living nearby, looked after her six-year-old son until she returned. Years later, the younger son referred to himself as one of the original "latch-key children." When Lela Leibrand became a marine, she sent her six-year-old daughter back to Kansas to live with her grandmother. Sometimes a yeoman (F) would ask for leave in order to be with a sick child. One woman asked, for example, for six days of leave, "as I have been offered a sea-trip . . . and . . . feel that my young daughter's health would be greatly benefited."

Some women even asked to be disenrolled in order to take care of their children. Lola Williams Duncan, for example, asked for release from active duty because her nine-year-old daughter was leaving school and would need her care. The records reveal very few such requests, and nearly all appear to have been granted.[4]

Accounts of romances and subsequent marriages appear frequently in records and memoirs. One woman who was beginning to realize how thoroughly the navy could regulate her life married her fiancé as soon as he returned from Europe. She didn't know if the navy would let her get married, so "I didn't ask," and she kept the marriage secret until she was released from active duty six months later. Others were less reticent. One woman proudly told her children that she had been married in uniform; both she and the groom had three-day passes. Another woman officially asked for two weeks of leave, which was granted but somewhat grumpily: Her commanding officer agreed that her reason for being absent "should be given every favorable consideration." Nonetheless, he said, "the Bureau of Medicine and Surgery can ill afford to lose (her) services" and requested "a relief be furnished." In another case, all hands celebrated at the wedding of a yeoman (F) to the public works officer of the station to which they were both assigned.[5]

Having enrolled married women and allowed yeomen (F) to marry, the navy next had to determine what to do about women who became pregnant while on active duty. Navy officials kept no records of how many yeomen (F) became pregnant, but by the summer of 1918 some cases had occurred, and the navy had determined that the best course was to discharge pregnant women. The naval district commandants were directed to note on each pregnant woman's discharge papers whether or not they recommended her for re-enrollment.[6] Although her return to active duty would have seemed quite unlikely, a recommendation for re-enrollment confirmed that her performance while in service had been satisfactory. Nonetheless, a pregnant yeoman (F) could still pose an administrative challenge, as recalled by a former medical officer:

> He said, "There's a yeomanette coming in with the mumps, and we don't have any place here to take care of her. Can you help out?" . . .[W]hen she came into the hospital she was transported to my camp. . . . In the meantime I'd cleared out the brig and fixed it up. We had Navy nurses there to help us, so we made a pretty nice room for her. A couple of weeks went by, and she got along fine. One day one of the doctors . . . said, "We're going to have to change the diagnosis . . . she's pregnant."
>
> Well, in those days, whenever you made a diagnosis, you always had to put under origin whether the malady had been incurred in the line of duty. . . . Being good old Marines and Navy men, we decided "line of duty," and that's how her records read. For the good of the cause.[7]

Survivor Benefits

There are two aspects to military survivor benefits: how much and to whom. In 1912 Congress guaranteed to the designated beneficiary of any officer or enlisted person killed in the line of duty a gratuity amounting to six months of the deceased's pay. The gratuity could be paid to the deceased's "widow, and if no widow, and if there be no children, to any other dependent." This wording precluded the husband of a yeomen (F) (or a nurse) from being a beneficiary: He certainly would not be a widow, and just as certainly the law assumed that he would not *depend* on his wife financially.

A case in point: When Chief Yeoman (F) May Turner died in June 1917, she was survived by her husband and her widowed mother. The latter, who had been her daughter's dependent, wrote to the navy asking for the death gratuity. The navy asked for a ruling from its judge advocate general (JAG). He ruled that the husband could not receive the gratuity because he was not a widow, and it went instead to Turner's mother.[8] At most, she received a few hundred dollars.

Then, in October 1917, the U.S. government offered to all reservists, male and female, an opportunity to buy war risk insurance, which insured the purchaser against permanent total disability and death. The premiums were set at normal peacetime rates, with the government bearing the extra wartime costs; the insured required no medical examination and could choose to continue the insurance after leaving the service. The Bureau of Navigation strongly urged all reservists to apply for "not less than $4,500 and for as much larger amounts as possible."[9] This legislation pointedly rescinded the 1912 law. Had Turner been able to take out war risk insurance, she would have been able to leave as much as ten times the amount that she did.

Transfers and Promotions

Women were routinely transferred from one duty station to another within the same naval district and could be transferred from one district to another if they had agreed to that upon enrolling. However, the transferring office had to agree that the woman's services could be spared or that a satisfactory replacement could be found. Occasionally a commanding officer would ask permission to

transfer one or more women because their work was unsatisfactory: Let someone else deal with them. Sometimes women sought transfer for personal or
family reasons.

For example, one woman finally asked to be transferred "*anywhere* out of
Washington, D.C." after her three requests to be transferred overseas received
ambiguous replies. Her boss forwarded her letter with his own request that
she be given a *definite* answer, saying that the replies she had received so far
kept alive the idea that she might be sent overseas. Another woman asked to
transfer to "some branch of the Navy Department" located in Chicago because
her brother had died and she was her mother's only family.[10] The navy's pre-
vailing principle seemed to be that its own needs must be considered first, but
compassion for genuine hardships related to family or to health was also wise.
In short, it would consider reasonable requests favorably, but it did not want to
provide a yeoman (F)—or anyone else, for that matter—the means to relocate
at whim.

As in any bureaucracy, both pitfalls and opportunities abounded, as Yeoman (F) Rose Volkman's story illustrates. She enlisted in Honolulu in 1917 and
initially served at the Pearl Harbor Naval Station. When she was discharged in
1919 and asked for funds to travel from her duty station in New York back to
Honolulu, the Bureau of Navigation asked her commanding officer how she
had gotten to New York in the first place. It was all quite simple, she later wrote
to a friend:

> I was granted leave to visit the United States shortly after my husband was
> transferred to the New York Navy Yard. I was instructed by my boss Com-
> modore D. H. Mahan USN, Senior Officer at the 14th Naval District to
> report to Captain Graham at the [New York] Cable Censor's office for duty.
> Commodore Mahan then had my papers transferred. Period.[11]

The bureau also granted transfers to women requesting further schooling, like Yeoman (F) Helen Douglas, who found bookkeeping at the navy yard
"a little boring so I asked around for something else to do . . . [A] class for
radio operators [was] starting on the West Coast, so I asked to be transferred
to enter. I had just gotten my orders when the war ended and the classes were
canceled, I was so disappointed."[12]

The Marine Corps had little occasion to transfer any of its women marines from their initial assignments at its headquarters in Washington, D.C. One exception was Sergeant Martha Wilchinski, a graduate of New York University and a professional publicist. One of the first few women to enlist in the Marine Corps, she was transferred from Washington to the city of New York, then later to San Francisco.[13]

The matter of promotion for yeomen (F) was snarled from the beginning because local recruiting officers variously interpreted the general directive to enroll women. Different women, equally proficient, might be enrolled in quite different rates: One as a chief, another as a yeoman second class, yet another as a yeoman third class. The commandant of each district had to consider how many men, in what positions, he needed to replace, then see how many women, with what skills, might enlist. Since the navy yeoman's clerical duties and level of proficiency were similar to that of many civil service clerks, some districts accepted passing grades in the appropriate examination as evidence of proficiency. There is no way to tell how many of the yeomen (F) were over- or under-rated to begin with.

Notwithstanding these anomalies, the navy just absorbed the women into its promotion procedures for men, sometimes making special adjustments as needed. For example, men were nearly always promoted one rate at a time. However, navy records show one woman being moved up two rates at once, and another woman, three rates. These two women had probably been markedly underrated upon enrollment.[14]

Each district held quarterly examinations for enlisted men and women eligible to advance to the next rate. Eligibility to take the examination included proficiency, length of time in present rate, and a superior officer's recommendation, which was often a deciding factor. One man took up the cause of a yeoman (F) third class who was not promoted when she failed the examination. He noted that she had had nine years of previous experience and her work was very satisfactory: "Please reconsider." The navy waived one requirement for yeomen (F): They need not have a certain amount of sea duty to be eligible for promotion, as enlisted men did. Also, men were required to take training classes in the duties of their rating, but some districts excused women; however, if a woman requested training, she was obliged to attend class regularly. In at least one district, the classes met at seven o'clock PM two or three times a week for three months, which meant long days for the students.[15]

Discipline

With very few exceptions, the yeomen (F) behaved in exemplary fashion. The navy emphasized to them that it would take the same dim view of their infractions as it did of men's. Yet it had to accommodate the differences between the men and the women without appearing to favor the women to a degree that might cause resentment among the men. For example, partly to enhance the women's morale, the navy did not require them to wear uniform off duty, a privilege not granted to navy men in wartime. Discipline regarding the marine women had to take the opposite tack: They were so proud of their uniforms that they could hardly be persuaded to wear anything else.

Nearly all of the cases in which yeomen (F) were disciplined occurred over minor matters. Many women simply had no idea that the navy had a standard procedure for nearly every situation and that failure to follow the proper procedure was an infraction.[16] For one example, many yeomen (F) did not realize that they needed permission to be excused from work for any reason. Moreover, some had trouble distinguishing between "leave" and "liberty." Liberty was any absence under forty-eight hours, including Sundays and holidays, and was generally comparable to hours that civilians would recognize as outside of working hours; that is, evenings and weekends. Full allowances for subsistence were paid for liberty days. Liberty could be granted by a department head. Leave, on the other hand, could be granted only by the commanding officer and had to be applied for ahead of time, except in emergencies verified by the American Red Cross. Every navy member, from seaman to admiral, had thirty days' paid leave each year, plus sick leave for as long as needed if verified by a navy doctor.

Women new to the navy sometimes took time off for good reasons but failed to notify their supervisors and ask permission; they were, technically, Absent Over Leave (AOL). Such an infraction could not be overlooked, but most navy supervisors realized that the yeomen (F) had received no indoctrination or recruit training, and therefore an explanation and a reprimand solved most problems. For example, former Yeoman (F) Joy Bright Hancock once was three hours late, earning herself a reprimand. Nonetheless she ended her World War I service as a chief yeoman, was commissioned in 1942, and retired in 1953 as a navy captain.[17]

The time came when a woman could no longer claim ignorance of the law, as shown by the case of the yeoman (F) who complained when she and her command differed over the amount of liberty she actually took. She said she had asked only for Saturday and Monday off, but her boss pointed out that, in such cases, all personnel had been instructed that the intervening Sunday would also be considered a day off as well. When payday came, the subsistence pay (approximately two dollars a day) for days of extra liberty would be subtracted from the monthly total. She had in fact had three days of liberty, said her command, not just the Saturday and Monday she had asked for. Since the incident happened in mid-1919, and she was a yeoman (F) second class, her case was weak. Moreover, the Bureau of Navigation was still undermanned, with just as much work to do as during the war, but with 50 percent fewer workers. It could not afford, it argued in this case, to "grant liberty promiscuously." A day here or a day there might seem of little consequence, but they did add up.

In quite a different vein, Yeoman (F) Louise McKenna could claim that her discipline situation was peculiarly onerous. Only three months past her fifteenth birthday when she enlisted, she was accepted by the navy because her mother enlisted with her and they both worked at the censor's office in New York. Her mother became the office's master-at-arms and more than once had to bring her daughter before the officer of the day on charges of lateness.[18]

Some women's transgressions were not so minor. One navy doctor put it very bluntly to a civil service supervisor inquiring about a former yeoman (F): "As her work was not entirely satisfactory for various reasons, one of them being that she was indiscreet and allowed office matters to become known to outsiders for which she had been reported by various officers to the Commanding Officer, she was considered undesirable to fill the important position which was open in this office."[19]

One yeoman (F) was found to have knowingly affirmed that another yeoman (F) was present at her desk when the latter was in fact absent. Both were found guilty and fined. In another case, a yeoman (F) serving in France received a special court-martial (like a general court-martial, before a panel of judges) for "refusing duty"; the court declared that she was to be discharged immediately with a bad conduct discharge. Both her commanding officer and the senior officer in the area approved the sentence in June 1918.[20]

Serious as these charges were, the Navy Department may have overturned the verdicts and sentences. Secretary Daniels had already overruled the decision of a court-martial to demote a yeoman (F). He wrote to her commanding officer that he considered it "inadvisable to try female yeomen by court-martial, as in contravention to public policy." He understood that the public, regardless of any case's merits, might strongly protest punishment of a woman. To his diary he confided, "Cannot deal with women as with men."[21]

The decision not to subject women to military courts was evidently a good one, for no one protested (as undoubtedly they would today) that the navy was discriminating against men. Reprimands, small pay forfeitures, and restrictions were one thing, actual punishment another. However, the public could accept disenrollment as the military equivalent of being dismissed from a job, which might occur for reasons of family need, or health, or no further requirement for her services. It did not necessarily mean that she had been fired, although that might be the case.

Soon the districts were asking the Bureau of Navigation for advice about the few women who were not serving well, lacking ability or industry or amenability or some combination thereof. If they were not to be tried in a court-martial, should these women be disenrolled? Each district could dismiss up to 1 percent of its personnel for undesirability; now they wanted to know if they could apply this policy to women as well as to men. The bureau advised that, if a woman was no longer needed, the district should try to find another job for her so as to meet the overarching need to release men for sea duty. If she proved to have no aptitude for her work, the district should release her with an ordinary discharge and keep the bureau informed. The bureau warned the commandants not to release women just so they could get better jobs elsewhere *unless* they could be spared "without the necessity of obtaining reliefs for them."[22]

At least two women caused enough trouble to earn full investigations by the Office of Naval Intelligence (ONI). One of them apparently had a gift for causing controversy and contention. Allegations against her included unjustly treating 225 men under her immediate orders in planning and executing a Navy Relief Drive; using abusive language to thirteen men she was supervising; stealing money; and spending weekends and overnights with various men. The district commandant judged her "temperamentally unfit" for service, her head "turned with too much authority." Her congressman defended her, pointing out her patriotism and an "excellent reputation" that caused her supervisor to choose her for extra duties, although he had also been harsh and hostile toward her solely on the basis of "secret reports." She made numerous countercharges when she was discharged, claiming that she was a victim of gossip because she had refused to go along with the misconduct of a group of yeomen (F). She added that newspaper editors were begging her to tell her story. The commandant concluded, in a letter to Daniels, that the grounds for formally charging her with anything specific were insufficient, but she should be discharged for the good of the service.[23]

The evidence against the other woman was far stronger. Various sources and documents showed that many statements she had made in her application to join the navy were untrue; that she had fabricated events and relationships; that she had written to an imprisoned convict asking him to lie and withhold information from an investigator who was coming to question him; and that the one person who defended her was the beneficiary of her war risk insurance. The ONI investigator listed her faults as "verbose egotism, mendacity and unfailing confidence in the ability of her friends to exercise pull in her favor." The director of the ONI concluded that she was "thoroughly unreliable . . . and her character . . . is such as to leave her open to very serious criticism. . . . [S]he is not worthy of further retention in the Naval Service."[24]

When the Marine Corps began enrolling women in August 1918, headquarters instructed recruiters to explain to all women applicants that they would be subject to the same regulations and rules as men and that they could be dismissed if their services or behavior were unsatisfactory.[25] That turned out to be not quite so; a turn at KP (short for kitchen police, a broad term that included any kind of housecleaning) was much more usual, especially after the Marine Corps officers and noncommissioned officers found out how well it worked on women. One former woman marine recalled that only two weeks after enlistment,

[A] typical hard-boiled sergeant who just loved to do it, ordered us to sweep the floors and wash the windows in our office. Two pretty girls, from wealthy families, rushed to Col. McLemore's office and said they would not undertake such labor. He was very angry with them, reminding them that they had enlisted, that they couldn't change their minds about their duties. He ordered them to wash those windows and they did it. It was wonderful discipline for young girls and we came to love the Marine Corps better than anything in life.[26]

Another new woman marine, innocent about the marines' strict views on punctuality, wired to her boss from her home in New Jersey that she would return from furlough (equivalent to leave) three days later than planned and sent him her regards. As soon as she returned to headquarters, she was ordered to his office and told she had been Absent Without Leave (AWOL). Later she learned that this breach of discipline cost her a promotion, but first she was surprised to find that it made her something of a celebrity:

"There was a crowd of enlisted men waiting to congratulate me; the Marine Corps newspaper published the shameful story and I got letters from Marines all over the world, including China, telling me not to worry, and saying, 'Now you are a real Marine' . . . [but] I never became a sergeant."[27]

In March 1919 (possibly because it was the first spring after the armistice), General Barnett, the Marine Corps commandant, himself had to call the conduct of enlisted personnel to the attention of the USMC's adjutant and inspector, its paymaster, and its quartermaster: "Enlisted men and women on duty at these Headquarters have been observed skylarking together on the streets, and not infrequently have been observed walking arm in arm . . . . [S]uch practices must cease and . . . they must conduct themselves at all times in a dignified and soldierly manner."[28]

The general may have had a little more success with this campaign for marine law and order than he had enforcing the ban on the Sam Browne belts, but probably not much. The women seem almost to have taken pride in their brushes with marine discipline. One later told a reporter, "We have drilled, we

have saluted, we have been officially recognized and we have done K.P. . . .
Now that the war is over . . . we admit that some of us have had court martials.
We were certainly real Marines."[29]

Recreation

From pure necessity, the armed services are accustomed to incorporating sports
and other recreational activities into their regimens. Dances, outings, and competitive events help keep spirits high and use energies that might otherwise be
drawn to more pernicious pastimes.

The yeomen (F) and women marines needed recreation and relaxation too,
and many were eager to take part in service-sponsored programs. At various
stations, yeomen (F) organized teams for baseball, bowling, basketball, track,
and swimming. In Boston, the naval district's athletic committee held a women's
swimming meet; events included twenty-five- and fifty-yard dashes, thousand-
yard relays, and fancy diving. At a naval regatta on the Charles River, fifteen
women showed off their rowing skills racing wherries (lightweight rowing boats)
against one another. The women marines at Marine Corps headquarters in
Washington organized a basketball team to play against the Navy Department
yeomen (F) and proudly wore blue turtleneck sweaters emblazoned with
"USMC" in white letters.[30]

Both the yeomen (F) and the women marines enjoyed navy-sponsored
dances. In Boston, the one hosted by the USS *New Jersey* was particularly successful; one reporter noted that the women "showed their efficiency in the
terpsichorean art." In Washington, D.C., trolley lines that ran twelve to fifteen
miles outside the city helped to promote picnics and other local outings. The
Marine Corps organized dances, taking the women by train to the Marine Corps
base at Quantico, Virginia. Colonel and Mrs. McLemore chaperoned the first
group of women marines to attend a dance there, late in November 1918, after
the war ended. The event was a huge success, and weekend dances at the base
thereafter were well attended. *Leatherneck,* a Marine Corps magazine, became
a great cheerleader for the women reservists. It particularly heralded a vaude-
ville show that the women put on at Quantico in January 1919, which was so

well received that it was repeated a year later, even though the women were by then back in civilian life.[31]

To the Beat of a Drum

Parades are colorful and draw crowds. Military parades are particularly attractive; the uniformed troops, heads high, shoulder to shoulder, marching as if they were one body behind a color guard while the drums beat a cadence—that stirs the blood. Why not have our yeomen (F) march? So thought a number of naval district commandants. It might stir up Liberty Bond drives to have those women parading through city streets, reminding the public of how much women were contributing to the war effort. Moreover, victory would bring more parades: it was time to teach the women to drill.

Whether or not a woman learned drill and marched in parades depended on where she was stationed.[32] Commanding officers who just were not interested, or who could not afford to release the women from work, or who had only a few women in their units, bypassed the option. But in and near the large cities of the east and west coasts—Boston, Newport, San Francisco, Seattle, Washington, D.C., Philadelphia, Brooklyn, and New York—the navy trained hundreds of yeomen (F) to drill and parade.

The First Naval District (Boston) claimed to have formed the first such unit and noted in its official history of the World War I years that one hundred of its yeomen (F) took part, proudly watched by Secretary Daniels, the district commandant, and Governor of Massachusetts.

> April 9, 1918 was the first time in the history of the United States that women marched with the armed forces of the government, and as the yeowomen swung along the route of the parade in perfect step at a cadence of one hundred and twenty steps per minute, they were enthusiastically applauded by ... hundreds of thousands. ... [33]

The Puget Sound Navy Yard, just outside Seattle, claimed to have the "only original company of armed women in the U.S .... the pride of the Navy." The commandant of the Thirteenth Naval District, Rear Adm. Robert E. Coontz, was extremely proud of this unit. He had himself and his wife photographed with them and paraded them at every opportunity. He had them ferried to Seattle and sent by train to Spokane for the Washington State Fall Fair, at which they were greeted with great fanfare, including transport by limousine. Much of the credit for the fine showing they made was due to a male chief petty officer named Walker who "spent most of his waking hours conscientiously instructing his ladies in naval customs and courtesy . . . and close order drill which included the manual of arms." The nine-pound rifles were real enough, the same as the men used for drill.

"We did the whole deal—rifles over our shoulders," one former yeoman (F) told a reporter. "But I never fired one. They never gave us any ammunition. If they had, I expect we would have killed each other—and they couldn't spare us."[34]

In Philadelphia, the women could have benefited from the attentions of an earnest chief. Their marine drill sergeants trained them just enough to make a good showing in parades; sometimes their meager training proved an embarrassment. Joy Bright Hancock later wrote,

> We learned hardly more than "forward march," "halt," and the necessity of maintaining straight lines and keeping in step. No instructions were ever given to the effect that we were not to break step for any obstacle, but sometimes there was sharp provocation for changing direction, as for example, the time when we marched behind beautiful, high-spirited horses that had not been housebroken. After a particularly shabby performance, our instructor gave us explicit directions: "You don't kick it, you don't jump over it, you step in it."[35]

Recollections of the women marines in Washington, D.C., drilled by male marines from Quantico, make clear that the drill instructors had no easy time of it. Their students had enthusiasm, but not all had aptitude. One student remembered, "Some got it right away, to others it came harder. . . . We had several drill instructors and they all tore their hair and went crazy. Some even pleaded with us and tried to bribe us to do it better." Another agreed that the men "were perfectionists, even stinkers, but they were good." She was the pivot of her platoon, and one morning she caught her heel in wet earth and could not make the turn: "I got KP for that!" Another woman concluded that the men "were indignant to have been selected to teach drill to women. As a result they showed us no mercy," but another woman thought the instructors were "terribly frustrated . . . because they weren't allowed to swear at us." [36]

While the women marines drilled on the Ellipse in front of the White House mornings, before going to their regular assignments, yeomen (F) drilled there after their regular working hours. In November 1918 the Navy Department began drilling women from all its Washington, D.C., bureaus and offices to march in victory parades. The resulting unit, comprising four companies, was named "the Battalion." Ensign J. P. O'Neill served as the Battalion's commander.[37] The Battalion's keenest distinction was its members' pride in their uniforms. The special patch they wore on their right shoulders, a one-and-three-eighth-inch anchor (red for blue uniforms and blue for white uniforms) signified that distinction, but its substance was their devotion to all uniform regulations.

Not all women were happy to find themselves assigned to the Battalion. Two of them, keeping hidden behind shrubbery, trailed the women reporting to the Ellipse and watched them muster on the first day of drill. Since no one noted their absence, they never did show up for Battalion duty, remaining instead in their office to work.[38] Given their attitude, the Battalion was probably better off without them.

The Navy and Marine Corps initiated no more policy for the women than they had to: a simple and conservative approach that served them well. Josephus Daniels was utterly confident that enrolling the women would turn out well and would require few bureaucratic adjustments. So it proved. The services generally treated the women much as they treated the men. Whenever it was necessary to modify service practice, the U.S. Navy and Marine Corps carefully steered courses that would meet public approval yet remain consistent with their customs and traditions. The services remained "a man's world," and the women adjusted accordingly.

SIX

Fighting a New Enemy

We were winning the war in Europe, but for a few weeks Death
seemed to have put his awful finger on our capital city.

Mrs. Henry F. Butler, former yeoman (F)

WARTIME DEMANDED THAT the Bureau of Medicine and Surgery, responsible for the health care of all navy and marine personnel, not only expand its
existing resources but also modify some of them for women reservists. Then,
suddenly in mid-1918, another enemy appeared and inflicted so much damage
that the bureau had to adopt a drastic change of policy. All too soon the bureau
was stretched past its limits in fighting another war.

Women's Health Care

Throughout the women's service, the Bureau of Medicine and Surgery had to
decide when to treat them the same way it treated men and when to treat them
differently. For example, when the bureau mandated prophylactic injections—
"shots"—against typhoid and cowpox, it reminded the Navy Department that

women were to receive them as well as men.[1] Some dispensaries injected the upper leg rather than the arm, embarrassing a few women.

The standard routine for a navy man who woke up too sick to go to work was to report to "sick bay," the shipboard term for a medical clinic. If the doctor put him on the sick list, he was excused from work without being given liberty or charged for leave. The key decision, of course, was the doctor's, that the man was in fact too sick to work. In cases of minor sickness or small injury, the doctor dispensed some medication or other treatment (hence the other navy term for clinic, "dispensary") and sent the man back to work.

Once they understood the procedure, the yeomen (F) followed it, but two variants developed. The first arose from the fact that many of them lived at home and had family physicians to whom they were likely to turn first; navy doctors would accept a civilian doctor's word that a sick woman should be put on the list. The second variant came with the advent of the telephone. If the sick person telephoned the navy dispensary and the navy doctor put him or her on the sick list, that might suffice in some cases, but at least one commanding officer found it unsatisfactory; certainly it was subject to abuse.[2]

Faced with an ever-growing number of women, navy doctors found that their official manual on nomenclature of diseases did not include "diseases which are distinctively female." Until a revised version appeared, the bureau suggested that its physicians use "the usual terms accepted by the profession . . . and proper classification will be made in the Bureau." But if the condition were common to both, physicians were advised to follow strictly the current manual.[3]

In March 1918, the medical officer of the Norfolk Navy Yard documented his facility's inadequacies: It was built when the navy was "about one-fifth the size it is at the present time." It contained about two thousand square feet, had only one dressing room and one bathroom, and provided "no proper sleeping place for the medical officer or the hospital corpsman on duty." He urged that a building of about six thousand square feet be built as soon as possible.[4] The need for privacy for the growing number of yeomen (F) aggravated these crowded conditions.

The navy still had to accommodate those women not treated by their own physicians. It already had a few civilian hospitals under contract to provide care as needed, and navy medical officers worked closely with those hospitals' staffs. Since 1915, for example, Columbia Hospital in Washington, D.C., had been offering care to female dependents of navy men stationed nearby.[5] In addition, a hospital in Georgetown set aside some of its facilities for navy nurses; during the war it also served the two thousand yeomen (F) stationed in the nation's capital. When Yeoman (F) Agnes Carlson had a bad experience with the first of her three typhoid shots, she ended up there.

> About 3:00 PM I began to get chills but stayed until the office closed at 4:30. I had to take the Chevy Chase [trolley] car home and to assure myself of getting a seat, I boarded a Potomac Park car which would run to Chevy Chase on the return trip. . . . I lost my lunch. . . . The daughter of a minister living in that block took me home with her, where her mother called the Navy Dispensary. Commander Lowndes of the Navy Medical Corps took me to Georgetown Hospital where I stayed 5 days.[6]

In another instance, a sick yeoman (F) stationed in New Orleans sought treatment from her own physician, who put her in a civilian hospital with a navy contract. He and her medical officer agreed that he would continue to treat her and would allow the latter to see her "often enough to keep up the records."[7]

The women were also entitled to navy dental care, which, like the medical care, was free to every person on active duty. One woman found out that the care was not always the same for men and women.

> The young and personable dentist was alone in the clinic. I was embarrassed to be sitting there with my mouth gaping open so this handsome man could do the dental work. When he had finished, without saying a word, he suddenly pinned me in the chair and gave me one of the biggest, longest kisses I've ever had. . . . When I told the other . . . girls what happened, they all immediately made appointments to get their teeth cleaned and examined.[8]

Another War

The new enemy, influenza, first appeared at home, in the American heartland. It struck here and there and caused some trouble but was soon gone and nearly forgotten. Unknowingly, America exported it, most notably to Europe. There it grew in virulence and acquired a foreign name. Then, with the deadly speed for which it became infamous, it returned to America and attacked the nation so extensively and savagely that, for a few ghastly weeks in the autumn of 1918, the war effort faltered. There existed no shield against it, nor any weapon with which to attack it. The source of its terrifying power was barely understood, and nearly seventy years would pass before anyone could identify it precisely. Even today, were it to attack again, it is by no means certain that we are less vulnerable now than we were then. It killed no fewer than 555,000 Americans—some estimate as many as 675,000—43,000 of them young men and women in the service. Yet it has largely disappeared from public memory.[9]

Flu viruses have been around for a long, long time. Most people have contracted one or more cases of flu by the time they are adults, for it spreads quickly. Seldom does it kill or leave behind any obvious or great damage; victims feel terrible for a few days, then recover fully. Because flu was familiar and commonly nondeadly, it was not even considered a reportable disease. Thus the American public, as well as doctors and health agencies, hardly noticed the flu that spread around the nation in the spring of 1918, although "[t]hat spring it was observed that pigs and pig farmers in Iowa got sick simultaneously."[10]

Only a few reports of flu piqued any interest. One was that a thousand workers at the Ford plant in Detroit were so sick they were sent home. The eighteen severe cases of flu that occurred in a small town in Kansas would not have been recorded at all, except that three victims died. Prisons and the army, both of which were obliged to care for their sick, reported epidemics of flu in March and April, in which three more persons died. But such institutions more or less expected to experience epidemics of mild and infectious diseases. In preceding years the army's medical corps had so hugely improved military sanitation and hygiene that no one felt any cause for alarm, nor did anyone connect the subsequent epidemic of pneumonia—in those days nearly always a killer—with the flu.

The overarching reason that Americans barely noticed the flu in the spring of 1918 was that the war was fast approaching its climax. The flow of American men and arms to France that began in early 1917 had become a flood: In March and April of 1918, for example, 202,000 Americans embarked for the European battlefields. They thought they were going to meet an enemy; they didn't know they were already in battle. Historian Alfred Crosby noted that "the first cases of epidemic influenza in the spring in the American Expeditionary Force (AEF), which were among the very earliest, appeared at a camp near Bordeaux, one of the chief disembarkation ports for American troops. The date was about April 15. It may be that the doughboys were bringing more across the Atlantic than anyone recognized."[11]

In Europe, the contagion spread from one army to another—and to civilians —with notorious speed. One German commander blamed the flu for his troops' failure to overpower Allied forces in July 1918.[12] Soon British and European civilians began falling. Authorities tried to keep secret the true extent of the epidemic. They succeeded mostly because the monstrosity and extent of the battlefields' carnage dwarfed all else and also because, in wartime, they could censor news. But nonbelligerent Spain, lacking the wartime power of censorship, could not hide the fact that flu struck an estimated eight million of its citizens. Thus the disease acquired the name of "Spanish influenza."

Between May and November, one and one-half million Americans were shipped to Europe to live, fight, and die among hordes of soldiers and civilians from all over the world. These vast war migrations only enhanced the virulence of those organisms that caused the flu and those producing the secondary infections. War's confusion, overcrowding, and poor nutrition and sanitation ensured that the epidemic would become pandemic. Beyond Europe, normal trade among nations spread the disease. It struck so quickly that its victims could pass it on before they knew they had it. Thus, four months after it first arose in the United States, the flu had spread around the world. No one knew how it spread (by air, the hardest to control), nor did there yet exist any medicines to cure it or even ease its symptoms. By the time it returned to America it had gained a potency equal to its speed.

Influenza Strikes the Navy

Like the rest of the country, the U.S. Navy first got the flu early in 1918. In January the USS *Minneapolis* was stricken while in the navy yard in Philadelphia. In February, cases appeared on five ships in Boston and at the Naval Radio School in Cambridge, some of them complicated by pneumonia. Navy ships around the world also reported cases. More than half of the USS *Nashville*'s crew of nearly two hundred were stricken while that cruiser was in the Mediterranean. Several American submarines on patrol reported one-third to one-half of their crews sick.

This early epidemic had barely subsided when it reappeared in July, this time at a U.S. Navy base hospital in France. Alarmed, in early August the Bureau of Medicine and Surgery sent out a warning that described the symptoms and prevalence of the disease overseas. But unknowingly the navy had already brought the flu home. It took hold again at the navy's Boston facilities on 27 August, when two or three men reported it at sick call. Eight new cases appeared the next day, and fifty-eight the day after that. Two days later the disease reached its local peak—106 cases—and within two weeks two thousand navy men and women of the First Naval District had become ill.[13]

Rhode Island, a small state with a large influx of naval trainees at Newport, was now also in crisis. One navy nurse described the flu's coming to the Newport Naval Hospital as "a blast from the blue. The hospital accommodated 600 patients and we had 2,000. Our wards and pavilions filled up and tents were pitched on the grounds around the hospital. . . . This flu germ was deadly, very virulent, often causing death in three days. There was always room for those brought in from the outside, as so many were dying."[14]

On 28 September the State Board of Health recommended closing theaters, schools, churches, and other public gathering places and begged those with any symptoms of the disease to remain at home. War activities came temporarily almost to a standstill, because too few people were well enough to carry them out and too few were well enough to care for the sick. So great was the navy's need for nurses that it recalled to active duty some reserve nurses who had already returned to civilian life, and it kept some who had volunteered for the emergency beyond the dates when they wished to be released. The surgeon general acknowledged that these steps were very regrettable, for it lowered morale in stations where it occurred.[15] Lack of nurses brought forth what the *Newport Daily News* reported as

at least one case of heroism. . . . A naval officer attached to the mine force of the Second Naval District became ill with the disease and was sent to the Naval Hospital for treatment. It later was learned that his wife and

three children also had the disease at their home in Jamestown, and efforts
. . . to find someone who would care for them . . . were unavailing, until
finally a yeowoman, Miss Dorothy P. Swarbrick . . . volunteered to go to . . .
put herself under quarantine in the house [to care for the family].[16]

The large navy training station at Great Lakes, about thirty miles from
Chicago, reported its first flu victims on 11 September, and within a week its
hospital was swamped. Built to hold eighteen hundred, at the height of the
epidemic it held six thousand. One navy nurse reported, "Our Navy bought
the whole city of Chicago out of sheets. . . . We couldn't get enough caskets. All
[we] could give a dead boy was a winding sheet and a wooden box."[17]

By late October the West Coast was under attack. The naval hospital at
Mare Island, near San Francisco, reported housing its overflow in an encamp-
ment of one hundred tents that was being constantly expanded. Moreover, "The
local markets are able to supply us with only a small proportion of stores, drugs
and material of all kinds which we require. Usually local bidders and stores
buy in the East after we call for articles, and sixty to ninety days elapse before
delivery. We are often forced to pick up articles in many different small stores
scattered over a large area, in order to obtain the much needed supplies."[18]

Already, though, by the end of September, more than thirty-one thousand
navy men and women had been stricken, and more than eleven hundred had
died from the flu itself or from the pneumonia that often followed. The army
had comparable statistics, and civilians were succumbing just as rapidly. Even
though the war was reaching its climax in Europe and the Allies were preparing to mount a decisive offensive, draft calls scheduled for October were postponed. Secretary Daniels cautioned Navy Department employees against using
local swimming pools, because the flu was prevalent in the District of Columbia. At the same time the army and navy quarantined their camps and restricted
travel. As one historian put it, "The unthinkable was happening: something
had appeared of greater priority than the war."

Yet the war went on, consuming stupendous sums of money. Consequently,
the government launched yet another drive to sell war bonds to a sick and fright-
ened population that had already bought millions of dollars worth of them. The
"Liberty Loan" drive demanded meetings and rallies that herded civilians
together, increasing the risk of contagion.[19]

By the end of November, navy deaths in the United States rose to three thousand; total navy deaths of flu and pneumonia for calendar year 1918 were nearly five thousand.[20]

Navy and Marine Women Fight the Flu

Fifty-six women died while in navy service, most of them from influenza. Of the women marines, two, possibly three, died from the same cause.[21] Unknown numbers of former navy and marine women apparently recovered from the sickness but died later, many from pneumonia and tuberculosis or other conditions originally brought on or aggravated by the flu.

In Philadelphia, Loretta Walsh caught the disease in the fall of 1918. The city came close to collapsing before the disease ran its murderous course there, eventually killing almost sixteen thousand. The telephone system had so many sick employees that it refused to handle all but essential calls; hundreds of police officers, firemen, and garbage collectors failed to show up for duty. For a few grim weeks, there were too few embalmers and coffins, so that many bodies lay where they fell, sometimes for days. The war had already depleted the ranks of doctors and nurses.

Since doctors could offer no medicines, the lack of nurses to care for the sick and dying was more critical, and anyone who could care for them had to pitch in. Walsh, in addition to her regular duties of recruiting and selling Liberty Bonds, helped nurse sick men and women in the naval hospital. She never truly recovered from the flu. Weakened by lack of rest and grieving over her older brother's death, she developed tuberculosis and remained hospitalized until her death in 1925.[22]

If a yeoman (F) was absent over two days without reporting in, the navy sent a doctor and corpsman to investigate. That procedure probably saved the life of at least one yeoman (F) living alone in Brooklyn, her husband out at sea. She was found unconscious and rushed to a hospital. When one yeoman (F) got the flu in Houston, the four others who shared her room were carried off to the hospital with her: "We were all treated as though we were contaminated. ... I wasn't even sick and they made me lie down on a stretcher and carried me to the hospital in an ambulance."[23]

The women much preferred staying home or taking leave to travel home if at all possible. Fear of the hospitals was well founded. One woman sent to the naval hospital in Boston, much against her will, was told "there were three bed-pans for thirty patients," which energized her sufficiently to rise from her bed, seize her uniform, and escape. Waving down a car, she asked for a ride to the train station in order to get to her home in Brockton, nineteen miles away. When the driver learned she had just left the hospital with flu, he dropped her as fast as he could at the nearest subway stop. She made it home, where she recuperated for thirty days. Technically, she was absent without leave, since the hospital had not discharged her, and so she forfeited her pay for that time.[24]

Jessie Arnold found the Georgetown Hospital equally disturbing: "There were no beds and we were left on stretchers in the halls. One corpsman came along to look at me and said, 'Don't bother with her, she is as good as dead.'" A woman marine also hospitalized at Georgetown reported a breakfast with eggs so old they "were practically wearing feathers."[25] The navy's surgeon general did not mention these details in his annual report. He wrote,

> As the number of patients rose rapidly, the equipment and facilities at Georgetown Hospital were taxed to the utmost. . . . The second floor of Riggs Annex of the hospital was set aside immediately and shortly afterwards a large ward on the first floor of the same building. . . . Navy cots or bed and bedding were always procured by the commanding officer of the dispensary ahead of the necessity for them.[26]

With a severe case of flu developing, on 25 September, Yeoman First Class Julia Hicks reported to the naval dispensary, which quickly sent her to the Georgetown Hospital. Physicians there released her on 6 October but certified to her senior officer that she was still too feeble to return to work. Her sick leave was extended to another eighteen days. On 1 October, Yeoman First Class Sarah Rice reported to her office that she was sick with flu but failed to report to the dispensary. A civilian doctor treated her on 5 October and told her to return to her home in New Jersey to recuperate. She returned to duty sixteen days later. Failure to report to the dispensary and failure to request additional leave and permission to travel home meant that she had actually been absent without leave (AWOL) for three weeks. The navy's readiness to accept certificates from two civilian doctors—the one who sent her home and the one who sent her back to duty—suggests that during those crisis-ridden days it was quite willing to overlook procedural and even legal niceties: It was grateful to have its yeoman recovered and back at work. Another yeoman (F) who had been granted leave to go home because of a death in the family resigned on 30 September because she was too sick to return to work. That action was ill-advised or, more likely, not advised at all. Anxiety, grief, and sickness probably combined to keep her from realizing that she could have been granted an extension of her leave owing to sickness, then returned to duty when she was well, or at least postponed her resignation. As it was, she got no sick pay.[27]

In 1918, preventive measures to heighten immunity against flu were not yet available, nor were there any antiviral remedies for flu itself or antibiotics to deal with secondary bacterial infections. Yeoman (F) Helen Butler came early to the office every day to wipe down desks, chairs, and telephones with disinfectant; "Just the same, it seemed to me that every morning somebody else was missing from his or her desk, and all too often when I called a home phone number I learned that our clerk had died overnight."

The navy recommended that yeomen (F) and women marines caring for the sick wear gauze masks, but that had no effect. Equally ineffectual was the recommended daily shot of undiluted whiskey followed by black coffee. One survivor wrote that the flu was a "terrible plague that baffled the medical profession. . . . Each labored according to his own ideas. There were no rules." Nothing seemed to help except, possibly, good nursing care. You either caught the disease or did not, you either died from it or did not. A navy nurse who survived the flu remembered that she "ran a temperature of 104 or 105 for days, had an icecap on my head . . . neck . . . over my heart, which pounded so hard it rattled the ice, the chartboard and the [bed]spring."[28]

The courage of the navy women who nursed the sick and of the survivors who returned, grieving, to their duties, deserves the highest praise. The fear that pervaded their lives is suggested by one searing memory, that of seeing coffins stacked high. One yeoman (F) saw them at a train station as she departed on her three-day honeymoon; another viewed a similar pile outside her window as she lay in a hospital, recovering.[29]

By mid-November, when the armistice ended the war, the worst of the epidemic had passed through the eastern part of the country, leaving indelible memories. A journalist in New London, Connecticut, wrote on 12 November of seeing, for the first time in his life, the military funeral procession of a woman. All too familiar was "the sight of a flag-covered coffin passing through the streets in a ship-gray truck, with sailors marching beside it and behind. But when standing at the head and foot of the coffin are girls, and marching soberly beside the truck are girls, girls in the uniform of the American Navy—it all seems strange and unusual, and somehow very, very sad."[30]

Drastic Adjustments

The Bureau of Medicine and Surgery began to contract with civilian hospitals to accommodate women patients, whose number was growing rapidly, as nurses and yeomen (F) alike succumbed to the flu. Not everyone thought this was a good idea: One distraught mother informed the navy that she had taken her daughter out of the civilian hospital to which the navy had sent her because if the daughter "had stayed [there] she would not have survived a month." The navy investigated the mother's complaint, found it lacking merit, and directed that the young woman, whose condition was serious, be returned to the hospital.

As we have seen, conditions in many hospitals left much to be desired, so one cannot gainsay the mother's conviction that her daughter would be better off at home. However, the civilian facilities may have been notably better than anything else the navy's beleaguered medical system could offer at the time, and the navy considered the patient too sick to remain unhospitalized. Some civilian hospitals under contract soon ran out of room. One in Pasadena, California, which had agreed to accept twenty-five women patients, at one point had to wire the bureau that it would need at least ten more beds to meet its obligations.[31]

Most yeomen (F) recovered fully, but a significant number of them, already weakened, developed tuberculosis, as Loretta Walsh had. They might live only a few years, but until or unless they recovered, they needed medical care. The navy could not provide that care, yet it could not discharge them.

The situation developing at the naval hospital at Fort Lyon, in eastern Colorado, illustrates the navy's dilemma. At the time, physicians believed that the best treatment for tuberculosis was complete bed rest, preferably outdoors, in sites abundantly supplied with clean fresh air. Fort Lyon was one of several naval hospitals established to care for tubercular patients. When better courses of treatment were developed, the navy closed down these hospitals. Captain Barber, the naval hospital's commanding officer, wrote to the bureau in October 1918 that he had already sent one navy woman with tuberculosis to a civilian sanatorium, as the bureau had instructed him earlier. However, that sanatorium would not be able to make room for many more. Do you have plans, he asked, to modify naval hospitals so that they can accept tubercular patients, many of whom would be women?

The surgeon general considered the matter, asking the Bureau of Yards and Docks to prepare plans for "an additional pavilion ward . . . sufficient to accommodate about 100 patients," suitable for male or female patients. When Barber examined these plans, he commented on their adequacy, recommended some changes, and pointed out

> a most serious obstacle to be overcome in establishing this unit here . . . the retention of patients. They will be mostly young girls. Their mothers or near relatives will not be likely to let them come alone. There will be no accommodations . . . for these relatives. They will immediately note the presence of eight hundred young men living in close proximity to the quarters intended for these patients.

Also, within two weeks the ground would be frozen, so construction could not even begin for several months. Far better, he suggested, to use a sanatorium run by nuns in Manitou, Colorado.[32]

The bureau sent Lt. Cdr. Fred Bogan of the Medical Corps to investigate. Bogan visited the recommended sanatorium and three others. Inadequate, he declared: Their combined total available capacity would not meet the immediate need. However, he had found a better alternative, namely, a "large substantial modern hotel" in Manitou Springs. One wing could be set aside for navy patients, with "nursing and medical attendance . . . by members of the Nurse and Medical Corps." The hotel's chief advantage, Bogan pointed out, was that it could take fifty patients on twenty-four-hour notice, and its owner would be willing to keep one hundred beds available for the next eight months "without making it necessary for the Government to pay for this privilege."[33]

The Bureau of Medicine and Surgery successfully met the challenge of caring for women, but the flu epidemic nearly swamped it, inflicting immense damage and marking the navy for decades to come. During that terrible time, when home-front casualties almost exceeded those on the battlefields, navy and marine women shared the same dangers from the flu as did the men and took up a larger share of nursing the sick. Almost fifty women died outright. An unknown number of those who caught the disease never recovered fully, their lingering weaknesses delivering them to early deaths.

SEVEN

Active Duty Ends

*We were civilians again and very proud of having served our country at a time of
need. I have carried my original dog tag every day for 77 years.*

Helene Johnson Coxhead, former yeoman (F)

PEACE WAS INFINITELY PREFERABLE to war, and Americans celebrated its
arrival with as much joy as they could muster. But it brought its own problems.
The navy was faced with thousands of young men returning from war, eager to
revert to civilian life. Not the least of the navy's problems was deciding how best
to end the active-duty service of the first enlisted women. Most of the women
were eager to return home, while others wanted to remain in government service. Those still suffering from flu and its aftermath posed special challenges.

Armistice

The darkest hours proved a prelude to the bright dawn. Victory could not come
too soon, and the very expectation brought a "false armistice" on 7 November
1918, when crowds in New York used so much confetti in celebrating that none

was left when the real armistice was announced four days later. On 11 November, the White House officially announced the end of the war.

Washington, D.C., lit up the night with forty-eight bonfires—one for each state—on the Ellipse in front of the White House, where crowds soon massed. Impromptu processions formed, and Eleanor and Franklin Roosevelt joined one, "exactly as if [he] were not the Assistant Secretary of the Navy." In New York, the Statue of Liberty, which had been darkened since America's entry into the war, was relighted an hour before dawn. The whistles and steam blasts from ships in the great harbor, along with bells and horns—including shofars on the east side of the city where many immigrants lived in crowded tenements—ushered in what turned out to be a perfect autumn day. Schools, factories, and businesses closed, giving everyone who wanted to drink alcohol plenty of time to do so (until supplies ran out) and to throw money at soldiers and sailors. Perfectly respectable women celebrated by kissing every serviceman they could find.[1]

Yeomen (F) and women marines happily joined the celebrations. One woman remembered "wild excitement and tumultuous joy, that War had ceased, and as we believed that day, ceased for all time." Another woman remembered how she and some of her friends "all piled into the back of a pickup truck and drove up and down Pennsylvania Avenue screaming like a bunch of idiots; it was wonderful." A similar act of celebration ended tragically. As a truck filled with women rounded a corner at high speed, its side opened and the women fell out. One of them, Ella Galvin of Fall River, Massachusetts, was killed.[2]

Victory Parades

All the hard work of drilling paid off in the great parades and reviews of 1918 and 1919. In Newport, Rhode Island, the women marched in three large parades, much to the approval of bystanders. The first was in October 1918, to promote the fourth Liberty Loan drive, of which the *Newport Daily News* reported, "although there are not a great many women at the [Naval] Station, they were well represented, the yeowomen coming out especially strong," one of them riding atop a float pulled by eight sailors. On Armistice Day they marched again, and the same paper noted that "the company of yeowomen was a revelation to most Newporters, who had no idea there were so many in service in Newport."

Newport's final parade of the war took place in April 1919, when Admiral Sims, commander of the U.S. Navy's forces in Europe, returned in triumph to his home city with his wife. Along with battalions of soldiers from Fort Adams, coast artillery from forts along Narragansett Bay, sailors from the torpedo station, companies of recruits, and a band and bugle corps came a corps of yeomen (F), a chief yeoman (F) at their head. Meanwhile, the hundred yeomen (F) who had first marched in Boston in April of 1918 had swelled to a thousand in that city's victory parade on 12 November, "many of them having taken the places of men transferred to sea duty." Moreover, the commandant of the First Naval District credited the success of the Liberty Bond effort "to the zealous work of the women yeomen who had charge of [it]."[3]

The Navy Department's drill team of yeoman (F), "the Battalion," made its first public appearance in mid-February, when they met President Wilson and his party returning from Paris, then again a few days later for a great welcome parade in Washington, D.C. Navy and marine women formed honor guards and took up station in front of his reviewing stand at the White House; on that occasion, fatigue caused at least one woman to faint and others to drop out. In May the Battalion took part in a Victory Loan drive in New York. They traveled by Pullman coach, which also served as their quarters for the three nights they were away from Washington. Patriotic organizations feted the women, and one can imagine the excitement with which they marched up Fifth Avenue, then gave an exhibition drill at which they raised more than fifty thousand dollars.[4]

Their success evidently aroused envy in some souls who carped about the women's presence to such an extent that a popular columnist, Earl Godwin, took up the yeomen (F)'s defense. He reminded his readers that members of the Battalion were *ordered* to take part in the parade and belonged there as much as anyone else. Moreover, Godwin said, a glee club from Hampton Roads and a band from Great Lakes also took part in the parade, but no one had criticized their presence. He took the opportunity to scorn Congress for its unwillingness "to appropriate money to maintain the several thousand women sailors —and will then impose on someone the job of finding civilians to do the same work these patriotic women have been doing." The women, many of them mindful that they would soon be released from active duty (see below), greatly appreciated Godwin's gallant fight on their behalf.[5]

The Battalion's final review came on 30 July 1919, just before most of the yeomen (F) were to be released from active duty, in accordance with congressional mandate. Along with the women marines, they formed ranks for the last time at the Ellipse, on which they had learned to execute their maneuvers with such precision and dash. Both Secretary Daniels and Assistant Secretary Roosevelt reviewed them and posed with them for formal photographs. Daniels again expressed his "gratitude and appreciation for their splendid service and patriotic co-operation." One may wonder if, twenty-three years later, when President Roosevelt signed the legislation that created the navy's Women's Reserve (WAVES), he remembered the first women to march so proudly in navy blue. Two months later the Battalion reunited for their final public service, that of selling the official programs created to celebrate the return of General Pershing and the First Division.[6]

Those who participated would remember these parades as a highlight of their lives. One marine woman recalls parading on Pennsylvania Avenue in Washington, around the Treasury building, then, "twenty across, we made a perfect turn to go up on 16th Street," but another's recollection is chiefly of a parade route that was about five miles long, part of it over cobblestones. A yeoman (F) remembers "marching down Fifth Avenue, in New York City, holding a corner of a huge American Flag with people throwing money into [it]." On the morning of 11 November 1921, former sergeant Ingrid Jonassen marched with the Marine Corps Honor Guard escorting the caisson bearing the Unknown Soldier to his resting place at Arlington National Cemetery. Other women veterans were also among the large procession that followed the flag-draped casket.[7]

Release

Once the stirring sounds and sights of the victory parades faded away, a population grieving its dead, caring for its wounded, and weary of supporting war expenditures had little interest in its armed forces. It wanted its boys home immediately and its wounded carefully tended, but it failed to understand that releasing the healthy and tending the sick took time and cost money. First, the navy had to bring back to the United States the military personnel and remaining material it had earlier carried overseas to fight the war. The voyage home might take up to two weeks, depending on the weather. Off-loading passengers and cargo, refueling and restocking for the return voyage could take several days, so that a round-trip voyage might stretch out to a month. The ships that were assigned those tasks still needed their crew members.

Once back in the United States, those leaving active duty had to pass a physical examination, a procedure critical for both the individual and the service. If the individual incurred a chronic or disabling medical condition while on active duty, the service had to keep the person on active duty until he or she was mended. If the disability was permanent, the service had to accept liability for it and grant a monthly remuneration based on pay grade and degree of disability. The service then settled the pay accounts of those who passed the physical examination, gave them final instructions regarding benefits and obligations, if any, and provided money for their return home. Every release required hours of clerking, so the navy could not afford to let go of its reservists too early, especially its clerks, most of whom were yeomen (F).

On 4 November 1918, with victory imminent, the navy stopped enrolling women but took no move to release those it already had, although the Bureau of Navigation agreed to release any woman who had a specific reason for requesting it. For example, when Yeoman (F) Dorothy Wright asked for a special early release to marry an army lieutenant just returned from France, Daniels granted it and "gave me his blessing for a successful marriage." By early 1919, the bureau asked for yeomen (F) to volunteer to transfer to stations that were shorthanded. Some women welcomed this opportunity to remain on active duty but at a station closer to families that needed them.[8]

Fortunately for the navy, most of the yeomen (F) were very willing to remain, although they were quite aware that, on some not-too-distant date, all of them would be released from active duty and eventually discharged: What then? The commandant of the Fifth Naval District at Norfolk explained their concerns in a letter to the chief of naval operations. He wrote that the women reservists in his district were "perfectly satisfied to remain on active duty but are restive for fear they may be summarily released." Plenty of good civilian employment awaited them locally, he pointed out, especially as the Norfolk Navy Yard, and the newly established Naval Operating Base would require larger numbers of workers than before the war. Moreover, he doubted that civil service employees could be persuaded to fill those jobs at the present salary, especially as the new base was nine miles from Norfolk and transportation was poor. These concerns led him to ask if the navy had a policy for the continuation of the yeomen (F).[9]

De facto, the navy's policy was to hold on to as many reservists as possible without keeping any women against their will, which might displease the public. Moreover, Congress was anxious to stop paying reservists, whom it considered no longer necessary. The next navy appropriations bill would no doubt speak to the matter; best to start paring personnel now. In February, navy bureaus made ready to cut their reservists by half (although the Bureau of Construction and Repair exempted the yeomen (F) from the cut), and a month later Secretary Daniels ordered that clerks, messengers, draftsmen, inspectors, and other technical workers be cut from the rolls on or before 15 April. Meanwhile, the Bureau of Navigation stopped transferring women about to be released.[10]

The Naval Appropriations Act of July 1919 did in fact specify that female navy and marine reservists, except nurses, "as soon as practicable and in no event more than thirty days after the approval of the Act, be placed on inactive duty." Most of the women reservists were released by 11 August, the deadline date. Although no longer on active duty and free to accept other employment, they were not discharged from the Naval Reserve and were still subject to its rules and regulations. They were to keep their uniforms but not to wear them after release. The commandant of their local naval district would keep their health and enrollment records, and they were to advise him of any changes in their mailing address or residence. The government would pay them one dollar every month until they were discharged. It would also pay their way home or to the place where they enrolled, at the rate of five cents per mile. Thus Rose Volkman, serving in New York, was entitled to three hundred dollars in order to return to her home in Hawaii. That sum provoked the Bureau of Navigation to ask her boss how a yeoman (F) from Hawaii had got to New York in the first place. The explanation was simple (see chapter 5) but did not change the fact that the navy had brought her some six thousand miles to New York and now would have to pay to return her.[11]

That spring the Navy Department and Congress found a way to keep the extremely valuable services of the women reservists while at the same time releasing them from active duty: It would entice them into the civil service. In June, Secretary Daniels advised navy and marine officials that the upcoming Naval Appropriations Act would provide that "reservists . . . whose conduct, services and efficiency have demonstrated the desirability of their retention may, in the discretion of the secretary of the navy, be given temporary civil appointments in the Navy Department or Naval Establishment at the ordinary and usual rates of pay . . . provided such services are necessary."[12]

Those accepting appointments as clerks, messengers, or police would receive a bonus to offset the subsistence allowance they would lose when they left active military duty. The bonus was first set at $120 and soon doubled. Reservists who had already served six months would receive the bonus immediately upon release; those who had served for less time would receive it when their active-duty time plus time in civil service totaled six months. The people whom the U.S. Navy and Marine Corps needed most urgently at the time were those who dealt with records and correspondence. Nearly all those clerks were women. While nothing in the act excluded male reservists from applying, the Marine Corps told its reservists that men would be allowed to apply only in special cases.[13]

The temporary appointments would expire no later than June of 1920. Although reservists would have to pass the qualifying civil service examination to gain permanent appointments, they would receive some preference because of their active duty service. Realizing that civil servants might become disgruntled by this large infusion of reservists, Daniels directed that the pay grades approved for the incoming reservists be assigned with

> . . . the utmost care . . . taking into consideration the character of work engaged upon, the pay of the present civilian employees engaged upon a similar character of work and ability . . . in order that there may be no just grounds for complaint on the part of the present civil forces that reservists are given a higher rate of pay. . . .

Daniels asked the officials to survey their respective units to determine how many reservists would accept such appointments. Most of the reservists leaped at the offer: 87 out of 97 in one office; 113 out of 158 in another; 558 out of 630 in yet a third; and so on. Of the nearly 250 marine women still on active duty, almost half of them accepted a civil appointment.[14]

The women's eagerness to stay on *in service,* even though it was civil rather than military service, reveals that they much preferred their present situations to those that they had had before they were enrolled. Particularly pleased with the new opportunity were those who had few or no prospects of jobs at home that could offer them chances to advance—or that they liked nearly as much as they liked working in the government. Their uniformed service had given them experience and independence they might not have gained any other way, and civil service would give them chances to rise as they learned new skills and could accept more responsibilities.

For some who went home, the choice was not easy. Mary Price's fiancé was coming back from the war and she turned down government service: "We were glad the war was over and we wanted to go home. But I missed the navy— oh, yes, back to the drugstore, but it was dull."[15]

Discharge

Navy enlistment contracts, including those of the women, were for four years. By special act, the secretary of the navy summarily cut the women's enlistments so that they all would be discharged by 24 October 1920. The district commandants apparently did not pay close attention to this deadline, for when Daniels inquired in December, he learned that hundreds were on the navy rolls; for example, the Fifth Naval District (Norfolk) still had 1,025 reservists to discharge. At his prompting, the districts took up the task and by January of 1921 had discharged all their yeomen (F). At the Navy Department in Washington, a few remained in the enrolling office, which was responsible for the final processing of all discharge papers. By 20 July most of that work had been completed, and all the navy women at the enrollment office had been dismissed for lack of funds. The last yeoman (F) to be discharged is reported to have been Rose Collins of Philadelphia, in March 1921.[16]

Had it not been for the determination of Chief Yeoman Eunice Dessez and the swift action of Adm. Charles B. McVay, both fortunately situated at the right place at the right time, the Navy Department might have given "ordinary" discharges to all the yeomen (F). The navy routinely gave such discharges to men not recommended for re-enlistment. According to Dessez, who had spent her entire naval service in the Naval Reserve Enrollment Office,

> The matter of DISCHARGES generally was not brought up until the time came for the discharge of ALL FEMALE reservists [when] the Civilian Chief Clerk said that ALL YEOMEN F should be issued ORDINARY DISCHARGES and NOT RECOMMENDED for re-enlistment because WOMEN WOULD NEVER AGAIN be regularly enlisted in the navy. . . . I went to my Commanding Officer and said, "one's HONORABLE DISCHARGE has always been considered a recommendation for a civil position, and if I presented an Ordinary Discharge NOT recommended for enlistment, any prospective employer would think that I had committed an offense of some sort, and furthermore, why should the male reservists under my supervision be given HONORABLE DISCHARGES and the female reservists be given ORDINARY Discharges?" The Commanding Officer agreed with me but he was powerless to issue any orders contrary to those which the office had. . . . [A] close friend of mine was the private secretary to the Chief of the Bureau of Ordnance, Rear Admiral Chas. B. McVay, and she explained to the Admiral that all Yeomen F were about to receive ORDINARY DISCHARGES—NOT RECOMMENDED FOR RE-ENLIST-MENT. The kindly Admiral took it up with the Secretary of the Navy at once, and . . . orders were issued to give HONORABLE DISCHARGES to Yeomen F with creditable marks. As to the question of re-enlistment . . . on the YEOMEN F discharges . . . in the space "recommended for re-enlistment" there are two dashes, in other words, "They didn't say, 'YES' and they didn't say 'NO.'"[17]

Dessez wrote this remarkable letter, reproduced here with its original underlinings, capitalizations, and punctuation, in 1953 to a former yeoman (F) who had been given an ordinary discharge. Nearly forty years after the episode, Dessez was still clearly indignant and appropriately so, for the women's fortunes had been at stake. How many more such discharges may have been issued to the women reservists is not known, but when one considers the thousands of former yeomen (F) whose honorable discharges allowed them to enter civil service, it must be few.

Fifty-seven yeomen were never discharged; they went to their deaths first. Besides the woman killed in a truck accident on Armistice Day, four others died accidental deaths. In addition, two were suicides and four more died of causes not recorded. The remaining forty-four died of disease, most likely of the flu or complications thereof. The first yeoman (F) to die on duty was Chief May Turner, in September 1917 (see chapter 5); the last was Marion Perlstein, on 14 September 1920. Of the 305 women marines, at least two died on active duty.[18]

Care for Sick Women Veterans

But what of those women whom the Navy Department could not release or discharge because they were too sick to pass the physical exam? In February 1919 the Bureau of Medicine and Surgery advised all naval hospitals that the situation was very difficult. Sick and wounded officers and enlisted men of the regular navy and Marine Corps were returning from the battlefields and overseas base hospitals, and "Naval Hospital facilities must be conserved for their care."

Once released from active duty, reservists, regardless of gender, were *not* entitled to care at naval facilities, although exceptions could be made for "cases especially meritorious, or in an emergency endangering health or life where other means are not at hand [and cases of those] disabled or injured during the war, especially over-seas, and of cases which have been previously treated in and discharged from naval hospitals before complete recovery, and which require perhaps further treatment."[19]

In such cases, the surgeon general declared, the hospital was to admit the inactive reservist and report him or her as a "supernumerary" on its muster rolls. (Every unit is allowed only a certain number of persons. A supernumerary would not be charged against that allowance.)

Some naval hospitals that would still have women reservists under treatment on 11 August, the date specified for release of all reservists, asked for advice. The Bureau of Navigation repeated the surgeon general's earlier instruction: Release the women from active duty but keep them on as supernumeraries. One naval hospital, still strained and understaffed in the aftermath of the flu, unable to find competent civilian help, asked permission to keep some reservists on active duty past the deadline. The secretary of the navy denied the request, on the grounds that it would create an undesirable precedent—a response that did not help the hospital at all. The problem of what to do with sick reservists was not yet solved.

Navy truck driver Margaret Mullaney, for example, broke both her knees in a motor accident in early July of 1919. Two weeks later, on 19 July, all remaining yeomen (F) were discharged, but Mullaney stayed for five more months at the naval hospital in Hampton Roads as a "supernumerary." She described her care as "splendid" and credited the hospital staff with helping her to start walking with a cane.[20]

The Bureau of Medicine and Surgery, to reduce further strain on its facilities, in April 1919 instructed naval hospitals to discharge tubercular patients, as tuberculosis was a condition "not in the line of duty," and to refer them to the Bureau of War Risk Insurance "for further care and treatment."[21]

The navy hierarchy proudly displayed the yeomen (F) and the women marines in parades to celebrate the war's end but then was eager to revert to a man's world, in which the only women allowed to wear a navy uniform would be the nurses. Left with mounds of paperwork but no yeomen (F) to help, the naval districts charged with releasing the vast numbers of reservists and with nursing those too ill to be released were less happy.

Caring for those who might never recover was too large a task for a peacetime military. The army and the navy handed over responsibility for their health care to a separate government agency.

First of the first, Loretta Perfectus Walsh, enlisted on 21 March 1917, in a uniform designed by the man who enlisted her, Lt. Cdr. Frederick R. Payne, U.S. Navy, recruiting officer in Philadelphia.
Personal collection, James J. Walsh

Secretary of the Navy Josephus Daniels *(right)* and Assistant Secretary
Franklin Roosevelt, 1917. Daniels seized upon a loophole in the Naval Reserve
Act of 1916 to justify his order to enroll women in the navy to take the places of
navy men working ashore.
Naval Historical Center

Yeoman (F) First Class Amalie
Townsley poses in her summer uniform of white cotton shirtwaist and
white duck jacket and skirt, with regulation black navy tie and white,
brimmed straw hat.
Naval Historical Center

Adm. Victor Blue inspects yeomen (F) in winter uniforms in Washington, D.C.
Dark brimmed hats tied under the chin, ties knotted at the closed collars, and
skirts hemmed eight inches above the ground present a businesslike image, unmistakably U.S. Navy.
Naval Historical Center

Chief Yeoman Daisy Pratt Erd, wearing traditional navy "middy" blouse and tie. Although not part of the women's officially promulgated uniform, these blouses were popular with the women and widely used. *Naval Historical Center*

Pvt. Avadney Hea, U.S. Marine Corps Reserve, in winter green uniform, with overseas cap. Corps officials told marine women they were neither to wear Sam Browne belts nor to carry swagger sticks—prohibitions that appear not to have disturbed the composure with which Private Hea posed for this portrait. *U.S. Marine Corps photo*

Nineteen-year-old twins Genevieve and Dorothy Baker volunteered to serve in the Coast Guard and chose to wear dark dresses with broad cummerbunds in lieu of the regulation uniforms.
U.S. Coast Guard Historian's Office

Joy Bright (later Hancock) enlisted as a yeoman (F) in 1918, beginning an association with the navy that was to last all her life.
Naval Historical Center

Yeoman (F) Edna Schmieder Ceiley, wearing the tam-o'-shanter beret favored in some units. Modeled after the sailor's flat "pancake" hat, it was more likely than the wide-brimmed hats to stay put in a breeze.
Naval Historical Center

Yeomen (F) serving at the navy yard in Portsmouth, N.H., October 1918. Brimmed hats appear in straw, felt, and beaver, their bands adorned with the words "U.S. Naval Reserve" or, on the chiefs' hats, naval insignia. Ties appear tied high, low, at half-mast, or not at all.
Naval Historical Center

Yeoman Second Class Mary Louise Wilkinson models the cape so beloved
by many women, with its arm slits, dashing high collar, and frog closure of
black silk braid.
Women in Military Service for America (WIMSA) Memorial Foundation

Twelve of the fourteen smartly uniformed black yeomen (F) known to have worked in the enrollment office at the Navy Department in Washington, D.C.
Spingarn Library, Howard University

A quartet of yeomen (F) assembling primers at a munitions factory in Bloomfield, New Jersey. Secretary Daniels praised highly the accelerated production achieved by 340 yeomen (F) in a similar factory in Newport, Rhode Island.
National Archives

Marine women received no training in firearms, but USMC publicists fully appreciated the attention that a photo of a uniformed woman being coached at pistol practice would attract.

National Archives

Sailors in Newport, Rhode Island, help two yeomen (F) launch a campaign to sell Liberty Bonds in October 1918.
Naval War College Library, Naval Historical Collection

The male chief petty officer in the front row trained these yeomen (F) stationed at Whidbey Island, Washington, to drill so proficiently that the commandant of the Thirteenth Naval District, headquartered in Seattle, sent them to perform throughout the Pacific Northwest.
WIMSA Memorial Foundation

Aboard USS *Arizona,* at a city pier in New York in 1918, Cpl. Martha Wilchinski, USMCR, renders a snappy salute.
U.S. Marine Corps Historical Center

Yeoman (F) in a carefree mood.
WIMSA Memorial Foundation

On a pier in Philadelphia.
WIMSA Memorial Foundation

For its sesquicentennial celebration in 1926, the navy commissioned artist Ann Abbott to paint this composite portrait of three former yeomen (F). The portrait is now in the Navy Combat Art Museum in the Washington (D.C.) Navy Yard.
Naval Historical Center

Women marines and yeomen (F) flank Secretary of the Navy Josephus Daniels, Assistant Secretary of the Navy Franklin Roosevelt, and their aides on the occasion of the women's final parade review in July 1919.
National Archives

Former Chief Yeoman (F) Joy Bright Hancock, appointed a lieutenant in 1942, was promoted to captain in 1946 and then played a central role in developing the legislation that allowed women to embark on military careers. She retired in July 1953.
National Archives

Former Chief Yeoman (F) Helen G. O'Neill was appointed a captain in the Marine Corps Reserve in 1943 and designated assistant to Col. Ruth Streeter, wartime director of the women marines.
U.S. Marine Corps Historical Center, World War I Collection

Former marine Edith Silvermail in 1983, pointing to herself in a photo of women marines in World War I.
U.S. Marine Corps photo

Former yeoman (F) Frieda Hardin, 101 years old, speaks at the dedication of the Memorial to Women in Military Service for America (WIMSA), at Arlington National Cemetery, October 1997. At left is her son, Capt. Jerald Kirsten, USN (Ret.); at right is Brig. Gen. Wilma Vaught, USAF (Ret.), president of WIMSA Foundation.

USAF Ssgt. Reneé L. Sitler, DOD Joint Combat Camera Center

EIGHT

Women Are Veterans, Too

It is a pleasure, but by no means an unexpected one . . . to state that
the service rendered by the reservists (female) has been uniformly
excellent. It has, in fact, been exactly what the intelligence and
goodness of our countrywomen would lead one to expect.

Maj. Gen. George Barnett, commandant, U.S. Marine Corps

UPON DISCHARGE, THE NAVY and marine women became veterans, a status
that would entitle them to several significant benefits. However, most did not
think of themselves as veterans, certainly not as persons *entitled* to anything
beyond their countrymen's respect. Upon realizing that they had earned these
benefits, they applied for them gratefully. However, receiving some of the
benefits entailed struggles, some of which only succeeded because the women
had the backing of the American Legion. The only women legally entitled to
the military benefits were the nurses and the enlisted women of the U.S. Navy
and Marine Corps. Even the women serving overseas with the army as civilians were precluded.

The Naval Reserve Act of 1925, passed over the objections of women veterans, recklessly devalued their wartime services. The act's language not only

insulted the women veterans but would later, during a grave crisis, burden the navy itself.

The American Legion

In mid-March 1919, Lt. Col. Theodore Roosevelt, Jr., the son of the former president and himself a U.S. Marine, gathered a group of like-minded American soldiers in Paris to found the American Legion. Other veterans organizations soon sprang up as well, most notably the Veterans of Foreign Wars (VFW) and Disabled American Veterans (DAV). These organizations helped to keep their members from being forgotten in the economic tumult that followed the armistice.

At first, America greeted its returning veterans as heroes. Monuments and memorials appeared all across the country, and the government began to address its obligations to care for the wounded and rehabilitate the well. All too soon, however, the public began to regard its erstwhile heroes with less enthusiasm. The government had abruptly canceled its war contracts when the armistice was signed, and the armed forces released about two million men by mid-1919. Uniforms lost their luster, and veterans became just so many more unemployed civilians. The women veterans were such a tiny minority within the larger group of veterans that they might have been completely overlooked but for their membership in the American Legion.

From the beginning, women veterans and the American Legion had a mutual affinity. At its first convention, on 8–10 May 1919, in St. Louis, the Legion voted that all women who had seen service in the U.S. Navy and Marine Corps were eligible for membership. Women signed up enthusiastically. On 22 May 1919, in Washington, D.C., 247 navy women—some still on active duty—formed the second of all Legion posts to be organized, and the first all-woman post; its membership eventually grew to more than four hundred women veterans. At first named after Betsy Ross, it was soon renamed USS *Jacob Jones* Post No. 2, in honor of a U.S. Navy destroyer lost early in the war. The women marines were just as prompt: That same summer a group in New York applied for a post to be formed of women marine reservists. They named their post *Semper Fidelis* and elected Cpl. Ray Sawyer as its commander. At the time, she was the executive secretary of the New York State headquarters of the Legion.[1]

Other Legion posts composed wholly or overwhelmingly of women veterans soon appeared in New York, Connecticut, Pennsylvania, Virginia, Massachusetts, and Illinois. In smaller towns where women veterans were less numerous, many joined with male veterans to form posts. Although one former yeoman (F) living about twenty-five miles east of Cleveland would later report that her local Legion post did not want women members, women found a warm welcome at other posts. A woman living in Louisiana was invited to join the Legion's women's auxiliary but declined, saying that if she joined anything, it would be the Legion itself. She then became the first woman in that state to become a Legion member.

Women in the mixed Legion posts, far outnumbered by male members, benefited from the credibility (and celebrity) coming to them during and after the war. Two mixed posts asked women members to serve as parade marshals. The first to do so was Post no. 27 of Key West, Florida, at an Armed Forces Day celebration on 17 May 1958. Post members treated Lamonte Cates "like royalty," she said. Four honor guards, one from each service, marched beside the Cadillac convertible in which she rode, carrying the bouquet of red roses the post had presented to her. Her grandson was there to witness the occasion, being home on leave following navy boot camp at Great Lakes, making it, Cates said, "the thrill of a lifetime." Two weeks later the Legion post in Niantic, Connecticut, asked Edna Ferguson to serve as marshal for its Memorial Day parade.[2]

The Legion helped the women stay in touch with one another and also came to their aid in some important postwar situations. Many women Legionnaires attained high local, regional, and national offices in the organization, serving as delegates to state and national conventions as well as adjutants and commanders in their respective posts. Mary Price Carey, in her job as secretary to the Legion's national treasurer, traveled to England, where she met King George V and Queen Mary, and to France, where she attended a dinner hosted by the President of France. In 1995 the Legion named her an honorary life member.[3]

Postwar Benefits for Veterans

The government was very clear that women were to be included as "veterans." A proviso added to the Naval Appropriations Bill of 11 July 1919, stated that "the words 'enlisted men' shall not be construed to deprive women, enlisted or enrolled, of the pay, allowance, gratuities, and other benefits granted by law to the enlisted personnel of Navy and United States Marine Corps." Thus the law of the land entitled the women to burial in Arlington National Cemetery; award of the Victory Medal; eligibility for government insurance; a bonus of sixty dollars upon discharge; medical treatment and hospitalization under the Veterans Administration for service-connected disabilities; and 5 percent added to their earned ratings in examinations for civil service. They would also be eligible, like the men, to any adjustments in compensation later enacted, as well as any state bonuses if they were legal residents at time of enlistment.

Burial Rights at National Cemeteries

All veterans are entitled to burial in national cemeteries, of which several hundred are scattered across the nation. The first two hundred or so were established during the early and mid-1860s, chiefly to handle the half-million deaths caused by the Civil War. The best known is Arlington National Cemetery, which spreads over more than six hundred acres above the west bank of the Potomac River. For Americans, there is no more sacred soil than those wooded acres studded with white crosses.

At least twenty former yeomen (F) are known to be buried at Arlington, including one black woman and the two British women (see chapter 1). The navy explicitly ruled that funeral escorts were to be provided for "female members of the Naval Service in the same manner as applies to all other enlisted personnel."[4] While the Department of the Army is responsible for Arlington, nearly all the other veterans' cemeteries are now administered by the Department of Veterans Affairs.

The Victory Medal

The Bureau of Navigation at the close of the war issued a Victory Medal and clasp to recognize U.S. Navy and Marine Corps veterans of the "World War." The name, rating, and the station(s) where the men and women had served could be engraved upon its rim. All the women who served in the U.S. Navy,

Marine Corps, and Coast Guard were eligible for this medal. The bureau also issued the medal to women who had served in the Lighthouse Service of the Coast Guard during the war, after the secretary of commerce verified their eligibility.[5]

Some women were discharged before the medal was officially issued and found out about it later, learning that they could obtain it by writing to its manufacturer. Former Chief Yeoman (F) Joy Bright Hancock did not receive hers until she was once again in navy uniform, in 1942. But then she received it from four-star admiral Ernest J. King himself, who pinned the medal's ribbon on her new uniform. Soon after, an elderly admiral passed her in a hallway and admonished her for wearing a ribbon she had not earned. "But, Admiral," she answered, "I did earn it in World War I. Admiral King just pinned it on my uniform." Startled, he reevaluated his position, then said, "Ah well, there aren't too many of us left."[6]

Grace Clay Selleck also received her medal and discharge certificate long, long after they had been issued. The Third Naval District mailed her discharge certificate, along with her Victory Medal and service button, on 3 November 1920, to her New York address. But she had moved since leaving active service about eighteen months earlier, so the registered letter and enclosures were returned to the navy. Meanwhile, Clay filed away the temporary certificate she had been given upon release, using it to obtain the adjusted compensation certificates issued in 1925 (see next section). In due time, these so-called bonus certificates were paid off in bonds, and Clay received hers with no questions asked. She had no idea that her temporary certificate was not her actual discharge and thus never inquired about it. But someone in the Bureau of Navigation finally discovered her whereabouts and mailed the package to her. It reached her on 26 December 1939.[7]

The Adjusted Compensation Act of 1924

Representative John McKenzie of Chicago introduced a bill in 1924 to offer a cash benefit, or paid-up insurance in lieu of cash, to all male veterans of the war (an earlier bill had not included the word "male"). McKenzie's bill was introduced specifically to exclude women other than nurses from the benefits.

Alerted to this exclusion, women veterans in Washington, D.C., sought advice and help from Col. John Tayler of the Legion's Legislative Committee. While Senate and House committee members were meeting to reconcile their differences with respect to the bill, *Jacob Jones* Post Commander Helen O'Neill and Post Legislative Officer Ollie Clapp Steele paid a call on Senator David Walsh of Massachusetts, O'Neill's home state. When O'Neill explained to Walsh the kinds and amounts of services the yeomen (F) and women marines had performed during the war, "it put quite a different complexion on the whole thing."[8]

They also spoke to McKenzie, who said his original intention had been to exclude all reservists from receiving benefits because they had played so slight a role during the war. He had not been successful, however, because a few male reservists had performed distinguished service and some had performed quite arduously overseas. Still desiring to keep the costs of funding the bill's provisions as low as possible, he had focused on the women reservists as one group he could exclude. During committee hearings, he had argued that the women reservists had received fair compensation and that there was no reason to pay money to women who, as yeomen (F), had "made more money than they'd ever made in their lives." However, when O'Neill advised him that the women would not take such discrimination lightly, the bill's wording was changed to include them. O'Neill recalled, "McKenzie's assistant later told me the congressman said he could see my red hair getting redder all the time."[9] If Congress had excluded the women veterans, it would have had to reckon with the American Legion, a consequence that congressmen had already learned was undesirable.

President Coolidge vetoed the bill, on the grounds that it cost too much, saying that "we owe no bonus to able-bodied veterans ... the first duty of every citizen is to the nation." Congress repassed it, and he signed it on 19 May 1924. Known in short as the Adjusted Compensation Act of 1924, it provided that any individual serving between 5 April 1917 and 12 November 1918 was to be paid one dollar for every day of service in the United States, and $1.25 for every day served overseas. Those with service only in the United States could receive no more than $500; the rest, no more than $625. Career officers, midshipmen, cadets, members of the Reserve Officer Training Corps program, and anyone above the rank of navy lieutenant or army or Marine Corps captain were excluded. Eligible applicants could choose the equivalent of a twenty-year endowment insurance, with premiums paid by the government, in lieu of cash. Many of the yeomen (F) qualified for the $500 maximum, and a handful for the $625. Receiving the bonus was a happy surprise for most of them.

State Bonuses

Nineteen state governments also offered bonuses to their sons who had served under arms, some of them first inquiring of the navy whether their daughters who had given similar service should be included. Minnesota, for example, was offering fifteen dollars per month to all residents who had enrolled from there. Secretary Daniels told inquirers that the Navy Department believed the yeomen (F) could be defined as soldiers and were "therefore entitled to receive the bonus."[10]

Veterans' Health Benefits

Sick and disabled veterans found their government ill-prepared to care for them, despite its programs to expand the U.S. Public Health Service (USPHS), which was responsible for the medical care of the disabled. The USPHS had 1,548 beds. But the army had discharged 54,500 men for tuberculosis and mental illness alone by January 1919, and more than twice that number remained overseas and in army camps around the nation. The effects were devastating:

> Before long, many of the discharged, thrown into makeshift arrangements, suffered the terrible oversight. Some with TB contracted after the gas attacks [in Europe] and [after] long exposure, coughed their lives away. The mentally ill were housed in jails, and other patients were led to cots provided by the Legion posts.[11]

The veterans organizations mobilized to gain health care and employment for their members. They soon acquired a reputation for political independence and activism, to say nothing of large constituencies, and Congress saw the wisdom of streamlining the management of veterans affairs. In 1921 it relieved the USPHS of the responsibility for caring for the wounded veterans and established the U.S. Veterans' Bureau, consolidating the functions of the Bureau of War Risk Insurance (BWRI) and the Federal Board for Vocational Education. The new bureau soon became the Veterans Administration (VA). In 1924 Congress passed the World War Veterans Act, which codified and amended all pre- and postwar laws regarding veterans benefits. In 1989, the VA achieved cabinet status, becoming the Department of Veterans Affairs.

Postwar Health Care for Women Veterans

In 1919 the navy's Bureau of Medicine and Surgery had turned over responsibility for many of its sick and wounded veterans to the BWRI, which placed those veterans in hospitals run by the USPHS (see chapter 7). In 1920 the navy designated sixteen of its hospitals to set aside a total of more than 3,200 beds for the USPHS, along with the services of doctors, nurses, and hospital corpsmen. The principal facilities having reserved beds were the naval hospitals in Great Lakes, New York, Washington, D.C., Philadelphia, and Boston.[12]

The first navy women for whose health care the BWRI had assumed responsibility were those already admitted to navy hospitals. Most of the women in those hospitals, like Loretta Walsh, suffered from tuberculosis or other long-term complications of the flu. They were moved to USPHS hospitals or private hospitals under contract to the USPHS.

The rest of the women, with few exceptions, emerged from their navy and marine service in good health. Almost all had survived the flu and the long work hours required of them; some might even have been in better physical condition than when they entered the service. These women veterans would have little need for long-term medical care for another twenty or twenty-five years. Most resumed whatever system of medical care they had used as civilians. At that time, physicians who were general practitioners made house calls, and family members often met the need for care and nursing. The women were scarcely aware that the government should offer them the same medical benefits it was offering to male veterans.

However, some women who had served in the armed forces during World War I had—for whatever reason—little or no access to any civilian health care after the war simply because they could not afford it. When they suffered injury or illness and lost whatever slender income they had, they quickly became destitute. They were severely disadvantaged in the unemployment crisis of 1919–21, especially those who had few job skills or no work experience beyond their entry-level naval service. In 1923, a Legionnaire named Leroy Smith, employed by the newly organized Veterans' Bureau, wrote from Los Angeles, most eloquently, to the assistant secretary of the navy, Theodore Roosevelt, Jr. His words can hardly be improved upon:

> In this district ex-service women are experiencing acute suffering and embarrassment because they are ill and destitute yet do not fall under the purview of the Veterans' Bureau. Soldiers' Homes refuse these women, claiming lack of facilities to run what they call "Mixed Institutions." Yet, most domiciliary institutions in this country, both public and private, do exist as mixed institutions. . . . [T]hese women, often delicate and always sensitive, are the subjects of hit-or-miss philanthropy from friends, former comrades, municipal or county charity.
>
> All this because . . . the Soldiers' Homes were instituted for another day and generation, and are now anachronistic in this important regard.
>
> The percentage of unworthy claimants upon the custodial care of the Nation is indisputably higher among the men than among the women; we are, therefore, leaving the *most worthy* group to the uncertain consideration of private charity, with all of its attendant stigmata. This matter has been the subject of voluminous correspondence, interviews, and beseeching. . . .
>
> The Armistice was signed fifty-three months ago; the cases in question are piling up; the lapse of time is severing the threads of contact and sympathy; these worthy unfortunates have few powerful friends at court; the citizenry supposes that this their civic and patriotic duty is being adequately discharged by their chosen representatives. It isn't being so discharged.
>
> Meanwhile, what of the several hundred women in the United States who, with their sturdy brothers, answered their country's call, to find out that, broken in health, purse, and spirits, their country cares for their brothers but steadfastly refuses to care for them? . . . [this] bandying about of a presumably vexatious problem . . . is disastrous to many innocent folk.[13]

Smith's charge was well founded: Some navy women entitled to care were being wrongfully excluded. Roosevelt agreed that exclusion of the women was wrong, but remedies would be so expensive, he replied, that only Congress could help. However, he and his boss, Secretary of the Navy E. W. Eberle, did discuss with the secretary of the army whether their respective departments might somehow cooperate so as to offer help to women veterans.

Over the next few years, navy hospitals continued to insist that they had no room for women veterans and no money to provide any. The Veterans' Bureau pointed out that the army had set aside a few beds for women and asked if the navy could do the same in a naval district that contained three naval hospitals. No, said the navy, the best it could do was to carry out "the more simple laboratory tests [that] do not involve admission to or retention in the hospital."[14]

How could such a thing have happened? Why did the women *let* it happen? First, there were so few women veterans, about twelve thousand—slightly more if both army and navy nurses are included. The few hundred in need of help were scattered across a nation still somewhat shell-shocked from the number of deaths, mutilations, and lingering illness the war had cost during the nineteen months in which American troops had been engaged. In many parts of the country, no one even knew that women had served in the U.S. Navy and Marine Corps during the war. (At the beginning of the twenty-first century, some still do not know.) Also, many women veterans did not yet identify themselves as veterans. Those few who did were not, for the most part, inclined to be activists.

Domiciliary Care

As the women veterans aged, the number who needed medical care gradually rose. By 1933, more than four hundred former yeomen (F) were known to have disabilities for which they were entitled to compensation from the government. At least one veterans' hospital, the National Soldiers Home in Danville, Illinois, announced in 1930 that it had set aside special quarters for domiciliary care of former servicewomen. Long-term institutional care for needy women with debilitating illnesses raised a call for domiciliary facilities.

In 1935 the American Legion announced that the government planned to build five domiciles for women veterans: one on each coast and one each in the

Midwest, the Southeast, and New England. Plans included a single bedroom for each patient and all the usual hospital facilities. Where a federal home was not reasonably available, the announcement promised, the woman veteran could contract with a private hospital near her home, with the government responsible for payment. This privilege would not be open to men with disabilities not connected to service. Women would also be admitted to contract private hospitals not only for service-connected diseases but also for other health needs. Women veterans could also apply to VA hospitals for outpatient treatment, but only for service-connected disabilities. [15]

Most of the planned domiciliaries were never built, victims of the severe budget cuts forced by the Great Depression that began in 1929. State after state appealed to Congress to build these institutions, but the nation's economic crisis swept all before it, even reducing pensions and other veterans benefits. Over bitter protests of veterans, Congress passed the Economy Act in 1933, but it did allow women veterans treatment at private hospitals under contract to the VA, for treatment of diseases and injuries, whether service-connected or not.[16]

By the end of the 1930s, the older women who had answered the call to colors in 1917 were getting into their sixties and beyond. They did not enjoy the medical advances that women of the same age do today: Childbirth, disease, and accident took greater tolls then, all of those conditions exacerbated by the Great Depression. It is no surprise, then, to find that several hundred women veterans were hospitalized by the end of the decade, but only a few of them were in VA hospitals.

Some former Yeomen (F) did receive excellent care at some VA hospitals. For example, at the death of Lavene Broyderick, shipmate Helen Stolba MacBeth reported, "The excellent medical and nursing care she received at the VA hospital was a consolation to her family and friends who visited her."[17]

In general, however, VA records reveal very little about the quality or quantity of care provided to women veterans. In 1954 the national organization of former yeomen (F) found forty-one "shipmates permanently disabled or confined in domiciliary care" at seven different VA hospitals. Yet in 1972, when the same group asked every VA hospital to report how many women veterans it had enrolled in long-term care, only ten hospitals responded, reporting a total of seventeen women.[18] Some of the women counted in 1954 might well have died in the intervening years, but an equal or greater number might have entered, as well. It can reasonably be assumed that many more women veterans found their way to private hospitals, perhaps under contract to the VA, perhaps not.

As late as 1981 one former yeoman (F) escaped an anonymous burial in potter's field only because a fellow veteran moved quickly. Virginia Hall Wellwood, one of the first women to enlist in 1917, was a great-granddaughter of Lyman Hall, one of the signers of the Declaration of Independence. When she died at a Long Island hospital after a brief illness, all her family was gone, and only one friend even knew she had entered the hospital. That friend was Susan Davitian, also a former yeoman (F). Davitian called the local county offices of the New York State Division of Veterans Affairs, for whom Wellwood had worked for twenty-one years as a counselor to veterans. Wellwood's former supervisor quickly found that she had far more money than the twelve dollars found in her pockets at the hospital. One bank account held sixty thousand dollars. Arrangements were made for Wellwood's military burial at a nearby national cemetery. [19]

In any event, it is not surprising that the VA could not locate more women veterans under its care because, until 1980, it hardly noticed them at all. It kept no data on them and did little to care for them even when the women's maladies were clearly related to their military service.

Congress Catches Up

In the 1980s, Congress finally recognized that the nation had huge unacknowledged debts to its women veterans; by that time there were many more of them.

In World War II, almost four hundred thousand women served in the U.S. armed forces. Like their World War I predecessors, most of them did not realize that the VA owed them health care after the war. The few who tried to claim the benefits to which their service entitled them had been gruffly denied, with the same old story: no room at the inn.

But the feminist movement of the 1960s and 1970s had raised the consciousness of women to question and to protest. Moreover, the armed forces of the eighties—partly because they had become an all-volunteer force—welcomed women more than ever before. Old legal and political restrictions succumbed to new realities, allowing women to enter nearly every field of service and rise to higher ranks. Participation in numerous overseas combat situations finally made the general public aware that servicewomen—a great many of them—did exist.

The General Accounting Office (GAO) reported in 1982, however, that many VA hospitals did not admit women and lacked obstetrical and gynecological facilities. The GAO called upon the VA to prepare for increased numbers of women patients, to ensure that they be given equal access to all health benefits, and to make available care for specifically female conditions other than pregnancy and delivery.

The 1990 census showed that about 1.2 million women had served in the armed forces and comprised about 4 percent of all veterans; by 2010 they could comprise more than 10 percent. Legislation in 1992, 1994, and 1997 addressed remaining shortfalls in VA health care for women veterans.[20] The VA today offers them better care than it did, partly because a newer generation of health-care specialists and VA administrators are better attuned to serving both men and women.

Even so, the VA's coverage of women veterans throughout the nation is still so thin that in some places they have virtually no access to it. For example, the VA's mammography centers today number forty-five, scattered across twenty-two states. Civilian centers are authorized to offer care to women veterans, but often there are long waiting times for appointments, and many local facilities do not meet VA standards of certification. As of September 1998, the Department of Veterans Affairs noted that thirty-six women veterans of World War I were still receiving benefits; how many are former yeomen (F) and how many are army or navy nurses is not known.[21]

The Naval Reserve Act of 1925

Early in the postwar years, the former yeomen (F) sustained a stinging defeat. The wording of the Naval Reserve Act of 1925 was changed to limit membership in the Naval Reserve to "male citizens of the United States," except for nurses. The former yeomen (F) had appeared before the Senate Naval Affairs Committee to complain that the exclusion cast a slur upon their wartime service. This point so impressed Senator Oddie of Nevada that on the Senate floor he moved to strike the word "male" from the bill. Senator Wadsworth of New York responded scornfully to Oddie's move, stating that it might open the way for women to serve in the Army Reserve as well. None of his colleagues supported Oddie; perhaps they shared Wadsworth's implied assumption that women in the army and navy reserves was an absurd idea. Even more telling was the failure of U.S. Navy officials to speak on the women's behalf at this juncture, despite the many words of praise that they had showered upon the yeomen (F) for their contributions to the war effort. Finding no support, and unwilling to hold up passage of the bill, Oddie withdrew his proposed amendment.[22]

An opportunity to amend the bill arose in 1938. By that time, more than eighteen years had passed since any women other than nurses had appeared in navy uniform, years during which the public had nearly forgotten the navy and marine women's wartime service. The American economy was barely pulling out of the Great Depression, while totalitarianism in Europe and the Far East menaced world peace. Even though President Franklin Roosevelt's personal secretary, Marguerite (Missy) LeHand, had been a yeoman (F), the implications of retaining "male" in the 1938 bill went unnoticed. Four years later, with America once more at war, the secretary of the navy could not enlist women as easily as Josephus Daniels had; first he had to ask Congress to amend the 1938 act that still carried the 1925 folly. This caused the navy a six-month delay in recruiting much-needed women into the U.S. Navy and Marine Corps after Pearl Harbor.

In the short term immediately following the war, the government provided to the women veterans of the U.S. Navy and Marine Corps the same benefits it did to men. But it failed to include them in any provisions for long-term health care. Official concern for male veterans developed and expanded over the ensuing years, but similar concern for women did not keep pace. In many cases, it was not so much that official policies failed to include women, but rather that those policies were implemented haphazardly or not at all. Not until the 1980s did an ever-increasing number of disregarded women veterans—plus the plight of some male veterans—arouse sufficient public interest to effect improvements.

NINE

Keeping in Touch
National Yeomen F and Women Marines Association

To foster and perpetuate memory of [their] service.

National Yeomen F Charter

THE AMERICAN LEGION'S PUBLICATIONS helped the former yeomen (F) gain news of one another, and its annual conventions gave them much-treasured opportunities to meet. By 1924 the women had determined to form their own national organization. The National Yeomen F (NYF) had three main goals: to keep in touch, to support patriotic enterprises, and to preserve their memory. The first two they accomplished. For some time, the third eluded them, despite many individual and collective efforts. Now, however, memory of their service seems on its way toward restoration.

The women marines of World War I did not form an organization after their discharges but remained in touch informally. In 1960 they happily joined up with the women marines of World War II and after, who had formed the Women Marines Association.

Founding the National Yeomen F

The defeat at the hands of Congress in 1925 (see chapter 8) gave the former yeomen (F) a sad lesson in how easily their historic contribution to the nation might be overlooked. One immediate result was renewed interest in forming a national organization. The early women's American Legion posts were instrumental in sparking that interest.

As commander of the USS *Jacob Jones* Post No. 2, Helen O'Neill in the summer of 1924 invited members from various posts to a meeting in New York to discuss the matter. By the time of the Legion's eighth annual convention in Philadelphia, in 1926, the idea was well formed. Members of the all-women Legion Post No. 50 hosted a meeting of two hundred other former yeomen (F) attending the convention for further discussion. The group met again in September to form the National Yeomen F (NYF) and elected Cecelia Geiger its first commander. The new organization held its first annual meeting in Atlantic City in July 1927. Members from New York, New Jersey, Connecticut, Pennsylvania, and the District of Columbia attended. On 3 August 1928, the NYF was incorporated under the laws of the District of Columbia. By that year's end, the NYF had its own insignia, designed by O'Neill: a gold anchor superimposed on two gold crossed quills, reminiscent of the navy's rating badge for yeomen. An official flag soon followed: a replica of the insignia on a field of blue silk. The NYF's most significant initiative was to establish a quarterly newsletter, the *Note Book*. The first issue appeared in November 1928.[1]

Rather than forming posts, chapters, or branches, the NYF divided itself into several regions across the country, each region with its own officers, including representatives to an executive council. The strong connection with the American Legion facilitated contact among the NYF members; figuratively speaking (and to some extent literally), each organization waved the other's flag. At post meetings, news of the NYF could spread readily to other women Legionnaires.

Thus the NYF was launched with the vigor and style that would characterize its entire existence, and it trumpeted its mission immediately. One of the earliest issues of the *Note Book*, that of September 1929, voiced the women's overriding concern that their service not be lost to history. Members were asked to contribute stories from their service days. "Let it be true," was the advice given. "Say it in your own words . . . let's put this wonderful story of ours in black and white for future generations."

Official recognition came quickly. The NYF was invited to march in the inaugural parade for President Hoover in March 1929. Thirty-five very proud former yeomen (F) marched behind their flag—its first public appearance. They were no doubt well aware that no other group of thirty-five women in the country could be assembled on short notice and *march* in proper military style in such a solemn, official parade.[2]

Gaining a Charter

Issues of the *Note Book* appeared every three months, encouraging all readers to contact the women with whom they had served and solicit their membership in the NYF. By 1930 members numbered 435 from twenty-eight states, plus two living in the Territory of Alaska and one each in Canada, Italy, and the Territory of Hawaii.

In 1936, more than six hundred members, from nearly every state, Puerto Rico, and the Territories of Hawaii and Alaska, petitioned Congress to grant the NYF a national charter. Congressman William P. Connery and Senator Francis T. Maloney sponsored the petition. President Franklin Roosevelt signed Public Law 74-676 on 15 June 1936, using two pens, one of which the NYF's legislative officer later framed.[3] (See appendix A.)

The charter first named all the signers of the petition, then added,

> and their associates and successors are hereby created a body corporate and politic, in the District of Columbia, by the name of 'The National Yoemen [*sic*] F,' for patriotic, historical, and educational purposes; to foster and perpetuate the memory of the service of Yoemen (F) in the United States Naval Reserve Force of the United States Navy during the World War; to preserve the memories and incidents of their association in the World War by the encouragement of historical research concerning the service of the Yoemen (F).

Clearly, one of the newly chartered organization's first educational duties was to teach Congress how to spell "yeomen."

The charter allowed the NYF to have no more than fifty thousand dollars worth of assets; in reality, its annual budget usually ran to less than three thousand dollars. Annual dues were set at one dollar and remained there until doubled in 1971. The charter also instructed the NYF to submit a report annually to the secretary of the Smithsonian Institution, who in turn was to communicate to Congress "such portions thereof as he may deem of national interest and importance," a requirement later dropped. Finally, the Smithsonian was to permit the NYF to deposit its "collections, manuscripts, books, pamphlets and other materials for history." The final provision resulted in the Smithsonian having a complete file of the *Note Book,* including three bound volumes, from the first edition through 1985.[4] Without this collection, much of the history of the yeomen (F) would have been lost, for the U.S. Navy's own records are meager, scattered throughout the files of numerous navy offices and bureaus.

Camaraderie and Loyalty

Almost every event, large or small, in the NYF's existence manifests its major themes of mutual support, loyalty to the national institutions that had brought them together in the first place, and preservation of their place in history. The *Note Book* gave news of travels, work, and hobbies. Best wishes, condolences, congratulations, and affectionate greetings filled up the four, six, or eight pages of each quarter's leaflet. Every issue carried a list of donations made to the organization by members to celebrate a "shipmate's" birthday or memorialize her death. The amounts ranged over the years from one dollar to (rarely) twenty-five.

A primary responsibility of the national commander during her two-year term was to visit every region as well as preside over the annual convention, which moved from city to city. By bus and train they made their journeys, exchanging news and views. They were quick to pass the word about members' activities, worrisome illnesses, and the inevitable deaths. When Lavene Broyderick died in 1960, her sister wrote of "the host of loyal friends from 'Yeoman F' days who remembered Lavene in her last days. Such lasting remembrance after 42 years is typical of the bond of loyal comradeship which has strengthened with time among those of us who still survive."[5]

These women were not wealthy, yet they gave faithfully to support many causes. They looked after the orphans of deceased yeomen (F) and created awards and scholarships for young people in service to the nation or their communities, as well as for those most in need of help and encouragement. At the same time they were loyal American Legion members, accepting responsibilities within local posts and at the national level, often scheduling their own meetings with the Legion's. On patriotic holidays they planned festivities, marched in parades, raised funds, and enjoyed social events. Histories of Legion posts frequently reveal names of the same women accepting leadership positions in both organizations. NYF members marched with their respective Legion posts in all Legion parades. In the mid-1930s, the NYF was invited to send representatives to the National Council on Defense, an organization that convened annually to discuss national defense. They responded immediately and soon made their mark there. O'Neill became the council's treasurer, certainly adding to NYF's prestige and recognition.[6]

Uniforms

A theme that runs throughout the organization's history is its members' enduring pride in their uniforms. Over the years the *Note Book* reminded members that their uniforms were valuable, and should they wish or need to dispose of them they would find ready takers in federal, state, and local museums. The Smithsonian Institution was pleased to receive several women's uniforms and has displayed them from time to time. In addition, authentic uniforms were made available, for example, for state library exhibits in New York, Rhode Island, and Connecticut and also to museums in Oregon, Louisiana, and California. In 1925 Madeline Ann Knight Johnson named a twenty-two-inch doll "Madeline," then dressed it in a uniform she had manufactured from her own, including shoes, gloves, purse, buttons, and badge—memorializing it in her own way.[7]

In 1925 the U.S. Navy offered a more permanent memorial to the yeomen (F) uniform when it celebrated its sesquicentennial in Philadelphia, by commissioning artist Ann Fuller Abbott to paint a portrait of a yeoman (F) in winter uniform. Three NYF members posed for the portrait, their faces blended into one composite: Charlotte Berry, Helen O'Neill, and Ulla Tracy. O'Neill donated a brass plaque for its frame. After the celebration, the portrait hung for years in the building known as "Main Navy" on Constitution Avenue in Washington, D.C. When that building was torn down in 1971, the navy lent the portrait to the naval station at Bainbridge, Maryland, where enlisted navy women recruits then received their basic training. It subsequently moved to Orlando, then back to Washington. Newly cleaned and renovated, the portrait now hangs at the navy's art gallery in the Washington Navy Yard.[8]

The navy's Historical Department actively solicited donations of uniforms from NYF members and received several. In return, at one point the department was willing to lend uniforms to NYF members for special occasions. One member reported in 1969 that she had recently borrowed one, having "signed the required receipt and received acknowledgment of the return in good condition."[9]

Remembering Josephus Daniels

If the American Legion was the NYF's birthplace, Josephus Daniels was its father, revered throughout their lives by the women he brought into service. Often the NYF invited him to speak at reunions. He accepted these invitations whenever he could and promptly sent regrets when he could not. Numerous former yeomen (F) corresponded with him, some addressing him as "Dear Uncle Joe." To one member who asked him to autograph a copy of one of his books, he replied on 28 March 1945,

> *My dear Mrs. Stafford,*
> *It gives me very great pleasure to autograph a copy of "The Wilson Era" for you. As you know, I always feel very close to all the yeomen "F." They were pioneers in rendering a great service. They laid the foundation for the larger contribution which women are making in this war. With my high regards, I am,*
> *Your old friend and shipmate, Josephus Daniels.*

He died in 1948, after having served as the U.S. ambassador to Mexico. The

NYF sent flowers to his funeral and mourned his passing. Upon the commissioning of the USS *Josephus S. Daniels,* DLG 27 (destroyer leader guided
missile ship) in May of 1965, NYF Commander Mary King, accompanied by
twenty-five other members, presented a bronze plaque to the captain and
crew. Following the commissioning ceremony, they ate lunch with the crew in
the ship's mess (dining hall), where they could view, now installed and shining
in all its spit-and-polished glory, the tangible tribute of their affection. It read:
"In Memoriam of Honorable Josephus Daniels, Secretary of the Navy during
World War I, who made it possible for women to serve their country in 1917."
Ships are scrapped, or go out of service, or are sold, but the yeomen (F)'s
memories of Daniels stayed green. Fifteen years later, Irene Malito Brown, an
NYF founder, happily joined other NYF members living at the Sailors Home
in Gulfport, Mississippi. She wrote to her "shipmates": "Little did I think,
when I enlisted in 1918, that the Navy would do so much for me in my 'old age.'
. . . Yes, I am grateful to . . . Daniels, who made it possible for us to serve our
country."[10]

Memorial to Loretta Walsh

Loretta Walsh died in 1925, months before the NYF was formed. Her death
and what she symbolized as the first of the women to have enlisted in the U.S.
Navy were integral to their sense of preserving the memory of their service.

When the NYF sought to have her remains reinterred at Arlington, the
government gave them a single plot, as it did for others buried there. The women
petitioned for a second plot next to the first, allowing enough room for a monument that would stand in honor of all the navy women who had served. When
every effort to secure the second plot failed, the women had to abandon the
project.

In Walsh's hometown of Olyphant, Pennsylvania, this historic figure was
already interred at St. Patrick's Cemetery in an unmarked grave. When members of the American Legion Raymond Henry Post No. 327 in Olyphant learned
of her burial site, they undertook to raise a memorial dedicated to her memory.
They of course invoked the help of the NYF to make a general patriotic appeal

to all veterans to subscribe to a fitting memorial. Raymond Henry Post raised a little more than half the funds to purchase a grave site and build the memorial, and the women veterans contributed the remainder.

Two thousand people attended the memorial's dedication in October 1937. High officials of the Legion attended, as well as state government dignitaries. NYF Commander Irene Malito Brown and Past Commanders Geiger, O'Neill, and Maybelle Bond attended and gratefully acknowledged contributions received from more than a thousand former yeomen (F) throughout the country, literally from coast to coast.[11] On Walsh's gravestone, in addition to her name and dates of service, are engraved these words: "Woman and Patriot, first of those enrolled in the United States Naval Service, her comrades dedicate this monument to keep alive forever memories of the sacrifice and devotion of womanhood."

In 1940 the NYF petitioned the navy's Bureau of Ships to name a ship after Walsh. Admiral Randall Jacobs, chief of the bureau, denied the request, explaining that U.S. Navy ships could be named only for persons who met certain strict requirements. Walsh met none of them.

The Stamp

From 1935 onward, the NYF repeatedly petitioned the federal government to issue a stamp commemorating its members' services. The frustrations of Mary Dwyer, chairman of the NYF stamp committee, boiled over in the *Note Book* of September 1968. She noted how many friends and supporters of the NYF, including the U.S. president, had urged the U.S. postmaster general to award the stamp. The powerful American Legion had twice passed resolutions at its national conventions to that effect. Nonetheless, wrote Dwyer,

> Again come the disheartening letters from the Post Office Department, saying "Our Citizens Stamp Advisory Committee gave very serious consideration to your request, but. . . ." and now, after they have turned us down for our 50th anniversary, they advise that "since the anniversary year has passed, apparently it will be necessary to wait for another significant date to further pursue the proposal." . . . [T]o each one of us, every year is

significant! . . . Surely, in the evening of our lives, [ours] is not an unreasonable request! . . . Commemoratives have been given to honoring dogs, flowers, birds, and clowns—undoubtedly all good causes—then what is wrong with ours?

But the unkindest cut of all came when the Women Marines were honored with a Stamp to mark their 25th ANNIVERSARY [of the USMC Women's Reserve in 1943, during World War II].

She closed by listing the names and addresses of eleven members of the Stamp Advisory Committee, urging every member of the NYF and their friends to write to the postmaster general and his committee, asking "Why? Why? Why?" Given what we know of the yeomen (F), we can reasonably assume the named persons received some blistering mail. In the next fifteen years, more supporters joined their voices to the request, including sitting presidents, a sitting secretary of the navy, and a former chief of naval operations.[12]

Regrettably, the yeomen (F) have yet to be honored with even one stamp, despite a news report in 1968 that the U.S. Postal Service had run out of subjects to honor and named subjects that had been honored more than once.

New Recognition, New Strength

At first the NYF members could not understand why the newspapers so wrongly (and loudly) proclaimed the army and navy women of World War II as a new phenomenon. But identification with the WAVES and other servicewomen helped the former yeomen (F) to see themselves as they too might have been. Daughters of NYF members who had become WAVES rapidly fostered friendships between members of WAVES units and their predecessors. When the WAVES celebrated the first anniversary of their creation on 30 July 1943, NYF members were on hand to celebrate. The members of Post No. 50 in Philadelphia marched with the WAVES in the navy women's first anniversary parade in that city.[13]

The contributions that the WAVES made to the war effort and their popularity with the general public helped the former yeomen (F) to reassess their own service. Many became more willing to be publicly identified as participants in an historical event then thirty-five years past. One consequence was a renewed interest in the organization. NYF membership increased over the two and a half decades following the end of World War II, reaching a peak of about thirteen hundred in 1969. That number was well above 10 percent of those eligible, a statistic of which the members boasted, knowing that it was the largest percentage in membership of any of the veterans' organizations.[14]

Having been so generally overlooked during World War II stung the former yeomen (F) into realizing that historical oblivion was still a threat. Even the youngest among them were as old as the century itself, and they began finding a new urgency about ensuring an accurate record of their service. When the Women's Armed Forces Integration Act of 1948 allowed women to have full careers in the nation's regular armed forces, it reaffirmed the older women's identity as military veterans and they grew more willing to claim recognition. For example, in 1963, after a very popular television talk show broadcast a story giving the impression that no women had served in the military during World War I, NYF Commander Mary Dwyer called network officials to task. They explained how the facts had "been garbled," then invited the NYF to give them advance notice of its next anniversary. Thus Dwyer and one other NYF member appeared on the show in June 1963. The resultant publicity delighted the women and helped to compensate for other oversights. When the 1965 *World Almanac* failed to mention the yeomen (F), NYF Commander Mary Margaret King wrote to its publisher, who apologized and assured her that the next edition would amend the error.[15]

Neglect by the public press was one thing; neglect by the Department of Defense (DOD) another. In 1981 DOD failed to invite NYF dignitaries to services paying tribute to veterans of World War II and the Korean conflict. NYF Commander Margaret Faglon Schutt wrote to the army major general in charge of the affair, advising him of the oversight.

> His office replied that at that time there were no tickets available to us. This was the start of a real tear-jerking correspondence which resulted in our receiving two front row center tickets and a . . . VIP parking space . . . [A]lthough it was a sad and solemn occasion we felt proud and happy to represent N.Y.F., and to have our floral wreath placed with others at the tomb.[16]

As others had before him, the major general learned that snubbing the NYF was not a winning move.

Memorial Contributions

During its lifetime, the NYF made several memorable contributions to good causes that notably combined its main objectives. Two examples follow.

United States Naval Academy

In section 32 of the Navy–Marine Corps Memorial Stadium in Annapolis is seat no. 23, donated by the NYF. The Naval Academy's Index of Memorials lists that seat under "Memorial Chairs (Miscellaneous)" and notes its donors as "The National Yeomen F, World War I." NYF Commander Margaret Schutt later recalled, "As we were the first women to be enlisted in the Navy, we had the honor of having a seat bearing our NYF insignia installed there."

That honor, however, was insufficient to keep the academy from over-looking not only the yeomen (F) of World War I but all other women who had served in the nation's armed forces: When the new stadium was dedicated in 1959, the academy described it as "a perpetual reminder of the Navy and Marine Corps as organizations of *men* trained to work hard and play hard...." [emphasis added][17]

Cathedral of the Pines

The Cathedral of the Pines is a beautiful and unique place of worship in Rindge, New Hampshire. Situated on a spectacular mountain site, it is a humble and gentle gathering place. Douglas and Sybil Sloane began it in 1945 to memorialize their son Sanderson, killed a year earlier in action over Germany. In 1963 a memorial bell tower was built at the Cathedral's entrance, dedicated to all American women—from pioneers to those serving in the modern armed forces —who had died in the nation's wars. Famed illustrator Norman Rockwell and his son Peter were among the tower's designers. Women from all the armed services took part in its groundbreaking, and in 1967 the NYF donated a bronze plate to the Cathedral's pulpit.[18]

Histories: Perseverance and Preservation

When she learned, probably in 1930, that histories of the early years of USS *Jacob Jones* Post No. 2 had been lost, Helen O'Neill prepared a chronicle up through 1929. Twice more she added to the chronicle, the last entry being September 1943. Many entries shed light on NYF activities as well as those of the post. No more reliable person could have been found to document so much of that early history, since she was an eyewitness to or participant in most of it.

During their lifetimes, several other former yeomen (F) attempted to compile histories, but few manuscripts survived. Some were lost or never finished, while others went to archives no longer in existence or were absorbed under another name, virtually untraceable.[19]

Two published memoirs have survived. The first is a fourteen-page booklet written by former Yeoman (F) Helen Butler, published by the Naval Historical Foundation in 1967, titled *I Was a Yeoman (F)*. Butler enlisted after graduating from college in 1918, and her generally accurate account is enlivened by some tart observations. Far better known is Joy Bright Hancock's autobiography, *Lady in the Navy*, published by the Naval Institute Press in 1972. Recollections of her childhood and of her unique and invaluable subsequent naval service give a broad perspective to her account of her days as a yeoman (F).

Only in the mid-1990s did the largest documentation of yeomen (F) become available to researchers. Its author was a woman who had died in 1974 with perhaps only 10 percent of her huge amount of research published. "I am devoting these years of my life to PRESERVING for posterity the memory of our PATRIOTIC WOMEN of World War I . . . I am still an old maid and have no ties that bind . . . all of my time is devoted to this work of love." So wrote former Chief Yeoman (F) Eunice Dessez to a friend in December of 1956.[20]

Dessez came from a family with a record of military service dating back to the American Revolution. Her brother ended his career in the Marine Corps as a brigadier general. In 1917 she was a spirited young woman who owned and rode an Excelsior motorcycle. She was the second woman in the District of Columbia licensed to drive a motorcycle; one of her friends was the first. "Our brothers taught us to drive our own machines . . . on roads not as good as they are today. Many a time I fell off on a slippery road but never suffered any injury because I was so thin I fell under the machine and the pedal kept its weight off [me]."[21]

When the war broke out, she sold her motorcycle and enlisted in the navy. She served in the enrollment division of the Navy Department, where she was able to raise a distress signal to her commanding officer in time to prevent the yeomen (F) from being given ordinary discharges (see chapter 7). Following discharge, she remained in the department as a civil servant and continued to live in Washington, D.C. She was one of the earliest members of USS *Jacob Jones* Post No. 2 and, in 1923, its commander. She never married.

Like many former yeomen (F), Dessez had noted with dismay that during World War II the public press hardly—if at all—mentioned the yeomen (F), as if they had never even existed. By 1953 she had begun to collect information for herself:

> I wrote to the National Yeomen F, various [American Legion] post com-
> manders and the commandants of the several Naval Districts asking for
> information. The result was very disappointing, in fact in many instances
> no replies were received; then I made up the form letters and sent out sev-
> eral thousands, only a few [replies] were received. . . . I have worked very
> hard to get "something" on the record about the yeomen F and have spent
> most of an inheritance. The result has been discouraging. A [Legion] Post
> Commander from . . . Norfolk promised to send me some material several
> years ago but nothing happened. Soon I will be *too old to work on this proj-
> ect* and have been anxious to complete the job before I get unable to type.[22]

She faced a vast and difficult task. Her own personal acquaintanceship, though large because of her Legion connections, covered only a fraction of the nearly twelve thousand women she intended to reach; moreover, it did not always include addresses, and marriage changed many women's last names.

Over the next few years she sent out more than five thousand question-naires and answered all who responded; to some she sent further queries. All this was at her own expense and with no more support than her typewriter and liberal supplies of bond and carbon paper. Some women who received the questionnaires were dubious about them, wondering just who Eunice Dessez was and why she wanted all this information. When she explained that no organization or branch of the government was sponsoring her inquiries and her sole purpose was only to write a history of the yeomen (F), most at least completed the questionnaire.

Among her frustrations was that not all those surveyed understood the point of her question, "Do you recall the names of any other Yeoman (F) with whom you served?" Several merely answered "Yes," while a few others said "Several" or "Many." Moreover, she found that many people apparently believed there was some official list of yeomen (F) to be found someplace in the navy's records. She assured her correspondents that there was no such list. In fact, she explained, "Few people know it, but there is VERY LITTLE information about the First Enlisted Women . . . in Washington D.C."[23]

To their credit, numerous navy commands, including more than half of the existing naval districts, answered with lists of women who had served. Where they had no official records, they sent the names of women who they believed could help. While several of those women were extremely helpful, notably in Pennsylvania and Connecticut, others were not. Lack of response to her queries to a woman in Massachusetts, where so many had served, led Dessez to write to a friend that she "did not feel very happy about the land of the Pilgrim fathers."[24]

In 1955 Dorrance and Company of Philadelphia agreed to publish her book, titled *The First Enlisted Women*. Noted writer and naval historian Capt. Walter Karig praised it highly: He wrote that she had not tried to create a "literary *chef d'oeuvre,* but rather to record what had happened through the eyes of a participant." The first printing sold out completely, and a second edition appeared in 1956. Still, Dessez was disappointed in the book as published. The publisher had insisted upon huge cuts, omitting the more than five thousand names and dates and places of service. Thus the book contained only a very small portion of the invaluable material she had collected. It was out of print by 1958, and Dessez held the few remaining copies for former yeomen (F). These she sold to eligible customers for $2.50, plus nine cents postage.

Numerous former shipmates expressed appreciation for her labors, and some even offered to help with her expenses, offers she firmly refused.[25]

The information continued to trickle in, even after the book's publication. Dessez at first assembled it alphabetically by last names (a procedure complicated by marriages) but soon had to subdivide further. Thus she began recording information alphabetically by states, then by last names. She did not have, of course, modern technology to facilitate sorting and organizing information. Nonetheless, over the years she annotated her thousands of typed entries with clippings, letters, and occasional pictures, some of them received after the volumes in which they belonged were bound. Her diligence and attention to detail give the papers an authenticity that far outweighs the pages' irregular and even amateurish appearance. At her own expense, she bound six volumes in blue leather with gold lettering. These were not, she emphasized, for sale.

It is due to Dessez's efforts that the records of two former yeomen (F) born in London who later became American citizens were preserved. She sent copies of their war records to the Imperial Museum in London. These women had been buried in Arlington National Cemetery, and their homeland might otherwise never have known that they too had experienced naval service similar to that of the British women who served in Women's Royal Naval Service during World War I.

In 1963 she submitted the first two volumes to the Library of Congress. The first volume included some general background about U.S. participation in World War I, interspersed with clippings and photos, then proceeded with her earliest collections of names. The second volume contained a state-by-state list. The library rejected her offering, deeming it "not worthy of inclusion in the collections of this [Manuscript] division."[26]

We hear no more from Dessez on the subject. We can only imagine the vast disappointment, even embarrassment, she suffered at this refusal. She might have been comforted had she known that the information, stored in six bound volumes and a folder for what she probably planned for the seventh, would one day come at last to a safe harbor. After her death in 1974, her brother stored these boxes of irreplaceable information in an attic, where they languished until his death. His granddaughter found them and donated them to the Naval Historical Center, where they became available to researchers early in the 1990s.[27]

Declining Years of the NYF

The *Note Books* of the 1970s and 1980s report more and more illnesses, and of course, more deaths. Membership dropped off sharply; in 1979 it was just over 552, less than half of what it had been at its peak a decade earlier. Increasingly conscious of their mortality, more members began contributing to the *Note Book* their own stories of service. Brief though they are, these stories often reveal a lively flash of the young women the authors had been—their sense of urgency to enlist, their families' reactions, their adventures in finding (or not finding) housing.

The women's pluck and mutual support probably gave to the NYF a few more years of life than it might otherwise have enjoyed. The navy helped by welcoming several dozen eligible navy women to its retirement home for enlisted men and women in Gulfport, Mississippi. When NYF treasurer Germain Lovejoy and her husband Al celebrated their sixtieth anniversary at the home in 1980, the governor of the home gave the celebrating couple a surprise luncheon, at which he noted that such a happy event "has never before happened in the more than 150 years of the Naval Home."

Navy women stationed nearby often remembered and honored the former yeomen (F) living at the Gulfport home. On the NYF's sixtieth anniversary in 1986, thirteen active-duty navy women stationed nearby came to visit, surprising their hostesses by bringing them individual corsages and a large, decorated cake. Another center of NYF unity and energy was Connecticut, where local members hosted an annual luncheon attended by members from near and far, who signed the guest notebook that had been signed by attendees every year since 1944.[28]

But the inevitable ending was at hand.

A Noble Ending

The NYF's demise was foreshadowed in August 1984 when Commander Anne Kendig announced that its upcoming annual reunion would have to be canceled because "infirmities of our age have taken their toll of many, making traveling long distances not feasible." In the *Note Book* of April 1985 the word "disbanded" appeared for the first time: "When our organization is to be disbanded, important memorabilia, such as our Charter, will be turned over to the Smithsonian. . . ." At the time the NYF had a paid-up membership of 210, a checking account balance of $3,153.68, and a memorial fund of several hundred dollars.[29]

Kendig named Gertrude Howalt chairman of the NYF's committee for disposition of the organization's funds and memorabilia. Howalt had enlisted very early—2 April 1917. She was rated a yeoman second class and later advanced to chief yeoman. Athletic and competitive, she was captain of the First Naval District's championship basketball team of 1918–19 and later won the Army-Navy Medal in Boston as a runner. A longtime member of the NYF, she was for many years its Southern representative and a prodigious recruiter for new members. She keenly appreciated the imminent need to plan for the NYF's disbandment.

In 1979, she had made a fateful journey to the Smithsonian Institution in Washington, D.C. There she met with Dr. Harold Langley, then curator of the Smithsonian's Naval History Division. The meeting went well. He assured her of the division's interest in uniforms, photos, newspaper clippings, and any other materials relating to the yeomen (F). Howalt later reported to NYF members that he gave her a tour "and explained there may be a display showing a waterfront street with a Yeoman F buying a 5-cent hot dog from a pushcart or 'snitching' a piece of ice from an old ice wagon, also showing the old gas lights, etc., from 1917." Since her first meeting with Langley, she and her husband had maintained a correspondence with him. He had already mounted several temporary exhibits of yeomen (F) uniforms.[30]

As the committee considered their options, they discussed several possibilities, including dividing their assets between the Navy Relief Society and the Smithsonian. Howalt argued otherwise: "I feel strongly that giving the funds to the Smithsonian with the stipulation that they be used only toward the erection of a lasting memorial . . . would be of greater benefit to all members. . . ." Her idea prevailed, and soon she and her husband were discussing with Langley how best to proceed. A generous provision of six thousand dollars from the Howalt family launched the Smithsonian Yeomen (F) Memorial Fund. The NYF's final material contribution to the nation was to donate to the fund all its cash assets. Contributions from some of its 266 remaining members brought the fund's initial deposits to approximately twenty-two thousand dollars, drawing interest. Only the fund's interest and principal above the original six thousand dollars may be spent.[31]

The Smithsonian's curator for naval history administers the fund, which is dedicated to preparing exhibits and publications featuring the yeomen (F) and supporting historical research focused on them. Thus far the fund has made possible one permanent exhibit case featuring the yeomen (F) and a grant to the authors of this book.

In the *Note Book* of December 1985, NYF Commander Anne Kendig announced the organization's dissolution: "The average age of our members is between 85 and 90, and traveling to places for our annual and other meetings has become difficult, if not impossible, for some of us. Much as we dislike to admit to infirmities of age, we must face reality." In that same issue was an announcement that may have been the saddest ever posted in its more than two hundred editions:

THIS IS THE FINAL ISSUE OF THE NOTE BOOK. THE NATIONAL YEOMAN F WILL BE DISBANDED AS OF JANUARY 1st, 1986. THEREFORE, PLEASE DO NOT MAIL OBITUARIES OR CHECKS FOR DUES OR DONATIONS TO ANY OF THE OFFICERS.

Once a Marine, Always a Marine

The women marines of World War I did not formally organize after the war as did the yeomen (F), although they kept in touch. Many of the more than two hundred who had served at USMC Headquarters in Washington, D.C., stayed on in civil service. The rest scattered to their homes, many up and down the Eastern Seaboard, some in the West. Some joined the American Legion and the Marine Corps League. In World War II, at least five returned to service, this time as commissioned officers (see epilogue).

In World War II, the Marine Corps' Women's Reserve brought nearly eighteen thousand women into the Marine Corps. Those veterans, too, kept in touch with their wartime comrades and met for reunions. At one such reunion in Denver in 1960, 105 marine women—both active duty and veterans—formed the Women Marines Association (WMA), electing Lt. Col. Genevieve Dooner as its first president. At the WMA's first annual convention, in 1961, member Emma Holmes took on the task of finding the women marines of World War I. She vigorously pursued all leads, including a 1919 roster of fifty names and hometowns forwarded by Lela Leibrand. By 1976, Holmes had made contact with, or could account for, 134 women of the 305 who had served.[32]

Holmes carried out her task with considerable energy and creativity. During her chairmanship, several imaginative, positive events focused on the "One-derfuls," as they soon came to be called. At the WMA's ninth annual convention, twenty of them attended, the highest percentage of any group present. An active-duty marine in dress blues escorted each to her table, then her 1918 likeness flashed on a screen, together with a review of her service highlights. On one evening in October 1974, the commandant of the Marine Corps swore in five women recruits, and this time each was escorted by a World War I veteran. In February 1979, twenty WMA members, including eight One-derfuls, held a reunion aboard a cruise ship to the Caribbean. One chapter named itself after one of its World War I members, Edith Macias Vann, choosing to "honor the past in the person of our namesake."[33]

Final Musters

In early 1980, Daisy Lingle died after a month-long battle with pneumonia. Aged ninety-seven, a former historian and bibliographer, she had been the oldest surviving woman marine of World War I. By 1986, thirty-two World War I veterans remained on WMA membership rolls, their average age eighty-nine years. At that time, this prayer appeared in the WMA newsletter: "Send me forth unto the days that lie ahead with a gallant heart, that I may live to the end of my days as it becometh one who bears the title 'Marine.'"[34]

Some of them were remarkably active, working in their retirement homes, holding American Legion offices, some still living independently. *American Heritage,* an historical magazine, had just published an article by Elizabeth Linscott, aged eighty-six. Journalist and poet Violet Lopez, also eighty-six and a former president of the Women's Press Club of New York City, still served as public relations officer for other volunteer organizations and had just proudly published her first book. Two years later Lopez was still attending writers' conventions and had won a thousand dollars for one of her poems. She died in November 1992 and was buried at Arlington with full military honors. The last surviving woman marine of World War I was Maybelle Hall, who died in October 1995, at age 106.[35]

Memory Set in Stone in the Nation's Capital

On 17 October 1997, former Yeoman (F) Frieda Hardin, aged 101, addressed the thirty thousand people assembled for the dedication of the Women in Military Service for America (WIMSA) Memorial at Arlington National Cemetery. Hardin's words captured the indomitable spirit of the yeomen (F) as her still-strong voice rang out her wishes to those women considering or already embarked on a military career: "GO FOR IT!" Then former Yeoman (F) Anne Pedersen stood next to the vice president of the United States as they cut the ribbon formally opening the memorial. At that time, only a handful of yeoman (F) and no World War I women marines were known to be alive.

With the raising of the memorial, dedicated to *all* women who have served in the U.S. armed forces, the historical tribute that the yeomen (F) had long sought at last stood in stone at one of the nation's most sacred sites. In the archives of the WIMSA foundation, more than 350 yeomen (F) and women marines of World War I were already registered, most of them posthumously.[36] Registrations from the families and friends of others continue to arrive at the WIMSA offices. As a final tribute to its One-derfuls, the WMA registered at least sixty of them in the WIMSA registry. Thus today's researchers have immensely more resources than did this book's authors when they began their studies of the yeomen (F) in 1981.

The women veterans' organizations were invaluable in helping the women to keep alive the camaraderie that they had found in wartime. Some of their many efforts to gain the recognition they had earned as the nation's first enlisted women were successful; others were not. Their newsletters contain firsthand glimpses of their unique and historic experience. At the century's end, these doughty, resourceful, patriotic women remain the first and the few, but no longer are they the forgotten.

TEN

Epilogue

WHAT BECAME OF THE women veterans of World War I? Only a handful became public figures, and most of those few were noted for accomplishments not connected with their military service. Overwhelmingly, the later contributions that these women made to their country and communities were little recognized outside the circle of their families and friends. Only a few of their stories are known from the annals of the National Yeomen F (NYF), letters, obituaries, and interviews with family members, and a few surviving yeomen (F). This epilogue summarizes some of their later experiences, but the reader will understand that these are only a tiny sample of these women's post–World War I lives.

Another Call to Colors

Women who were attracted to military service in World War I might have been expected to seek service again in World War II, and in fact some did.

Navy

One of the women who returned to service, Joy Bright Hancock, had a truly distinguished naval career. Discharged from the Naval Reserve in 1920, she transferred to the civil service at the Cape May Naval Air Station, where she married Lt. Charles Little, one of the navy's earliest aviators. In August 1921 he was killed in an airship crash. The young widow moved to Washington and went to work for the navy's newly formed Bureau of Aeronautics, editing its newsletter and setting up personnel files for its growing numbers of naval aviators, many of whom became lifelong friends. In 1924 she married Lt. Cdr. Lewis Hancock. He, too, was killed, when the airship *Shenandoah* crashed in September 1925.

To overcome her fear of airplanes, she learned to fly. Rediscovering a childhood aptitude for changing automobile tires and repairing bicycles, she found that the best part of flight school was taking aircraft engines apart and putting them back together. She returned to the Bureau of Aeronautics in 1930 as the civilian head of its General Information Section, where she made friends among legislative staffs, reporters, and leaders in the fast-growing aviation industry.

As war loomed in Europe, very few navy planners could foresee the need to employ women. Hancock, however, was part of the group in naval aviation that made very explicit plans for recruiting, training, housing, and assigning up to twenty-three thousand of them. The bureau's detailed plans helped others in the navy to accept the need for women. The law signed by President Franklin Roosevelt on 30 July 1942 created the Navy's Women's Reserve. The navy sought and soon found an acronym that suitably described this new entity: WAVES—Women Accepted for Voluntary Emergency Service. This description was readily accepted by the navy, the public, and the women themselves.

Hancock reentered naval service in October and stayed right where she was as Lieutenant Hancock. She was one of the small group of women officers advising Lt. Cdr. Mildred McAfee, the peacetime president of Wellesley College, appointed to serve as director of the Women's Reserve. Hancock, the only officer in that group who could "speak navy," was able to explain to the others how to get things done the navy's way. McAfee, well accustomed to appraising women leaders, fully appreciated Hancock's unique contributions, and they formed an effective team.

Hancock visited nearly every naval aviation facility, seeking places for navy women to be trained and employed. Thanks chiefly to her, thousands of navy women were trained alongside men in specialized skills to become flight simulation instructors, air traffic controllers, and aviation mechanics, to name but three of an ever-expanding list of technical fields. By 1944, every naval aviator had received a part of his instruction from a WAVES member, and by the war's end in 1945, about one-quarter of the navy's eight-five thousand WAVES had served in aviation.

In 1946 the U.S. Navy named Hancock the director of the Women's Reserve and promoted her to captain. For two years she led the planning—and the struggle—to establish a permanent place for women in the navy. One important lesson of the war, hammered home by Hancock's team and other key supporters, was the need to maintain a nucleus of women. That nucleus was to explore the fields in which women could best serve and thus be prepared for emergency expansions. Strongly supported by wartime leaders such as Admiral Nimitz and Generals Eisenhower and Vandenberg, the Women's Armed Services Integration Act of 1948 was signed on 30 July 1948, establishing a permanent place for women in America's armed forces.

The legislation allowed women other than nurses to serve in the regular navy, thereby abolishing the Women's Reserve. Hancock became the first incumbent of the new office of assistant to the chief of naval personnel for women (ACNP(W)) and remained such until her retirement in 1953, at age fifty-five. She led the effort to maintain and—judiciously—expand the beachhead now gained. During the hostilities in Korea, the number of women in the navy nearly tripled between 1950 to 1953, from about three thousand to almost nine thousand, fully validating the nucleus concept. No other service branch came as close to meeting its expansion goals.

In 1954, Hancock married Vice Adm. Ralph Ofstie, who died two years later. She outlived him by thirty years, dying in 1986, at age eighty-eight.[1]

Other women returned to naval service, though they did not achieve the stature of Hancock. For example, Esther Hall Beckett, one of the NYF's earliest members, was commissioned in 1942 as a lieutenant (junior grade) in the navy's Supply Corps. She had worked for the navy for twenty-three years as a civilian, traveling widely abroad and in the United States, working with casualties, missing persons, and their families to expedite claims and accounts. She performed similar services for prisoners of war held in the United States. In 1946 she helped establish the Veterans Administration's services west of Denver.

When Eunice Whyte reported as a lieutenant to the Naval Air Station in New York (better known as Floyd Bennett Field) as assistant personnel officer in 1944, she found her "new" boss was in fact her old one. He was Rear Adm. John McCain, grandfather of U.S. Senator John McCain, USN (Ret.), former prisoner of war in Vietnam. She had been Admiral McCain's secretary in 1918, when he had been a commander serving in the Navy Department.

Hazel Young was a civilian psychiatric nurse working with navy medical officers, training naval personnel in psychiatric nursing. During the war years, she trained more than eight hundred hospital corpsmen, forty-four WAVES, and seventy-two registered nurses.[2]

The military service of some World War I women extended beyond World War II. Thanks to the Women's Armed Forces Integration Act of 1948, a few women veterans did, like Joy Hancock, return to the armed forces, some of them for full careers. Once more in uniform, Helen Harney served as master-at-arms at the women's barracks in Newport, Rhode Island, and Bainbridge, Maryland. A woman officer described her as "truly a salt of the first order." When she marched in John Kennedy's Inaugural Parade in 1961, she made headlines as "the oldest WAVE [*sic*] in the Navy."

The war in Korea brought back to active duty another former yeoman (F), Madeleine Gratrix. She stood at attention and saluted when her old shipmate, Capt. Joy Bright Hancock, reviewed the women on duty at the Naval Air Test Center at Patuxent River, Maryland, in 1957.[3]

Marine Corps

Helen O'Neill's numerous contributions to the creation and growth of the NYF, to the American Legion, and to fellow yeomen (F) were detailed in the preceding chapter. She remained in Washington and continued her work in the Navy Department as a civil servant. She served as private secretary to four successive assistant secretaries of the navy. In 1935, Col. Henry Latrobe Roosevelt, the acting assistant, remarked to an admiral with whom he was reviewing proposed Naval Reserve legislation that it made no provision for women. The admiral replied that the Marine Corps would have no women in the next war. Roosevelt said, "You will so, and"—pointing to O'Neill—"here's one sitting right here."[4]

Returning from Pearl Harbor, where he had inspected the damage done to ships and facilities by the enemy attack on 7 December 1941, Secretary of the Navy Frank Knox turned over to O'Neill the top-secret notes that were the basis for his report to President Roosevelt. Although the navy had already identified O'Neill as an ideal instructor for the flood of reservists being mobilized, she could not leave her position until she had completed work on the report. "Besides," she later said, "I'd already been spoken for."[5]

By 1943, the Marine Corps commissioned her as a captain, assigned to assist and guide Maj. (later Col.) Ruth Streeter, newly appointed to direct its Women's Reserve program. Later the USMC transferred O'Neill to San Francisco, and by the end of the war she was a lieutenant colonel. Released from active duty in 1946, she returned to civilian life as administrative officer in the Office of Naval Research. She remained active in the Marine Corps Reserve until she retired in 1959.[6]

Lillian O'Malley Daly was one of the first former women marines to return to duty in early 1943. The USMC commissioned her and sent her immediately to Camp Pendleton, California, to facilitate the growth of the USMC Women's Reserve on the West Coast. By the time the war was over she had been promoted to the rank of major.

Martrese Thek Ferguson was in the first class of women marines to be trained as officers. She graduated at the top of her class, eventually rose to the rank of lieutenant colonel, and was in charge of more than two thousand women serving at Henderson Hall in Arlington, Virginia.[7]

Other Services

Edith Warren Quinn called herself a three-timer, having served with the yeomen (F) in World War I, with the WAC in France in World War II, and in the National Guard Reserve in the Korean War. Similarly, Jean McLeod Cook joined the army in 1943, served two years in Texas, then later served in the Air Force Reserve for fifteen years.

Former marine Ruth Byer DePass had already served twenty-two years in the postal service when she heard in 1942 that the armed forces were looking for postal officers. Lack of a college degree disqualified her from a navy or marine commission, and she was too old to enlist. The army, which had different requirements, quickly accepted her and trained her as a postal officer, then assigned her to its air forces. In 1948 she transferred to the newly created U.S. Air Force as a captain. Similarly, the Marine Corps did not reenlist Edith Macias, so she joined the army and, she said, "served her time proudly." All four of her sons and her stepson became marines. The WMA chapter to which she later belonged named itself after her.[8]

Edna Loftus Smith's husband was a naval aviator, and she received her commission from the Marine Corps. After the war, when the USMC selected author Robert Sherrod to write a monumental work entitled *History of Marine Corps Aviation in World War II*, he turned to Major Smith for help. Her intensive efforts and long hours of painstaking research working side by side with Sherrod won his admiration. In the book's preface he wrote, "Major Smith has been the heart and soul of Marine Corps Aviation History since this book was first conceived (and before I got into it)."[9]

On the Home Front

Millions of American women supported their country on the home front during World War II, and the veterans of World War I were typical in this regard. A few examples follow.

When the draft was instituted in September 1940, Ann Frame, the NYF's membership chairman, was asked to act as supervisory registrar of a board of fifteen women Legionnaires, who were also all NYF members. They worked seven-hour shifts to register draftees in the District of Columbia. These volunteers were believed to be the only draft board to consist solely of women.[10]

Dorothy Sullivan played a quiet but key role in the creation of the navy's Women's Reserve by helping Rep. Melvin Maas draft the necessary legislation. From 1943 to 1946 she was a first lieutenant in the American Red Cross Motor Corps. She was wearing her World War I ribbon on her uniform when a young naval officer stopped to tell her she should not wear her husband's or son's campaign bars. She told him it was hers by Act of Congress, but he wouldn't believe her, saying there were no women in the military in World War I.[11] He was certainly not alone in that bit of ignorance. Even today he would not be alone.

From the West Coast Etienne V. Scheier reported to the NYF *Note Book* in April 1944 that women in the West were "thoroughly content that they are working hand and spirit across our country's great miles with other members of the NYF. Many blood donors have given a quart or more." Scheier herself was serving her third year as an air-raid warden responsible for a sixteen-block neighborhood. The ground floor of her home became San Francisco's first designated casualty station. She took first-aid and nutrition courses from the American Red Cross and later instructed others in the same skills.[12]

What Charlotte M. Bis could not do herself, she encouraged other women to do. The navy's recruiters sent her a certificate of merit for sending them more than ten women who applied to become WAVES.[13] Loretta Walsh would have been proud of her.

Blue and Gold Star Families

Literally millions of American families sent men—and women—to the armed forces in World War II. The *Note Books* reported that many World War I women veterans sent their sons to war and that not all of them returned. To mention just one such former yeoman (F) is to honor all the others.

Samuel B. Roberts, son of former Yeoman (F) Edith Derrick Roberts, became a naval hero when, as coxswain of an assault boat, he was killed during the battle for Guadalcanal in September of 1942. He was awarded the Navy Cross citation for his intelligent, effective, conspicuously brave deeds. His actions were instrumental in rescuing a sizable group of marines who had been cut off and nearly surrounded by the enemy.

The navy's response to Roberts's action was swift. In January 1944 his mother, Edith Roberts, christened a destroyer escort named after him. When that ship was lost in the battle of Leyte Gulf, the navy named a second ship after him, also christened by his mother. The navy retired the second USS *Samuel B. Roberts* in 1971. In 1986, the navy named a *third* ship after Roberts, a remarkable recognition of his heroism. As his mother had died, the new ship was christened by his sister. Its wardroom proudly displays Roberts's Navy Cross.[14]

Government Service

Hundreds of former navy and marine women remained in the civil service after the war, many completing careers of decades or more. Sara M. Nolan, for example, served as chief secretary to eighteen successive commandants of the Boston Naval Yard, over a period of forty years. In 1957, the navy estimated that at least a hundred former yeomen (F) were still among its employees. Many women veterans also spent decades of service in state governments.[15]

Agnes Meyer Driscoll graduated from Ohio State University in 1911, studying mathematics, music, physics, and foreign languages. She enlisted as chief yeoman (F), assigned to the Code and Signal Section of Naval Communications. She remained in the same job upon discharge; then, in 1920, navy officials invited her to join an office that was working on early cipher machines. She cracked a Japanese code early in the 1920s and from then until the U.S. entry into World War II "taught an entire generation of navy cryptologists" whose later exploits would greatly facilitate American victories in the Pacific. Her major cryptanalytic achievement was determining that retrofitted Japanese warships could attain speeds much higher than those of American battleships. As a direct result of this information, the Navy Department raised the required speed of its modern ships. Driscoll also took charge of the navy's research efforts against the German codes. She retired in 1959, having devoted forty-one years to exemplary work critical to national security.[16]

Ruth Caheel also began her career in counterintelligence as a yeoman (F) assigned to the Brooklyn Navy Yard. After release from active duty in 1919, she worked with the intelligence offices for more than thirty years, with assignments in Canada, Japan, New York, and all over the Far East. She met her husband, a British King's Courier and undercover agent for England, in Kyoto. After he died in 1941, she returned to the United States. In 1961 President John F. Kennedy recognized her with a Presidential Citation, "In recognition of devoted service and selfless consecration to the service of mankind in the armed forces of the United States."[17]

Edna Burdine Casbarian stayed with the navy after her discharge. Whenever the navy determined to name a new warship after a deceased hero, she researched that person's family tree in order to find the nearest kin. To the closest female relative or descendant is given the honor of christening the ship. In 1938, Casbarian herself was asked to christen USS *Saury,* a submarine, at New London. On that occasion, the secretary of the navy called her "The Mother of Naval Sponsors."[18]

Marguerite LeHand was Franklin Roosevelt's personal secretary for twenty-two years. He relied heavily on her judgment and absolute discretion and called her "a real genius for getting things done." Known widely as "Missy," a nickname bestowed on her by the president's daughter, she accompanied the family to the White House in 1932, residing in her own suite and joining in many family activities. Until chronic heart trouble forced her resignation in December 1942, she supervised a corps of fifty stenographers. She died in 1944.[19]

Professions

Many World War I women veterans made their marks in the various professions. For example, Dorothy Frooks began her life brilliantly and never stopped. A child prodigy from a large family of lawyers, she became accustomed to speaking in public at impromptu political rallies. President Wilson gave her a medal for having recruited an estimated thirty thousand men, primarily for the navy, and then recruited *her* for the navy. She stumped long and hard for women's suffrage, earned her law degree from Hamilton Law School in Chicago and then a master's degree from New York University, and later became the first full-time lawyer for the Salvation Army. There she learned firsthand of the plight of the poor, which led her to pioneer free legal clinics and small-claims courts. She prodded the New York legislature to establish aid to dependent children, which later became a national program. In 1986 she married J. P. Vanderbilt, heir of the well-known wealthy family. At the time she would have been in her late eighties. She claimed she was born in 1901, although others said it was 1897. During World War II she served in the Judge Advocate General Corps in the Army.[20]

Anne L. Kendig was one of the first five women to attend National University Law School in Washington, D.C., which had opened its doors to women when the men went off to fight in World War I. For four years she served in the navy and took classes six nights a week. After discharge, she worked in the Office of the Postmaster General, then for the Post Office and Post Roads Committee, under Senator Townsend of Michigan. She moved to Chicago after marriage and worked for the Veterans Administration.[21]

Frances Strover was a journalist, employed at the *Milwaukee Journal* for forty years. At her death in 1967, she had earned a high reputation as a feature writer, art critic, and expert on the city's history. Violet Van Wagner Lopez went to work for AT&T in 1928 and stayed for thirty-seven years. An active member of the Women Marines Association, she published poetry until her eighties. She was at one time the president of the Women's Press Club of New York City. She died in 1992 and was buried with full military honors at Arlington.[22]

Arts and Entertainment

A number of women who had distinguished themselves in navy or marine service went on to win recognition in creative endeavors.

Theater

After World War I, Lela Leibrand returned to Hollywood as a screenwriter. When her daughter, Ginger Rogers, entered the theater, Lela became her business manager. For some time, she ran a workshop in East Hollywood called the Hollytown Theatre, where aspiring actors had opportunities to train and perform. Officials of the RKO movie company invited Leibrand to shift her workshop activities to the Hollywood Playhouse on the RKO lot, so that she could coach its contract players, together with her other students. Studio producers often dropped in to observe new talent appearing there. Among her pupils were such stars as Lucille Ball, Betty Grable, Leon Ames, and Tyrone Power.[23]

Fiction

Author Lillian Petersen Budd wrote both adult and children's fiction. She was the author of a trilogy about Scandinavian immigrants in the United States

(*April Snow, Land of Strangers,* and *April Harvest*), of which the first is the best known. Some of her children's books are still found in libraries today. They concentrate on American Indian life and lore, drawing on oral legends from diverse tribes throughout the United States, from the Passamaquoddy in Maine to the Panamint in central California. For example, *Full Moons: Indian Legends of the Seasons* relates the tales of how each of the year's thirteen full moons derived its name.[24]

One writer overcame formidable barriers to become a well-known and much-loved American novelist. Born in Manchester, England, Taylor Caldwell came with her family to the United States when she was seven years old. At age twelve she submitted her first novel to her grandfather, then on the staff of a major Philadelphia publishing house. He dismissed it, refusing to believe a child could have written it. By the age of fifteen she was working full-time by day and going to high school and later the University of Buffalo at night. She left school to enlist in 1918.

Caldwell married early, had children, and worked throughout her marriage to help support the family. At one point she worked as a court stenographer. She eventually finished her college degree and put her husband through school as well. In 1938 she achieved instant literary fame with the publication of a novel, *Dynasty of Death.* She followed that triumph with several more best-selling historical novels, including *Dear and Glorious Physician, Great Lion of God,* and *A Pillar of Iron.*[25]

Music

Mabel Vanderploeg Pease became a gifted musical performer, playing opera roles on stage and on radio in Chicago. She also played the piano and the organ for her church. In her later years, she entertained at Veterans Administration hospitals.[26]

Crafts

Partly inspired by the many statues and monuments she saw during her wartime service in Washington, D.C., Mabelle Linnea Holmes determined to weave a series of tapestries illustrating the nation's history. She designed her own loom, learned to create her own dyes, and visited nearly all the sites she ultimately depicted. Forty years later, she completed her work, a series of twenty five-by-six-foot panels titled "The Pageant of America." The panels display America's history from the landing of the Vikings to the landing on the moon.

In 1981, when Yorktown, Virginia, celebrated the two-hundredth anniversary of the decisive battle of the American Revolution, Holmes's series was a featured exhibit. The panels then toured the country. One school superintendent declared that her tapestries taught him more American history in one hour than he had been able to absorb in sixteen years of schooling. Holmes later donated the series to the State of Virginia as a nucleus and foundation of its historical art center in Yorktown. Of this donation, Holmes said, "Like Cornwallis at Yorktown, I 'surrendered'... but Cornwallis *had* to surrender, whereas I was happy to. Where could I have found a more fitting place?"[27]

Community Service

Many of the women veterans worked selflessly for their communities. After serving again in World War II, with the Coast Guard Transportation Corps, Edythe Radis Dallas learned a new skill. When she was immobilized in a body cast after an accident, a friend offered to teach her how to transcribe printed books into braille. A year later, she passed the Library of Congress examination to become a certified transcriber. She was very proud when a young law student for whom she had transcribed some books passed the Pennsylvania Bar exam, among the first two hundred out of eight hundred. When she moved to California in 1957, she taught braille at an adult school program. After organizing the braille classes, she solicited funds from business clubs in Monterey to purchase machines. Then she taught braille to lifetime inmates in California prisons. When she moved to the Naval Home in Mississippi, she learned she was the only person in that state certified to teach braille; she soon began to teach others.[28]

Other yeomen (F) served their communities through religious organizations. Former Yeoman (F) M. O'Halloran was one of several women veterans who became nuns and devoted their whole lives to assisting others. Many of them maintained membership in the NYF.[29]

In a League of Her Own

When Marjory Stoneman Douglas died in 1998, at the age of 108, *Time* magazine called her "the ever vigilant empress of the Everglades."[30] Jon Mills, former speaker of the Florida House of Representatives, said that the Everglades, although millions of years old,

> was an orphan until [she] adopted it. . . . [T]he Everglades has lost its mother. She put the life of the swamp in moral terms and made us all . . . focus on the value of the environment to our children in a way no one else has. Others talk about pollution in parts per million. Marjory talked about the ecosystem the way a mother would talk about a child.[31]

Thousands of people mourned her death and paid her tribute, while hundreds who had known her personally and worked with her spoke of her extraordinary energy, power of expression, and devotion to her cause. Opponents grew to respect—and sometimes fear—her depth of knowledge, passion, and wit. Handsome, spirited, intelligent, she graduated from Wellesley College in 1912 and took up journalism, the career she practiced throughout her long life.

Douglas returned to journalism after her discharge from the navy and, in the late 1920s, embarked upon the great love affair of her life. She began to visit with friends the Tamiami Trail, recently hacked through the heart of the vast Everglades Swamp. Soon she was helping to lead the committee struggling to establish a national park to preserve the 1.6 million acres lying just west of Miami. Long before the word "ecosystem" came into popular use, she realized that the so-called swamp was in fact a wide, shallow river of fresh water moving slowly southward across a low, grassy plain. Moreover, that river was the wellspring of the Biscayne aquifer, the source upon which the life of southern Florida depended.

In 1943, when the editor of a series of books about the rivers of America asked Douglas to write a volume about the Miami River, she declined because, she said, that river was "only about an inch long." She proposed instead to write about the Everglades. Her book, *River of Grass,* was published in 1947. It has remained in print ever since, being both an anthem to the area's beauty and a powerful argument for preserving its purity.

The Everglades became a national park that same year, but vigilance was still required as Florida rapidly developed. For example, in the late 1960s a developer proposed putting an oil refinery on the shores of lower Biscayne Bay. No sooner was that project deterred than another group proposed building a jetport in the same sensitive swamp habitats.

With urging from friends, in 1970 Douglas started an organization named "Friends of the Everglades." Soon she was making speeches to every organization that would listen. In two years her group had more than a thousand members and soon after, three thousand. She later wrote that the Everglades had become "a central force in my existence at the beginning of my eightieth year." Over the years, "Marjory's Army" faced off against many opponents, including, among others, ever-present, voracious developers, the Army Corps of Engineers promoting flood control, and sugar farmers contributing to the pollution of Lake Okeechobee.

Until well into her nineties she continued to write and travel, producing several nonfiction books. By 1990, the year of her centennial, her name had been given to several buildings, most notably a high-rise of gold glass in Tallahassee that houses Florida's Department of Natural Resources. Schools, parks, and a long stretch of Sunset Drive in Miami also bear her name. The governor of Florida named her a Great Floridian in 1987, and in 1993, President Clinton awarded her the Medal of Freedom, the nation's highest honor.[32]

These examples give only a taste of the later lives of the World War I women veterans. The memory of their service is mainly carried in the hearts of those they knew. The Women's Memorial at Arlington Cemetery also honors these women as it honors those who have followed them into military service.

APPENDIX A

The Act To Incorporate The National Yeomen F
Public—No. 676—74th Congress [S. 16871]
AN ACT
To Incorporate The National Yeomen F.

Be it enacted by the Senate and House of Representatives of the United States of America in Congress assembled, That Eva H. Clarke, Beatrice Brown Dwyer, and Mary J. O'Donnell, of Arizona;

Ruby Busse Anglim, Lottie Sessions Barrett, Philome Lucy Cavanagh, Stella Austen Clark, Pearl Bonham Clerk, Lillian Koeber Neumann, Harriet Jane Dodson, Alma Simmermacher Dreyer, Stella Neumann Elberson, Ola Belle Emmner, Edna Crumpler Estes, Mirian Mathews Everett, Katherine Driscoll Fallon, Kathleen Vance Hatch, Eva Wilson Hay, Ellen Keefe Heady, Ruth Hemphill, Myrtle Kinsey, Anna Geisler Kirkpatrick, Katherine Brown Lightner, Margaret Dannagger Lovelace, Lillian Catherine McCarthy, Gladys Farmer McCool, Laura Landes Metcalf, Louise Vickery Mowers, Ruth Manahan Neal, Gladys D. Nelson, Madeline O'Leary Peggs, Caroline Peirce, Sara Craddock Sasser, May Gesner Schaefer, Billie Browne Schank, Rita Beauton Schaub, Etienne V. Schier, Louise Williams Sears, Williams Shumway, Florence Kelly Sparrow, Laura V. Waldron, Agnes L. Walker, Gladys Spaulding Wheless, Evelyn Lyon Wiberg, and Muriel Andrews Zerangue, all of California;

Gladys Yeager Briggs, and Blanche Marion Curry, of Colorado;

Grace Pascoe Agard; Julie Sternberg Aichler, Mary Sweeney Alling, Sara Hinchey Barry, Anna Kilroy Bean, Kathleen Moriarity Begley, Anna Lyons Bergin, Ethel Cornet Bolles, Anna McDowell Brown, Mary MacKenzie Carson, Lucy Galvin Cavanaugh, Rose Reiger Chapman, Dorothy Sara Clifford, Monica Cecelia Clifford, Sadie Connelly, Marjorie Murray Cormack, Martha Swirsky Cotton, Marion McEntee Cox, Ione Disco Cunningham, Katherine Lyng Donovan, Margaret Bess Dordelman, Marguerite Driscoll, Mae Sheehan Dwyer, Ruth Lawson Euster, Katherine Frances Fagan, Ethel Clendenen Fargo, Gertrude Selesnitzky Feinberg, Elisabeth Tagliabue Fields, Helen Buckley Fitzgerald, Irene Catherine Fitzgerald, Anna Campbell Forsythe, Anna J. Gaughan, Mary Penders Gillis, Mary Agnes Grady, Theresa Madeleine Hamill, Alice Mary Harrington, Florence Hulbert Hermanus, Ella Veronica

Houlihan, Deborah Pickett Kane, Frances Walsh Keenan, Margaret O'Brien Kennedy, Hazel Merwin Lander, Elizabeth Mallon Leighton, Agnes Carlson Lukens, Catherine Gertrude MacKenzie, Clara Armstrong MacKenzie, Edna Murray Manchester, Mary Driscoll Markham, Regina Martin, Josephine McAuliffe Martin, Bellerose Meunier, Mazie Rogers Miller, Elsie Reichert Moon, Winnifred Patricia Nagle, Isabelle Dickson Peterson. Lucy Riley Pfannenstiel, Jewel Perkins Pitt, Eleanor Donahoe Reilly, Elizabeth Kepes Reynolds, Ida Reed Sanders, Alice Savage, Mildred Mabel Schwartz, Margaret Hogan Seaman, Ida Selesnitzky Stone, Agusta Strand, Caroline Wyllie Waterman, Juliana Augusta Weske, Helen Weinhusen, Louise Arnold Wiley, Selina Lee Winter, Margaret Hardiman Wrisley, Mary Connors Wundrack, and Marie Deering Yeager, all of Connecticut;

Norma M. Albers, Lucille Loveless Allan, Gladys Elizabeth Allen, Sarah Jarvis Andrus, Edith Ober Armstrong, Mary Hough Barber, May A. Barrett, Nettie Neitzey Beach, Mary Munday Becker, Esther Hall Beckett, Anne Curtin Belt, Charlotte Louise Berry, Jeannette L. Bishop, Alice Boland Bloomfield, Amelia Boberg, Beulah Holtzscheiter Bosworth, Jane M. Breen, Kate Knight Briggs, Eloise Broaddus, Helen Sprague Brown, Lola Carlisle Strailman Browning, Rose Flood Buice, Annette Louise Burton, Gertrude Bange Butts, Mary Callen, Daisy House Campbell, Ella Echols Chambers, Emma S. Collie, Maude V. Cowan, Jane Regina Cox, Catherine Crowley, Reva S. Darrell, F. Pearl Delaplaine, Eleanor Marie Downey, Alice M. Downie, Cora Laughlin Drake, Anna Cecelia Dunn, Emma Schroder Dyer, Bessie London Faine, Elizabeth Waters Fallis, Anna Schultz Frame, Barbara Spence French, Agnes Monia Gallagher, Annie Ellen Gilson, Eleanor Mary Griffith, Mary Derouda Hall, Amy F. Hammond, Adelaide Ruth Harbers, Dorothy B. Harper, Carolyn Hardesty Herman, Nellie Grant Hinson, Mary E. Jones, Claire Keefe, Kathryn Gallagher Kendrick, Ann Kilmartin, Hope Knickerbocker, Louise Elender Koester, Mary Beall Kolhos, Helen Lucinda Leonard, Edith Kite Lewis, Mary Dove Loughrey, Marie B. Luebkert, Lillian Allen Brubaker Luther, Helen Horigan Maisel, Laura Garcia Martin, Louise Greenwald Matthews, Helen C. McCarty, Geraldine Clark McGovern, Lois B. McRae, Ellen Russell McWilliams, Eloise Sanford Davison Miller, Mary Kurth Moler, Alice Alford Morgan, Anna Lochte Murphy, Margaret Elma Naylor, Edna Meier Nielson, Margaret Broderick Nolan, Alice F. O'Neal, Helen Geraldine O'Neill, Helen Linkins Opitz, Netty Baxter Parker, Blanche C. Paul, Anna Viola Phelps, Annie Skidmore Powers, Sue Gould Prentiss, Edith Warren Quinn, Lillian Louise Reagan, Edna Marie Robey, Estelle Richardson Ruby, Ethel Clark Rule, Louise MacDonnell Ryan, Elizabeth Ivey Sage, Marion Trumbo Skinner, Jessica Randolph Smith, Margaret Grady Smith, Mabel F. Staub, Emily Steele, Nellie Rollins Stein, Edith Herndon Summerson, Mary Sullivan Tatspaugh,

Marion Crawford Thur, Mary Killilea Tracey, Margaret Mills Vaughan, Eva Young Virtue, Olive Wrenn Walter, Genevieve F. Wedding, Mary Z. Weide, Lena Kathryn Willige, Pansie Casanave Willson, Ethel M. Wilson, Faith Clements Windsor, Amy Owen Wood, Lena Rigby Woolford, Myrtle Stephens Wright, and Mary Crook Yates, all of the District of Columbia;

Marie Roberts Bevis, Zella Prunty Byrd, Lamonte Oliver Cates, Demerise Labbe Cleveland, Ida Matthews Eichenberger, Loyce Davis Hackett, Mabel Williamson Jacobs, Madeline A. Jacobson, Idele Torrance Jamison, Adele Mead Kendrick, Josephine Mack Miller, Lois Clappison Morse, Almeda Fink Murphy, Roxana Anne Post, Agnes Towson Shelton, Daisy Ruth Westerlund, and Elsie Tuttle Wright, all of Florida;

Anna Elizabeth O'Connell, of Georgia;

Alta Sebree Wardwell Donovan, of Idaho;

Elsie Ericksen Biever, Nora Pomeroy Darling, Grace Alma Dunbar, Anne Rourke Durst, Virginia Stoddert Moore Grottee, Nell Weston Halstead, Edna Benton Hann, Cornelia M. Huennekens, Elizabeth Ann McCoy, Mary Louise Minton, Josephine MacFarland Moran, Mable Vander Ploeg Pease, Hester Smith Rasmussen, Agnes Foertsch Rohlfing, Marie Healy Simpson, Evelyn Jackson Skavlan, Constance Strong, and May Gilligan Sutherland, all of Illinois;

Donna Zimmer Akin, Bessie Fisher Bogwell, Hortense Lee Goldsmith, Mary Parker Harris, and Minnie Tryon Ryan, all of Indiana;

Maud Lowell Ayers, of Kentucky;

Sarah Flaherty Gallagher, and Gladys Ilsley McKnight, of Maine;

L. Dorothy Devey Brunken, Lucille Bonita Garrett, Fannie Grigat Laut, Grace Ryder Mead, Katherine Marie Page, Lillian Deters Tabor, Effie Van Horn Thomas, Edna Josephine Yorker, and Anna Kaer Yust, all of Maryland;

Mary Lee Aylward, Marion L. Bain, Florence K. Barry, Anna E. Beers, Helen I. Blake, Mary C. Breslow, Adelaide Mary Bresnahan, Gladys Bruce, Isabel Kehoe Burk, Aileen J. Burke, Elizabeth Helen Burke, Dorothy Leighton Cady, Alice Elinor Carey, Helen Carman, Mary A. Carroll, Mary Chisel, Mary Warner Colombo, Mazie Conley, Kathryn J. Connor, Anita Ryan Connors, Mary M. Conroy, Ellen Bernadette Corbett, Catherine A. Corcoran, Winifred Burns Cox, Lizzie Glidden Crowley, Madeleine Galvin Delano, Elinor Kyle Devine, Sally Ryan Devlin, Mary F. Doherty, Jane E. Dolsen, Mary Dowd, Eleanor Marion Drew, Alice Driscoll, Mary Joyce Duggan, Mollie Catherine Dundon, Margaret Murphy Faherty, Helen Farrell, Helen Mary Farrell, Catherine Woodward Feeney, Bernice W. Fortin, Patricia Gleason, Marion E. Grady, Mary E. Grady, Anna Mary Hegarty, Ethel Hickey, Dorothy Drew Horan, Elizabeth A. Horgan, Marie Lambert Johnson, Anna Riley Joyce, Agnes

Keanneally, Ellen E. Kearns, Bessie Josephine Kelly, Violet Elizabeth Kirkland, Ethel Lally, Genevieve Adrienne Lane, Lucy Marshall Lanigan, Ellen A. Lannigan, Leonore Learson, Julia B. Lehan, Marie Alice Long, Gertrude Lorton, Emma Macaulay Lyle, Helen Stolba Macbeth, Gertrude Catherine Macdonald, Margaret Mehlman Maguire, Anna Marie Mahan, Genevieve A. Maher, Mary Louise Marcille, Marie Kathryn McAuliffe, Anna McCarthy, Helen F. McDonald, Catherine McDonough, Marion Mary McElaney, Anna Marie McGuire, Esther McCall McLaughlin, Agnes Murphy McLean, Anna L. McNulty, Ruth Desmond McSweeney, Bertha Erickson Mead, Irene Florence Michel, Yvonne Michel, Margaret Isabelle Mitchell, Margaret Louise Murphy, Helen Adelaide Murray, Elizabeth McDonald Myers, Helen Barr Nickerson, Eleanor Teresa O'Brien, Marguerite Catherine O'Brien, Ria Minehan O'Brien, Margaret Lonergan O'Brion, Helen O'Brien O'Connor, Elizabeth M. O'Donnell, Mary Bull Owens, Olive T. Parsons, Mary Fielding Rawling, Mary McGunigle Redmond, Elizabeth Foley Regan, Mary Lane Regan, Ellen Riley, Helen O'Brien Riley, Anita Roberts, Mary Myers Robinson, Alice Mahan Saunders, Gladys Mary Saxton, Mary Elizabeth Scalley, Julia E. Shine, Elizabeth Stander, Mary Catherine Sughrue, Madeline O'Brien Sullivan, Harriet Mussinan Swearingen, Mary Gross Thayer, Grace M. Tomasello, Madeline Robillard Treloar, Isabel Catherine Wall, Lulu Veronica Walsh, Ethel May Ward, Agnes O'Brien Welch, Esther Marie Werme, Margaret Gertrude Wholly, Alice M. Williams, Lillian Everette Williams, Lucy M. Winn, and Maud C. Young, all of Massachusetts;

Theresa Bean Ballenger, Lilla Mary Bellinger, Gertrude M. Camp, Pauline Cassidy, Grace Schoenhur Conway, Marie Rossley Kalt, Gladys Webster Mallett, Helen Moran, and Margaret Morton Mullaney, all of Michigan;

Ethyl Ryan Maly and Gertrude O'Connor Trestrail, of Minnesota;

Gladys Thames Hubbard of Mississippi;

Sophie Polenska Coleman, of Missouri;

Davidson, Edyth Plummer, and Dorothy Mauck Wehrman, of Nebraska;

Christina Sander Anderson, Anna Elizabeth Conroy, Gertrude O'Neil DeBrunner, A. May Erwin, Alice Catherine Fairbrother, Kathleen Mary Field, Anne Pedersen Freeman, Marguerite B. Geiger, Lillian Helena Hannold, Julia Hicks, Anna V. Kane, Dorothy May Lee, Corrine Dextroze Mahanna, Anne Marie McCormick, Mina Klein Morrison, Marie Burke Oetmann, Ann B. Shinnick, and Catherine Waters, all of New Jersey;

Sara Russell Imhof, of New Mexico;

Mary Ducey Archer, Laura Dayton Ball, Esther Berkowitz, Rose Brancato Biagi, May Anne Blazina, Ruth Nethaway Bouck, Harriet Eldridge Robins Brandt, Josephine Mitchell Brosseau, Irene Malito Brown, Regina Burke, Frances Jedlicka

Campbell, Rowena Margaret Campbell, May Flaherty Carroll, Veronica Marie Cherry, Mary L. Clark, May Cecilia Collins, Ada Howe-Webster Dailinger, Julia Flynn Dorner, Alice Leahy Everard, Dorothy Winifred Ferrier, Elinor Valentine Foley, Marie McElroy Forte, Anna Gallagher, Margaret Katherine Garland, Florence Wilson Goulden, Alice Miriam Govenor, Elizabeth Anna Gridley, Mildred Berryman Hall, Mary Mahoney Halwartz, S. Dorothy First Hayes, Alice Gieseking Johnson, Angela Lyons Johnson, Marie Elizabeth Kelly, Carrie Klinger, Leonore Lawson Koellsted, Lucile Alzamora Lacey, Mary Gray Langford, Esther Martins Law, Hortense Lersner, Gertrude Long, Isabel Margaret Lynch, Nellie Mahoney, Ruth Evelyn Manning, Matilda Foeth McDonald, Agnes Murphy McGovern, Mary McMahon, Lillian Forsberg Miller, Maud Amelia Mittern, Blanche Babbitt Moeller, Frances Donahue Molloy, Mina Walden Mullen, Lulu Muller, Mary Elizabeth Noel, Lillie May Nohowec, Mabel Dorothy O'Connell, Betty A. Peifer, Frances L. Phair, Anna Reisman, Julia White Robbins, Marion Flannery Savage, Gertrude Evelyn Sawyer, Margaret Faglon Schutt, Mae E. Shuttleworth, Ethel Linwood Sickles, M. Grace Siegmann, Alice Clyde Stafford, Jeannette Gartland Sturla, May Agnes Sullivan, Lillian Browne Swanson, Dorothy Bradford Thomson, Irene M. Tynan, Rita Regan Wallis, Florence Kelley Walters, Irene Hallan Webb, Julia Woodroff Wheelock, Sally R. Wolf, Sarah Gibbon Yeoman, and Henrietta Yunker, all of New York;

Cooper Miller Correll, Willa Tritt Coward, Virginia Dockery Crow, Lassie Kelly Cunningham, Ethel Harwood Fuller, Estelle D. Gordon, Velma Moody Horne, Annie L. Londeree, Arabella Johnson Milligan, Rebecca Adams Nichols, Mary Allen Pearce, Kathleen Rogers Tate and Edith Singer Weibel, all of North Carolina;

Neita Russell Christian, Evelyn Evans, Mary Pow Hartman, and Mae E. Hickey, all of Ohio;

Helen Jane Bringier and Bessie Hittle Groff, of Oklahoma;

Anna Lenz Seaton, and Evelyn V. Youngs, of Oregon;

Marie R. Ahern, Mary Kemp Anthony, Laura Anderson, Sue Rohland Arishoff, Lillian Young Armour, Minnetta Collies Bentz, Lillian LeVene Blackman, Maybelle M. Bond, Anna D. Boyle, Gertrude Margaret Bracken, Winifred Brooks, May McCormick Bullock, Emma Engel Bunte, Margaret Rebecca Burdell, Mary Gallagher Campbell, Margaret M. Collins, Mae McConnell Conlin, Mary E. Cross, Mrs. James Crumlish, Anna Maguire Culliton, Mary Cavanaugh Daly, Claire Dougherty Dever, Helen.M. Devery, Anna Marie Devine, Elizabeth Gray Doran, Helen Dunne, Helen Coty Easterby, Anna Viola Edmonds, Dorothy Elma Evans, Florence Monberger Fedor, Sylvania Israel Garner, M. Cecelia Geiger, Gertrude White Gilkes, Fanny Goldscheider, Blanche Miller Grimes, Catherine Stanfield Gutenberger, Emily Hacker, Beatrice B. Hamer, Agnes E. Hamill, Marion Manahan Hammill, Claire V.

Harkins, Bertha M. Harris, Mary English Harvey, Freda Forster Hawsey, Kathryn Johnston Hazzard, Charlotte King Hedden, Jane Orr Heilig, S. Elizabeth Holmes, Effie C. Innes, Sue Altemus Jones, Anna Elizabeth Jourdan, Marie A. Kelly, Marie V. Klase, Emma Edith Lapeus, Sophia Levin, Mary M. Long, Laura Harrison Love, Anna Elizabeth Magee, Helen Marshall, Esther Nichols Martin, Cecilia McHale, Elizabeth Marie McNamee, Anna, J. Meara, Mary Burton Morris, Rosaline K. Moscony, Helen Hannigan Myers, Sara Myers, Florence Fischer Nicholson, Vesta Kaufman Niedt, Sylvania W. Oberholtzer, Anna Florence O'Connor, Constance O'Hara, Catharine G. O'Neill, Margaret Elizabeth Paul, Anne M. Perry, Cora Felter Phillips, Molly Dever Purcell, Mary A. Raith, Sara Ada Rice, Isabel E. Rosenfeldt, Anna M. Ross, Lillian White Schumacher, Prudence McCullin Sheperla, Rachel Emily Shultz, Aida Holz Skelly, Mabel Melville Slifer, Marjorie L. Slocum, Mary T. Smith, Caroline Steinbock, Mary M. Taylor, Agnes Finley Tieman, Ida Carver Townsend, Gertrude Martin Voigt, Katherine Frances Walsh, Mary Warren, Elsie E. Weaver, Amy Maria Weems, Annette Kirby Weirbach, Margaret Rowena Wellbank, Joanna Ferguson Wittman and Elsie Richards Whitmore, all of Pennsylvania;

Jennie Carter Aldred, Elisabeth Louise Baxter, Lydia York Brown, Lylian Annette Callis, Lillie Reeves Campbell, Olive Mather Clark, Theresa Margaret Dunphy, Helen MacDonald Garnett, Matilda Eglinton Grady, Dora Bucklin Helwig, Catherine Freeman Hunt, Monica Monaghan Keenan, Margaret Ruane McCartin, Effie Crowther Meeker, Mary Littlefield O'Mara, Jennie Cavanaugh Peffer, and Agnes Wheeler Smith, all of Rhode Island;

Bertha Avaunt Frischkorn, Sara Quinn Harrington, Rosa Wade Holland, Florence Idella Larasey, Mary Sinkler de Saussure McQueen, Ida Marie Stoesen, and Mamie Elizabeth Verdier, all of South Carolina;

Antonio Shuster Bunger, Sue Lou Rutledge Corbin, and Louisa Daniell Shepherd, all of Texas;

Esther Laubach, of Utah;

Nellie Leland Cutler and Minnie Bliss Sweetser, of Vermont;

Bertha Tyler Carwithen, Columbia Taylor Conway, Mary Anne Eike, Janet Rishell English, Dorothy Knight Fannon, Pauline Taylor Groves, Peggy Oakes Marable, Ethel Ward Montagne, Rose Nelson O'Hara, Anna Smith Reynolds, Josephine M. Senerchia, Maude Lois Smith, Mayme E. Smith, Mary Phillips Spiers, Margaret C. Thomas, and Ulla Rathbun Tracy, all of Virginia;

Sadie Conely Babcock, Margaret Powell Bidlake, Calla Layton Henley, Betty L. Reynolds, Emma Rogers Shriver, Lillian M. Squier, and Agnes Bell Williams, all of Washington;

Elsie Jane Beaty, Beulah Bess Carper, Ada Drown Childers, Mabelle W. Clinton,

Alberta Herren Davis, Selma Price Deyo, Cora Byrnside Haynes, Mabel Claire Hes-
lep, Hazel Hodge, Pauline Miller Howard, Tillie Haley Hull, Elizabeth Van Hoose
Hurt, Helen Southworth Lanterman, Hope Parker Oesterle, Naoma Hawkes Parsons,
Mary Louise Price, Kathaleen Dellinger Ridgley, and Wafie Calebaugh Robinson, all
of West Virginia;

Mrs. Wallace A. Giffen, Laura V. Hall, Eleanore Walters Herdrich, Ada Hosford,
and Sophia Keller Ormond, all of Wisconsin;

Susan Barnes Turney, of Wyoming;

Wilhelmina Mezger Farvin Woofter, of Alaska;

Katherine Patee MacMillian, of Canada;

Rose O'Connell Shaefer, of China;

Laura Finnegan Cheatham, Margaret MacEachern Edwards, Marie Murray
Grant, Lillian Cooper Harrington, and Julia Weber, all of Hawaii;

and their associates and successors are hereby created a body corporate and
politic, in the District of Columbia, by the name of "The National Yoemen F", for
patriotic, historical, and educational purposes; to foster and perpetuate the memory
of the service of Yoemen (f) in the United States Naval Reserve Force of the United
States Navy during the World War; to preserve the memories and incidents of their
association in the World War by the encouragement of historical research concerning the service of Yoemen (f); by the promotion of celebrations of all patriotic
anniversaries to cherish, maintain, and extend the institutions of American freedom;
to foster true patriotism and love of country, and to aid in securing for mankind all
the blessings of liberty.

SEC. 2. That said organization is authorized to hold real and personal estate in
the United States so far only as may be necessary to its lawful ends, to an amount not
exceeding $50,000, and may adopt a constitution and bylaws not inconsistent with
law, and may adopt a seal.

SEC. 3. That said organization shall report annually to the Secretary of the
Smithsonian Institution concerning its proceedings, and said Secretary shall communicate to Congress such portions thereof as he may deem of national interest and
importance. The regents of the Smithsonian Institution are authorized to permit
said national organization to deposit its collections, manuscripts, books, pamphlets,
and other material for history in the Smithsonian Institution or in the National
Museum, at their discretion, upon such conditions and under such rules as they
shall prescribe.

Approved, June 15, 1936.

National Yeomen (F) Commanders

1. 1926–27 Miss Cecelia Geiger
2. 1928–29 Miss Helen G. O'Neill
3. 1930–31 Miss Helen Wienhusen
4. 1932–33 Helen Murray McGuinness
5. 1934–35 Miss Marjory M. Cormack
6. 1936–37 Miss Maybelle Bond
7. 1938–39 Mrs. Irene Malito Brown
8. 1940–41 Mrs. Charlotte Berry Winters
9. 1942–43 Mrs. Marie Ruggles Steele
10. 1944–45 Miss Mary Kemp Anthony
11. 1946–47 Miss Lulu V. Walsh
12. 1948–49 Mrs. Adele Meade Kendrick
13. 1950–51 Mrs. Mae Shuttleworth
14. 1952–53 Miss Margaret Collins
15. 1954–55 Mrs. Mary Sullivan Tatspaugh
16. 1956–57 Miss Sara Myers
17. 1958–59 Mrs. Margaret F. Schutt
18. 1960–61 Miss Margaret Wellbank
19. 1962–63 Mrs. Mary E. Dwyer
20. 1964–65 Mrs. Margaret Mary King
21. 1966–67 Mrs. Mabel Vanderploeg Pease
22. 1968–69 Mrs. Marguerite B. Geiger
23. 1970–71 Mrs. Estelle R. Ruby
24. 1972–73 Mrs. Catherine C. Larkin
25. 1974–75 Mrs. Mabel Vanderploeg Pease
26. 1976–77 Mrs. Rose M. Volkman
27. 1978–79 Mrs. Margaret Mary King
28. 1980–83 Miss Marjorie Slocum
29. 1984–85 Mrs. Anne L. Kendig

APPENDIX B

Numbers of World War I Yeomen (F) by State

State	Number	State	Number
Alabama	21	Nebraska	11
Arizona	3	Nevada	4
Arkansas	12	New Hampshire	80
California	557	New Jersey	352
Colorado	17	New Mexico	1
Connecticut	315	New York	2,324
Delaware	5	North Carolina	190
District of Columbia	1,874	North Dakota	10
Florida	31	Ohio	207
Georgia	30	Oklahoma	33
Idaho	6	Oregon	79
Illinois	210	Pennsylvania	1,067
Indiana	45	Rhode Island	235
Iowa	47	South Carolina	143
Kansas	32	South Dakota	11
Kentucky	35	Tennessee	53
Louisiana	128	Texas	107
Maine	72	Utah	4
Maryland	418	Vermont	20
Massachusetts	1,324	Virginia	1,071
Michigan	47	Washington	179
Minnesota	80	West Virginia	137
Mississippi	36	Wisconsin	92
Missouri	40	Wyoming	2
Montana	13	U.S. Possessions*	63

*Includes Hawaii and Alaska.

Source: "General Information: Enlisted Personnel Strength," Folder NA3, Box 277, Record Group 45, National Archives, Washington, D.C.

APPENDIX C

Legislation Affecting U.S. Navy and Marine Corps Women of World War I

Naval Act of 1916	Public Law 241	Allowed "all persons who may be capable of performing special useful service for coastal defense" to be enrolled in the Naval Coast Defense Reserve Force
War Risk Insurance Act Amendments of 1917	Public Law 65-90	Established pensions for U.S. military personnel
Vocational Rehabilitation Act	Public Law 65-178	Established Federal Board of Vocational Education to provide training for veterans
World War Adjusted Compensation Act of 1924	Public Law 68-120	Provided adjusted compensation for active service
World War Veterans Act of 1924	Public Law 68-242	Established Veterans Bureau, combining the Bureau of War Risk Insurance (BWRI) and the Federal Board for Vocational Education
Naval Reserve Act of 1925	43 Statute 1080	Changed the Naval Reserve enlistment requirement so that only men were eligible to enroll
Veterans Administration Order of 1930	Executive Order 5309	Veterans Administration established, taking over the work of the U.S. Veterans' Bureau
The Act To Incorporate The National Yeomen F (1938)	Public Law 74-676	Chartered an organization in the District of Columbia, to foster and perpetuate the memory of the service of Yeomen (F) in the United States Naval Reserve Force

NOTES

Abbreviations

Daniels Papers	Josephus S. Daniels Collection, Manuscript Reading Room, Library of Congress
Dessez Papers	Papers of Eunice Dessez, Navy Operational Archives, Washington, D.C.
National Archives	National Archives and Records Administration, Washington, D.C.
National Archives (College Park)	National Archives and Records Administration, College Park, Md.
Naval Historical Center	Naval Historical Center, Washington Navy Yard
Naval History Collection	Naval History Collection, Naval War College Library, Newport, R.I.
Navy Archives	Navy Operational Archives
PC	Personal Collection, Personal Papers Section, U.S. Marine Corps Historical Center
USMC Historical Center	U.S. Marine Corps Historical Center, Washington Navy Yard
WIMSA	Women in Military Service for America Memorial Foundation, Arlington, Va.

Chapter 1. Breaking with Tradition

1. J. Stanley Lemons, *The Woman Citizen: Social Feminism in the 1920s*, pp. 4–19.

2. *Annual Report of the Secretary of the Navy*, 1 December 1917; letter from Secretary of the Navy Charles J. Bonaparte to Senator Eugene Hale, Chairman, Committee

on Naval Affairs, 15 January 1906, file 3842, entry 22, box 74, Record Group 125, National Archives.

3. Public Law 241.

4. Memo from Chief of the Bureau of Navigation to Judge Advocate General, 7 March 1917, document no. 28550-45, file 28550, Secretary of the Navy General Correspondence, 1916–1926, Record Group 80, National Archives.

5. *Newport (R.I.) Herald,* 21 March 1917, p. 4; letter from Lt. Cdr. F. R. Payne to Cecelia Geiger, 1 February 1933, National Yeomen F Papers, box 2; notes listed under "P," Dessez papers, box 3, Navy Archives.

6. A summary statement about the yeomen (F) released by Navy Department Historical Section, 19 April 1923, folder NA3, "Women in the USNR Force—Employment as YN(F)," subject file 1911-27, Record Group 45, National Archives; Harold T. Wieand, "The History of the Development of the United States Naval Reserve, 1889–1941," Ph.D. diss., University of Pittsburgh, 1952, Navy Department Library; Hearings before the Senate Committee on Naval Affairs on Public Law 241, August 1916.

7. Bureau of Navigation Circular Letter, 19 March 1917, subject file 1911-27, "Women in the USNR," Record Group 45, National Archives.

8. "America's Forgotten Heroine," by James J. Walsh, 1992 monograph including photocopies of contemporary newspaper accounts, copy found in Philadelphia Maritime Museum; letters from Lt. Cdr F. R. Payne to Cecelia Geiger, 19 January and 1 February 1933, National Yeomen F papers, Navy Archives; *New York Times,* 22 March 1917, p. 2.

9. Correspondence to the Bureau of Navigation, 27 March–12 April 1917; letters from Bureau, 15–16 April 1917; Bureau of Navigation General Correspondence, 1913–25, subject file 9878, files 9878-1313 and 9878-377, Record Group 24, National Archives.

10. *Newport (R.I.) Daily News,* "Women Yeomen Enrolled in the Naval Reserve Will Not Have Duty With The Fleet," 28 March 1917, p. 5; letters, 28 May 1917, and 5 June 1917, file 9878-1281:1, Bureau of Navigation General Correspondence 1913–1925, Record Group 24, National Archives.

11. Carol Everts, "Keystone resident has a past to cherish," *Gainesville (Fla.) Sun,* n.d., stamped 1984, folder "Women in the Navy"; *Your PBX,* published by Chesapeake and Potomac Telephone Company, n.d., copy found in box 4, Dessez papers, Navy Archives.

12. Navy Department memorandum, 21 December 1917, file 9878-2791, Record Group 24; memo from Principal Clerk, Aviation Division, 30 October 1918, file 0154-509, Records of the Bureau of Aeronautics, General Correspondence 1917–1925, Record Group 72, National Archives; papers of Mary Change Clancy, membership no. 145905, and of Mary Rexrode Lacey, membership no. 314041, WIMSA Registry.

13. *Note Book,* September 1980. The *Note Book* was the quarterly publication of the National Yeomen F, an organization of former Yeomen (F) chartered by Congress that existed from 1926 to 1986 (see chapter 9). The Museum of American History of the Smithsonian Institution maintains a complete file of these newsletters.

14. Obituary of Bernice Tongate, *Washington Post,* 27 January 1990, and an undated clipping from the *Memphis Commercial Appeal,* folder "Women in the Navy, WWI," Navy Archives.

15. "History of the First Naval District," folder no. 8, subject file ZPN-1, Record Group 45, National Archives.

16. Letters and memoranda March–August 1918, file 128377; letters of Dr. W. C. Braisted, Navy Surgeon General, and Dr. Rosalie S. Morton, 5 March, 17 May, and 19 May 1915, file 127038, General Correspondence of the Bureau of Medicine and Surgery, Headquarters Records Correspondence, 1896–1925, Record Group 52, National Archives.

17. Letter from Surgeon General to Commandant of Thirteenth Naval District, 2 August 1918, file 127038, General Correspondence of the Bureau of Medicine and Surgery, Headquarters Records Correspondence, 1896–1925, Record Group 52, National Archives.

18. Letter from Lt. Cdr. F. R. Payne to Cecelia Geiger, 19 January 1933; "Circular Relating to the Physical Examination of Women for Enrollment in the Naval Coast Defense Reserve," 24 March 1917, file 127644, General Correspondence of the Bureau of Medicine and Surgery, General Correspondence 1896–1925, Record Group 52; "Circular Relating to the Physical Examination of Women for Enrollment in the Navy and Marine Corps," 14 August 1918, file 1535–1555, General Correspondence 1913–1932, USMC Adjutant and Inspector's Office, Record Group 127, National Archives.

19. Letter from Martha Mulholland to Eunice Dessez, Dessez papers, box 6, Navy Archives.

20. Helen Butler, *I Was a Yeoman (F),* pp. 2–3.

21. Mary Price Carey interview.

22. Folder NA-3, "General Information, Enlisted Personnel and Strength," subject file 1911-27, Record Group 45, National Archives; *Note Book,* September 1960.

23. Kelly Miller, *History of the World War for Human Rights,* p. 596 [We wish to thank Richard Miller, who brought Kelly Miller's book to our attention, via an article in *Minerva,* Fall/Winter, 1995.]; Navy Department Personnel Muster Rolls, September and December 1918, "Muster Rolls 1860–1956," Record Group 24, National Archives; Alice Dunbar-Nelson, "Negro Women in War Work," in Emmett Scott, *The American Negro in the World War,* pp. 375–77, 384–96; Jack D. Foner, *Blacks and the Military in American History,* p. 124.

24. Jane and Harry Scheiber, "The Wilson Administration and the Wartime Mobilization of Black Americans, 1917–18," *Labor History,* Summer 1969; Army Nurse Corps Historian files, Center for Military History, Washington, D.C.

25. "History of the First Naval District, 1917–1918," pp. 222–23, folder 8, subject file ZPN–1, Record Group 45, National Archives; Courtland Milloy, "A Love Story of Historic Proportions," *Washington Post,* 20 December 1992, p. B-1; letter from John R. Shillady, 15 August 1918; letter from James J. Posey, 5 September 1918, AC 19,815, reel 62, Daniels papers.

26. Miller, *History of the World War for Human Rights,* pp. 597–98.

27. Muster rolls of Navy Department personnel for periods ending 30 September and 31 December 1918, and 30 September 1919, Record Group 24, National Archives; Miller, *History of the World War for Human Rights,* p. 597.

28. Richard E. Miller (grandson of historian Kelly Miller), letter to Jean Ebbert, 29 March 1996.

29. Letter from Commandant U.S. Marine Corps to Secretary of the Navy, 2 August 1918, Secretary of the Navy, General Correspondence, 1916–26, file 28550-402, Record Group 80, National Archives; Edwin N. McClellan (Major, USMCR), *The United States Marine Corps in the World War,* p. 86.

30. Linda L. Hewitt (Captain, USMCR), *Women Marines in World War I,* pp. 4, 6–7.

31. Ibid., p. 7.

32. Memo for Major T. H. Lowe from Assistant Adjutant and Inspector, 5 August 1918; circular letter from Bureau of Navigation, 14 August 1918; files 1535–1555, box 128, Record Group 127, National Archives.

33. Hewitt, *Women Marines in World War I,* p. 15.

Chapter 2. Joining the Navy

1. *New York Times,* 26 March 1917, p. 1; *New York Times,* 28 May 1917, p. 3; *Note Book,* September 1964, March 1967, December 1978, June 1980; *Newport News,* 24 March 1917, p. 5; *New York Times,* 19 July 1917, p. 11; interviews, Mary Price Carey, Mary Ann Longacre, Estelle Richardson Ruby, Gladys Carr Bolhouse, Phyllis Kelly Peterson, Anna Danhakl, Helene Johnson Coxhead, and Grace Schaffer; Elizabeth Dwyer Milliken letter; Jacque Devine, "World War I Yeomanette Will Be Special Guest," *Gosport* (newspaper of Pensacola Naval Air Station), 28 June 1974, p. 3; quotations from newsletter, the WIMSA *Register,* Fall 1990, p. 6.

2. Letter to Bureau of Medicine and Surgery from Medical Aide to the Com-

mandant of the Thirteenth Naval District, 12 July 1918, and letter to Commandant First Naval District from Commanding Officer U.S. Naval Hospital, Portsmouth, N.H., n.d., file no. 124942 (91), General Correspondence of the Bureau of Medicine and Surgery, 1896–1925, Record Group 52; "Historical Narrative of Activities of Navy Yard and Thirteenth Naval District, April 1917–March 1918: Register 13, Book I," pp. 28–33, folder ZPN-13, subject file 1911-27, Record Group 45, National Archives; newspaper clipping regarding Gertrude Murray, folder "Women in the Navy, WWI," Navy Archives; Ruth Fisher and Grace Schaffer interviews.

3. Records of the Bureau of Naval Personnel, General Correspondence 1913–25, file 9875-2371, Record Group 24, National Archives.

4. Statement of Margaret M. Telfer, Dessez papers, box 6, Navy Archives.

5. Story about Virginia Ralston, undated clipping from unnamed newspaper; Margaret Silsbee, article, "One of the First Women to Enlist," about Mabel Vanderploeg Pease, folder "Women in the Navy, World War II," Navy Archives; papers of Nan Harvey, membership no. 098041, WIMSA Registry; Edna Loftus Smith, USMCR (Ret.) oral history, interviewed by Bemis M. Fran, at USMC Historical Center, 7 May 1981.

6. Quotations from *Baltimore Sun*, 4 February 1918, folder 7, file NA-3, "Women in the USNR Force Employed as Yeomen (F)," subject file 1911-27, Record Group 45, National Archives; letter to Dessez from Frances Amelia Boyd, Dessez papers, box 6, Navy Archives; Ruth Fisher interview.

7. Ruth Fisher and Anna Danhakl interviews; papers of Nelia Rice, membership no. 0761594, WIMSA Registry.

8. Marjorie Stoneman Douglas, *Voice of the River*, pp. 112–13.

9. Mary Price Carey, Ruth Fisher, and Virginia Kennerly Tilghman interviews; remarks by Anne Freeman Pedersen, printed in *Government Issue*, July/August 1995, p. 26, copy found in papers of Margaret Backus, membership no. 316317, WIMSA Registry; letters to Eunice Dessez from Frances Bishop and Hazel Lander, Dessez papers, boxes 6 and 7, Navy Archives.

10. Helen Butler, *I Was a Yeoman (F)*; Grace Shaffer interview; Elizabeth Dwyer Milliken letter; papers of Rosemary Valla, membership no. 342470, WIMSA Registry; Gertrude French Howalt, WIMSA *Register*, Fall 1990, p. 6.

11. Grace Schaffer interview; Edna Loftus Smith oral history; Joy Bright Hancock, *Lady in the Navy*, p. 24; papers of Gertrude McGowan Madden, membership no. 057002, WIMSA Registry; Mary Ann Longacre interview and telephone conversation; Helene Johnson Coxhead interview; *Note Book*, June 1980.

12. Papers of Indra Dickerson Sayre, membership no. 024343, WIMSA Registry; Mary Price Carey interview.

13. Copy of orders from Recruiting Officer, Chicago, to Yeoman Third Class

Genevieve Galvin, dated 21 August 1918, authorizing her and nine other yeomen (F) put in her charge to travel at government expense by train to Washington, D.C., file 128377, Record Group 52, National Archives; letter from Amelia Bishop to Eunice Dessez, 6 October 1955, box 6, Dessez papers, Navy Archives.

14. Marcia Kincaid, "Mrs. Fish Recalls Service with Legendary Yeomen (F)," *Corpus Christi Times*, 23 January 1958, p. 18, box 1, Dessez papers, Navy Archives.

15. Hancock, *Lady in the Navy*, p. 24.

16. Mary Price interview; letter to Eunice Dessez from Rosella Hallisey, Dessez papers, box 2, Navy Archives; Mary Ann Longacre interview and telephone conversation; letters from Johanna Wilcox and Nina Rhoades to Eunice Dessez, box 6 and box 1 (latter under "H"), Dessez papers, Navy Archives; Marie Forde Bond telephone conversation—copy of notes given to WIMSA Registry.

17. Eunice Dessez, *The First Enlisted Women, 1917–1918*, pp. 22, 23.

18. Mary Price Carey interview; Lou MacPherson Guthrie, "I Was a Yeomanette," U.S. Naval Institute *Proceedings* (December 1984), p. 58.

19. Undated, unidentified newspaper article about Mabel Vanderploeg, folder "Women in the Navy, WWI," Navy Archives; Butler, *I Was a Yeoman (F)*, pp. 4, 11–12; Virginia Kennerly Tilghman interview.

20. Letter from Bureau of Navigation to Bureau of Medicine and Surgery, 20 August 1918, file 126003, Record Group 52, National Archives.

21. Jacque Devine, "World War I Yeomanette Will Be Special Guest," p. 3; "Twelfth Naval District," folder ZPN-12, subject file 1911–1927, Record Group 45, National Archives; note by Ann Ginter, *Note Book*, March 1982; Helene Johnson Coxhead interview; letter to Josephus Daniels from Mrs. Henry Davison, 6 August 1918, and Daniels's reply, 15 August 1918, file 28971, Secretary of the Navy General Correspondence, 1916–1926, Record Group 80, National Archives.

22. Lou MacPherson Guthrie, "I Was a Yeomanette," p. 60.

23. *Newport Daily News*, 17 May 1917, p. 5.

24. Estelle Richardson Ruby interview; Ardelle Humphrey letter, 6 July 1983.

25. Helen Douglas Coutts Saul interview.

26. John A. Stacey, "What Happened to This Man's Navy?" *Military Images*, July–August 1989, pp. 4–5; Hancock, *Lady in the Navy*, p. 23.

27. Naval History Collection, U.S. Naval Training Station series, *Newport Recruit*, April 1917, p. 21; May 1918, pp. 12–15, 49, 50; December 1918, p. 14.

28. Memorandum for Chief of Bureau of Navigation, 19 October 1918, AC 19,815, reel 55, container 517, Daniels papers.

29. Anna Danhakl interview; Kincaid, "Mrs. Fish Recalls Service"; Jean Gillette, "Uncle Sam's First Women Recruits," *Retired Officer Magazine*, July 1991, p. 40.

30. Hewitt, *Women Marines in World War I*, p. 25.

31. Ruth Dean, "Subway Ride Launches Career," Washington, D.C., *Sunday Star*, 9 August 1955, p. D9.

32. Hewitt, *Women Marines in World War I*, p. 25; *?Nouncements* April 1976, p. 5.

33. Ginger Rogers, *Ginger: My Story*, p. 32; Hewitt, *Women Marines in World War I*, p. 9; papers of Miller, Olive May, PC no. 981, box 2A27; letter from Marion L. Polli, Bond's daughter, to Curator of USMC Historical Center, 14 September 1984, USMC Historical Center.

34. News Release, USMC 1945, Folder, "Women Marines: Anniversaries"; Joan Ambrose, "21st Anniversary," *Leatherneck*, October 1965, p. 19, USMC Historical Center.

35. Letter from Mabelle L. Musser (Mrs. A. W. Hall) to Curator of USMC Historical Center, 29 June 1984, papers of A. W. Hall, PC no. 830, box 2A16; letter from Oagley printed in "Scuttlebutt, W. W. I, 1975," papers of Oagley, Pearl C., PC no. 788, box 3A24, USMC Historical Center.

36. Hewitt, *Women Marines in World War I*, pp. 76 and 17.

Chapter 3. Uniforms

1. Letter from Lt. Cdr. F. R. Payne to Cecelia Geiger, 19 January 1933.

2. Papers of Beulah Worrell Wilson, membership no. 99739, WIMSA Registry.

3. "Changes in Uniform Regulations, United States Navy, 1913, No. II," container 593, reel 80, AC 19,815, Daniels papers.

4. Comments by Dessez, box 2, Dessez papers, Navy Archives; speech by Ambassador Josephus Daniels to the thirteenth reunion of former Navy women, Chicago, 27 September 1939, *Note Book*, 30 September 1939.

5. *Uniform Regulations of the United States Navy*, Navy Department, Washington, D.C., 1913.

6. *New York Times*, 19 June 1917, p. 19; undated clipping, subject file "1911–1927," folder NA–3, "Women in the USNR Force"—Employment as Yeomen (F), Record Group 45, National Archives; Kincaid, "Mrs. Fish Recalls Service."

7. Letter from U.S. Comptroller to Pay Inspector B. P. DuBois, 24 May 1917, File 26254, Record Group 80, National Archives.

8. Letter from L. K. Karr to Auditor, Navy Department, 6 June 1917, file 26254; letter from Josephus Daniels to Commandant, Key West, 19 June 1917, file 26254, Record Group 80, National Archives.

9. Letter to Bureau of Navigation from Bureau of Medicine and Surgery, 13

September 1917, file 129185; Navy Department memorandum signed by Josephus Daniels, 20 September 1918, file 12985, Record Group 52, National Archives.

10. *U.S. Naval Administration in World War II: 14th Naval District,* vol. 1, p.142; *Note Book,* June 1981, reported that the Armistice Day photo had appeared in the April 1981 issue of the *Torch,* published by Veterans of WWI in the USA, Inc.

11. WIMSA photo collection; interviews with several former yeomen (F) by Jean Ebbert at U.S. Navy Home in Gulfport, Miss.; Helen Douglas Coutts Saul interview; *American Legion Magazine,* November 1977, p. 9; letter to Eunice Dessez from Jessie Arnold, box 6, Dessez papers, Navy Archives.

12. Mary Price Carey interview; Hancock, *Lady in the Navy,* p. 20; U.S. Naval Institute *Proceedings,* December 1957, pp. 1338, 1339; memo from commandant of Washington Navy Yard to Female Members, Naval Reserve Force, 14 May 1918, file 128377, Record Group 52, National Archives.

13. Bureau of Navigation Circular Letters 175-18 (23 September 1918) and 184 (22 October 1918); letter from Commanding Officer, Navy Department Personnel, to All Bureaus and Offices, 25 October 1918, file 128377, Record Group 52; letter from Bureau of Navigation to Commandant, Thirteenth Naval District, 20 November 1918, file General Correspondence, 1913–1925, and memo issued by Commandant of First Naval District, 2 November 1918, folder 5537, subject file E89, Record Group 24; letter to Bureau of Navigation from Bureau of Construction and Repair, 3 October 1918, and reply, 9 October 1918, file 16276, A-6, vol. 1, Record Group 19, National Archives.

14. Memo from Chief of Bureaus and Accounts to Secretary Daniels, 15 November 1918, folder 2641-2750, file 5537, entry no. 89, Record Group 24, National Archives; memo from Bureau of Navigation to All Bureaus and Offices, 12 December 1918, and memo from Commanding Officer, Navy Department Personnel to All Bureaus and Offices, 27 December 1918, copies in box 1, Dessez papers, Navy Archives; memo from Commanding Officer of Navy Department Personnel to All Bureaus and Offices, 21 January 1919, File 16276-A 6, vol. 1, General Correspondence, 1912–1925, Record Group 19, National Archives; orders releasing Yeoman Second Class Elizabeth Bacon Heterick from active duty, dated 19 June 1919, copy sent to Marie-Beth Hall by Heterick's son; Bureau of Navigation Circular Letter 237-18, 16 December 1918, file 128377, Record Group 52, National Archives.

15. Butler, *I Was a Yeoman (F),* pp. 6, 7; Estelle Richardson Ruby interview; interviews with former yeomen (F) at U.S. Naval Home.

16. Three-page typescript of remarks signed by Kate M. Clagett, former Chief Yeoman (F), Commander USS *Jacob Jones* Post No. 2, n.d., perhaps prepared for testimony before Congress, container 593, subject file "Reserves," Daniels papers.

17. Lee Ineson interview; Robert Rankin, *Uniforms of the Sea Service,* pp. 229–30.

18. *Note Book,* 30 June 1951, p. 4; Southern Oregon Historical Society, Jacksonville, Ore., Pauline Greaves Collection; Estelle Richardson Ruby interview.

19. From scrapbook of Yeoman (F) Kate Greene, author unknown, shown to Marie-Beth Hall during interview with Greene's daughter, Mary Ann Longacre.

20. *Note Book,* March 1951.

21. Norma Burd Jones Watson, membership no. 192927, WIMSA Registry; letter to Isabel Smith from Maj. Gen. John A. Lejeune, 14 October 1920, document no. 1535-55, Record Group 127, National Archives.

22. Hewitt, *Women Marines in World War I,* Headquarters, p. 21.

23. Ibid., p. 22.

24. Ibid., p. 24.

Chapter 4. Pulling Their Oar

1. Papers of Indra Sayre Dickinson, membership no. 024343, WIMSA Registry.

2. Navy Department press releases, 4 February and 14 June 1918, and Historical Section memo dated 19 April 1923, files NA–1 and NA–3, subject file 1911–1927, Record Group 45, National Archives; Walter Scott Meriwether, "The Many-Sided Naval Reserve: Plumber's Helpers, Naval Architects, College Professors and a Corps of Able Women," *Sea Power* (March 1918), p. 199; Susan Godson, "Womanpower in World War I," U.S. Naval Institute *Proceedings* (December 1984), pp. 62–63.

3. "Will Navy Commission Women?," *Army and Navy Journal* 55 (8 June 1918): 1569; box 6, Dessez papers, Navy Archives.

4. Ardelle Humphrey interview; Mary Ann Longacre interview; Russo, Cheryl, "Navy Vet," *State Times,* Baton Rouge, La., 25 May 1987, pp. 1C, 3C; *Note Book,* vol. 2, no. 2, June 1934.

5. *Note Book,* vol. 2, no. 8, September 1935, p. 3; letter to Dessez from Lucille Marguerite Alzamora, box 6, vol. 4, Dessez papers, Navy Archives; Helene Johnson interview.

6. Helen O'Neill interview.

7. Quote from Dolly Purvis interview; Ruth Fischer interview; clipping from Washington, D.C., newspaper, 13 August 1918, box 3, Dessez papers, Navy Archives; memo from Principal Clerk, Aviation Office, 30 October 1918, file 0154-509, Record Group 72, National Archives. Papers of Mary Change Clancy, membership no. 145905, WIMSA Registry; letter from Edna Benta Hann, *Note Book,* vol. 2, no. 5, March 1935, p. 8.

8. *Note Book,* vol. 36, March 1969, p. 7.

9. Portion of a speech given by Lillian Budd in 1986, printed in the *Register,* WIMSA newsletter, Winter 1996–97, p. 8.

10. Irene Malito Brown interview.

11. Papers of Della White Griffith, membership no. 364100, WIMSA Registry.

12. *Your PBX,* a brochure published by the Chesapeake and Potomac Telephone Company, undated (copy in Dessez papers), box 4, Dessez papers, Navy Archives; *Newport Recruit* (station newspaper), April 1919, p. 15, Naval History Collection.

13. Dessez, *The First Enlisted Women,* pp. 61–62.

14. Correspondence from 19 September 1918, to 18 October 1919, box 2, folder 20940-1233, General Correspondence, 1913–1924, Record Group 38, National Archives.

15. *Report of the Secretary of the Navy, 1918,* p. 494; Eileen Warburton, *In Living Memory,* Newport, R.I., Newport Savings & Loan Association/Island Trust Company, pp. 59–60; Hancock, *Lady in the Navy,* p.20; Josephus Daniels, "Women's Work in War," address to the Congressional Club in Washington, D.C., 7 February 1919, copy, Container 716, Daniels papers.

16. *Norfolk Ledger-Dispatch,* 30 October 1918, Virginia State Archives, Richmond, Va.

17. Nina Livermore Rhodes, "Women Who Were in War Tell Their Experiences," *Virginian-Pilot and the Norfolk Landmark,* 21 September 1921, copy, in papers of Margaret Mullaney, membership no. 281338, WIMSA Registry.

18. *Norfolk Ledger–Dispatch,* 30 October 1918; Mary Price Carey interview.

19. Letter from Lt. Cdr. F. R. Payne to Cecelia Geiger, 19 January 1933, folder no. 1, file "Loretta Perfectus Walsh," box 2, National Yeomen F Papers; clipping from *St. Petersburg (Fla.) Times,* 14 September 1986, folder "Women in the Navy WWI," Navy Archives; Susan Godson, "Womanpower in World War I," U.S. Naval Institute *Proceedings,* December 1984, p. 63.

20. Susan Godson, "Womanpower in World War I"; Lt. Cdr. F. R. Payne letter to Cecelia Geiger, 19 January 1933.

21. Lt. Cdr. F. R. Payne letter to Cecelia Geiger, 1 February 1933; Pauline Greaves collection, Southern Oregon Historical Society, Jacksonville, Ore.

22. Letter dated 12 July 1918, file General Correspondence, 1896–1925, Record Group 52, National Archives.

23. Memo from Acting Chief of the Bureau of Construction and Repair to Secretary of the Navy via Bureau of Navigation, dated 31 May 1918, file 16276-A6, Record Group 19, National Archives; *Washington Sunday Star,* undated clipping found in papers of Sophia Howard Thompson, membership no. 430323, WIMSA Registry.

24. S. R. Wilson, "The Womanly Art of Lighthouse Keeping," G-APA/83, copy found in Folder "World War I," USCG Historian's Office.

25. Letter from Daniels to House Representative Allen Treadway, 23 January 1917,

box 318, file 7014-319, Record Group 80; Navy Department memo to Commandants of Naval Districts, 1 October 1917; ZPN-1, folder 8, Record Group 45; Muster Rolls of Ships and Shore Establishments, vol. 2282; letter from Secretary of Commerce to Daniels, 28 April 1921, file 3104-237, Record Group 24, National Archives.

26. John A. Tilley, *A History of Women in the Coast Guard,* pp. 2–3, Office of the Commandant, USCG, March 1996; caption, U.S. Navy photo no.165-WW-598 B9, Photo Stills Branch, National Archives (College Park).

27. "Muster Rolls 1860–1956" and "Muster Rolls of Ships and Shore Establishments, January 1898–June 1939," Records of Bureau of Naval Personnel, Record Group 24, National Archives. *Note Book,* September 1964, p. 6.

Muster rolls pose some challenges. First, the chronological record is incomplete; some periods are missing for certain locations. Second, some are bound helter-skelter, neither chronologically nor geographically sequential. When searching for women's names, one cannot always be sure, especially with foreign names, whether the person listed is male or female. Also, formats and categories differ from one unit to another, and from one time to another. Therefore, not to find a person's name in muster rolls for a given location does not prove he or she was not present. However, the keeping of muster rolls was taken very seriously, as they provided the navy's primary source of accounting for individual payrolls, documenting promotions, ordering supplies, and other administrative requirements. Thus, to find a person's name on a unit's muster roll is very strong evidence that he or she was officially and physically present in the unit on the date(s) specified.

28. Letter from Mabel Jackson, box 2, Dessez papers, Navy Archives; Guam Muster Roll, Record Group 24, National Archives.

29. Muster roll for Radio Station, San Juan and St. Thomas; vol. 2465 (61), muster roll for Naval Air Station, Coco Solo, Panama Canal Zone, 30 June 1918–31 December 1918; vol. 2487, muster roll for 15th Naval District, Atlantic Section, 1 January–30 June 1919, Muster Rolls of Ships and Shore Establishments, Record Group 24, National Archives. *Note:* Vol. 2465 also carries the number 2461.

30. Muster Rolls, Base Hospital, Paris and Base Hospital, Brest; notes under headings "Pennsylvania" and "New York," boxes 2 and 3, Dessez papers, Navy Archives; John A. Stacey, "What Happened to This Man's Navy?", *Military Images,* July–August 1989, pp. 4, 5, copy in folder "Women in the Navy, WWI," Navy Archives.

31. Folders labeled "Base Hospitals"; "Doctors Aweigh: The Story of the U.S. Navy Corps in Action," a two-page, double-spaced typescript, no author, no date, in folder labeled "no. 5, Brest"; "Dr. James Talley, Lieutenant Commander (MC), USNR, A Navy Doctor in France 1917–1918," by Major R. W. Morgan, USMC, folder "World War I, Medical History Documents"; Surgeon General's Report, 1918, p. 103, Office of the Historian, Surgeon General, Bureau of Medicine and Surgery.

32. Muster rolls for U.S. Naval Forces in Europe (Paris) and U.S. Naval Headquarters, London; official Signal Corps photos, nos. 15,133 and 15,126, Record Group 80, National Archives (College Park).

33. List titled "Telephone Operators of the A.E.F.," WIMSA Collection; Dessez papers.

34. WMA *'Nouncements*, April 1987, p. 18; papers of Pearl C. Oagley, PC no. 788, box 3A24, USMC Historical Center; Ruth Dean, "Subway Ride Launches Career," Washington, D.C., *Sunday Star*, 9 August 1955, p. D9; R. R. Keane, "Skirt Marines?" *Leatherneck*, August 1993, p. 14–15, copies at USMC Historical Center.

35. Ginger Rogers (Leibrand's daughter), *Ginger: My Story*, p. 32; Hewitt, *Women Marines in World War I*, pp. 29, 32, 78–80; WIMSA photo collection; WIMSA *Register*, Fall, 1990, p. 6.

36. Joan Ambrose, "21st Anniversary," *Leatherneck*, October 1965, p. 19; *Recruiters Bulletin*, October 1919, p. 20; papers of Minnie Arthur Kinstler, membership no. 66089, WIMSA Registry.

37. Hewitt, *Women Marines in World War I*, pp. 28–29.

38. Major Streeter quoted in news clipping, date and paper unknown, in folder "Women Marines: News Clippings 1900–1969," USMC Historical Center.

Chapter 5. Navy and Marine Corps Policies for Women

1. Form filled out by Binnie Avalon Hick, vol. 6, Dessez papers, Navy Archives; Navy Department press release, 27 March 1918, "Women in the USNR," folder NA–3, subject file 1911–1927, Record Group 45, National Archives. *Note Book*, September 1939; "Will Navy Commission Women?" *Army and Navy Journal* 55 (8 June 1918): 1569.

2. Press Release from Committee on Public Information, 27 March 1918, subject file 1911–27, file NA-3, Record Group 45, National Archives.

3. Letters between Daniels and First Naval District Pay Director, 13 December 1917, and 3 and 26 January 1918, document 2488, file 26254, Record Group 80; History of First Naval District in World War I, p. 222, file ZPN-1, folder 1, Record Group 45, National Archives.

4. Robert Heterick letter and telephone interview; Rogers, *Ginger: My Story*, p. 32; request from Yeoman First Class Lola Williams Duncan, 19 March 1919, file 128377-33; various requests in file 128377, Bureau of Medicine and Surgery General Correspondence, 1896–1925, Record Group 52; requests from Mabel Shears, file 0154-223, and Marie Granger, file 0154-267, Bureau of Aeronautics General Correspondence, 1917–25, Record Group 72; National Archives.

5. Papers of Nelia Rice, membership no. 076154, WIMSA Registry; letter from

Hazel Louise Greve and first endorsement thereto, 23 May 1918, file 128377, Record Group 52, National Archives; Elizabeth Dwyer Milliken letters; *Periscope,* issue of 15 November 1918, folder 4, file ZPN-13, Record Group 45, National Archives.

6. Letter to Commandant of First Naval District from Bureau of Navigation, 8 August 1918, file 9878-3532, Record Group 24, National Archives.

7. Oral history of Admiral Kent Melhorn, U.S. Naval Institute *Proceedings,* December 1983, p. 138.

8. Correspondence among Secretary of the Navy, Bureau of Supplies and Accounts, Judge Advocate General, 16 and 23 October and 1 November 1917, file 26543-203, Record Group 80; Bureau of Navigation memorandum, 3 October 1925 (corrected to 1932), subject file 1911–27, folder NC-1, Naval Personnel Losses, Record Group 45, National Archives.

9. Eunice Dessez, *The First Enlisted Women,* pp. 36–37.

10. Correspondence of Yeoman First Class Ruth Schurer with Bureau of Navigation, files 0154-220 and -328, Record Group 72; letters to the Bureau of Navigation, files 0154-223, -283, -328, -384, Record Group 72; file 28550-563, Record Group 80, National Archives.

11. Muster roll for the 14th Naval District, 30 June 1917, vol. 2483, Record Group 24, National Archives; letter from Rose Volkman to Eunice Dessez, 14 January 1960, box 7, Dessez papers, Navy Archives.

12. Helen Douglas Coutts Saul interview.

13. *Recruiters' Bulletin,* July 1919, p. 19, folder "Women Marines: History," USMC Historical Center.

14. Memo to Commandant of Washington Navy Yard from promotion board, 19 June 1918, file Commandant's Office General Correspondence, 1917–1918, Record Group 181; memo to Bureau of Medicine and Surgery from Commanding Officer of USS *Triton,* 15 January 1918, file 128377, Record Group 52, National Archives.

15. Memo to Navy Department from Bureau of Medicine and Surgery, 17 January 1919, file 128377-1, Record Group 52; memo to Commandant of the Washington Navy Yard from Board of Examiners, 19 June 1918, Record Group 181; memo from Bureau of Navigation, 4 April 1918, file 2836-2900 (2874), subject file 9878, Record Group 24; memo from Bureau of Navigation to all Bureaus, 4 September 1917, file 128377-38, Record Group 52, National Archives; Dessez, *The First Enlisted Women.*

16. *Washington Post,* 21 March 1917, p. 1; *Newport Daily News,* 13 April 1917, p. 6.

17. Letter from Hancock to Eunice Dessez, box 5, Dessez papers, Navy Archives.

18. Correspondence between Yeoman Second Class Effie J. Thomas and the Bureau of Navigation, Document 28550-998, box 2528, Secretary of the Navy General Correspondence, 1916–1928, Record Group 80, National Archives; *Note Book,* June 1980.

19. Letter to G. L. Snyder, Twelfth Civil-Service District, from Commanding Officer, Fort Lyon, Colo., 12 July 1920, file 4942-7220, Record Group 52, National Archives.

20. Muster Roll, Base Hospital No. 2, vol. 2193, June 1918, Record Group 24; letter to Assistant Vice Chief of Naval Personnel, 17 December 1917, General Correspondence of the Secretary of the Navy, Record Group 80, National Archives.

21. Correspondence among Judge Advocate General, Secretary of the Navy, Bureau of Navigation, and Fleet Supply Base, South Brooklyn, N.Y., between March 25 and 5 May 1919, files 27217-3544, -2648, -3626, Record Group 80, National Archives; Josephus S. Daniels, *The Cabinet Diaries of Josephus Daniels, 1913–1921*, p. 253.

22. Letter to Bureau of Navigation from New York Cable Censor, 1 February 1918, file 2701-2800 (2763); letters from Bureau of Navigation to senior station commanders and district commandants throughout continental United States, 21 November 1917, file 9878, file 9878-2422, Record Group 24, National Archives.

23. Correspondence referring to Yeoman (F) "X," 16 February to 3 July 1918, file 20940-946, Record Group 38, National Archives.

24. Correspondence referring to Yeoman (F) "Y," 5 September to 17 November 1918, file 20941-189, Record Group 38, National Archives.

25. Circular letter from Marine Corps Headquarters, 14 August 1918, file 1535-1555, Record Group 127, National Archive.

26. Hewitt, *Women Marines in World War I*, p. 35.

27. Ibid., p. 36.

28. Former Cpl. Elizabeth Shoemaker Linscott, USMCR; memo from Major General Commandant, 8 March 1919, quoted in Hewitt, *Women Marines in World War I*, pp. 35–36.

29. "The Passing of the Marine Girls," *Leatherneck,* 8 August 1919, p. 1, USMC Historical Center.

30. Lettie Gavin, *American Women in World War I,* p. 12; "History of the First Naval District, 1917–1919," p. 222, folders 6-8, file ZPN-1, Record Group 45, National Archives; *Leatherneck,* 8 August 1919.

31. "History of the First Naval District, 1917–1919," p. 222, folders 6-8, file ZPN-1, Record Group 45, National Archives; Hewitt, *Women Marines in World War I,* pp. 37–40.

32. Papers of Theresa Bean Ballenger, membership no. 346204, WIMSA Registry.

33. "History of the First Naval District," file ZPN-1, Record Group 45, National Archives.

34. Base newspaper, *Periscope,* 13 September 1918, ZPN-13, Record Group 45, National Archives; WIMSA *Register,* eulogy by Donna Fournier; papers of Gertrude McGowan Madden, membership no. 057002, WIMSA Registry; Lois Cress, "'Yeo-

man Female' Recalls Life in Navy During WWI," undated clipping from Denver *Post,* and notes on Lila Naomi Watkins, folder "Women in the Navy, WWI," Navy Archives.

35. Hancock, *Lady in the Navy,* p. 25.

36. Hewitt, *Women Marines in World War I,* p. 32; personal papers of Edna Lee Freund, PC no. 868, USMC Historical Center.

37. Memo from Commanding Officer of Navy Department of Personnel to all Bureaus and Offices, 18 November 1918, file 0154-549, Record Group 72, National Archives; Dessez, *The First Enlisted Women,* p. 55.

38. Butler, *I Was A Yeoman (F),* p. 7.

Chapter 6. Fighting a New Enemy

1. Memo from Bureau of Medicine and Surgery to Second Naval District, 2 October 1917, file 128377-39; to Navy Department, 18 August 1918, file 128377, Record Group 52, National Archives.

2. Memo to all Bureaus and Offices in Navy Department, from Commandant's office, 16 January 1918, file 128377-5, Record Group 52.701, National Archives.

3. Letter to Bureau of Medicine and Surgery from Medical Aide to the Commandant of the Twelfth Naval District, 20 August 1918, file 123262; memo to Medical Aide, Third Naval District, 31 May 1918, file 125262, Record Group 52, National Archives.

4. Letter to Bureau of Medicine and Surgery from Medical Officer of the Yard, 29 March 1918, file 128780-8 (15), Record Group 52, National Archives.

5. Memo for the dispensary at the Naval Dispensary, Washington, D.C., from Surgeon General, 23 October 1915, file 125487-3:1, Record Group 52, National Archives.

6. Agnes Carlson, letter to Eunice Dessez, 3 November 1961, box 7, Dessez papers, Navy Archives.

7. Correspondence between Bureau of Medicine and Surgery and Commandant of the Fifth Naval District, 29 March and 5 August 1918, file 12870-8(15); between the Bureau and Naval Hospital, New Orleans, 12 and 15 August 1918, files 130107 and 126963(33), Record Group 52, National Archives.

8. Lou MacPherson Guthrie, "I Was a Yeomanette," U.S. Naval Institute *Proceedings,* December 1984, pp. 63–64.

9. The sources for this summary of events are Alfred W. Crosby, *Epidemic and Peace;* the Armed Forces Institute of Pathology's *AFIP Letter;* and Gina Kolata, *Flu: The Story of the Great Influenza Pandemic of 1918 and the Search for the Virus That Caused It.* Crosby's book is an excellent history of the epidemic that killed as many

Americans as the war did yet seems to have vanished from modern memory. Kolata explores the events and issues of the research that has answered some but not all of the many questions concerning the epidemic's exact origin and development. "The Dead Zone," by Malcolm Gladwell, *New Yorker,* 27 September 1999, pp. 52-65, examines current defenses against recurrences of the lethal virus.

10. *AFIP Letter,* p. 1.

11. Crosby, *Epidemic and Peace,* p. 25.

12. Ibid., p. 27.

13. *Annual Report of the Surgeon General, 1919,* p. 367. Crosby, *Epidemic and Peace,* pp. 26, 30-31, 39.

14. Papers of Helen Armand Fielding Spaulding Quin, membership no. 117535, WIMSA Registry.

15. *Annual Report of the Surgeon General, 1920,* p. 11.

16. "Outbreak Soon To Be Well in Hand," *Newport Daily News,* 28 September 1917, pp. 1-2, 5, 8.

17. Crosby, *Epidemic and Peace,* p. 57; "A Winding Sheet and a Wooden Box: A Navy Nurse Recalls the Great Influenza Epidemic of 1918," from an oral history of Josie Brown, *U.S. Navy Medicine,* May-June 1986, pp. 18-19.

18. Letter to Bureau of Medicine and Surgery from U.S. Naval Hospital, Mare Island, 19 October 1918, file 13017-D12, Record Group 52, National Archives.

19. Box 1, Dessez papers, bound vol. 1, p. 104, Navy Archives; Crosby, *Epidemic and Peace,* p. 49.

20. Crosby, *Epidemic and Peace,* p. 58; *Annual Report of the Surgeon General, 1919,* p. 391.

21. Bureau of Navigation memo, 16 October 1925, folder NC-1, Personnel Losses and folder 2, List of Women Killed; folder NC-8, Marine Corps Casualties, subject file 1911-27, Record Group 45, National Archives.

22. James J. Walsh, "America's Forgotten Heroine," unpublished typescript, copy held by Philadelphia Maritime Museum. Loretta's nephew James Walsh wrote a twenty-page manuscript in 1992 that incorporates several contemporary newspapers' photos and accounts of her naval service, illness, and death.

23. Kincaid, "Mrs. Fisk Recalls Service," p. 18; Rose Volkman, letter to Eunice Dessez, 14 January 1960, vol. 7, Dessez papers, Navy Archives.

24. Ruth Fisher Richardson interview; papers of Annette Feader, membership no. 98802, WIMSA Registry; Rosella Hallisey, letter to Eunice Dessez, 28 November 1955, box 2, Dessez papers, Navy Archives.

25. Jessie Frances Arnold, letter to Eunice Dessez, box 6, Dessez papers, Navy Archives; papers of A. W. Hall, PC no. 830, box 2A16, USMC Historical Center.

26. *Report of the Surgeon General, 1918,* p. 127.

27. Memo to Lt. Jackson regarding Hicks, 26 October 1918, file 0154-445; memo regarding Marie Granger, 16 October 1918, file 0154-451; memo regarding Sarah A. Rice, 16 October 1918, file 0154-479; and letter from Belfast, Me., regarding Yeoman Small, 1 October 1918, file 0154-436, Record Group 72, National Archives.

28. Butler, *I Was A Yeoman (F),* p. 12; Susan Godson, "Womanpower in World War I," pp. 63–64; Desscz, *The First Enlisted Women,* p. 63; "A Winding Sheet and a Wooden Box," pp. 18–19.

29. Correspondence from Elizabeth Dwyer Milliken to Jean Ebbert and Marie-Beth Hall, April 1995, regarding her mother, former Yeoman (F) Mary Sheehan Dwyer; papers of Rosemary Santos Valla, membership no. 342470, WIMSA Registry.

30. Gavin, *American Women in WWI,* p. 11.

31. Correspondence between senior medical officer at Mare Island and Bureau of Medicine and Surgery from 29 September 1918, to 5 December 1919, file 131000-D12-42, Record Group 52, National Archives.

32. Correspondence between the Surgeon General and the commanding officer of Fort Lyon Naval Hospital, 8 October 1918, to 28 March 1918, subject file General Correspondence, 1912–1926, file 131000-12, Record Group 52, National Archives.

33. Letter from Lt. Cdr. Fred Bogan to Commanding Officer, Fort Lyon Hospital, 9 December 1918, file 131000-D12, Record Group 52, National Archives.

Chapter 7. Active Duty Ends

1. The quotations and events in this and preceding paragraphs were drawn from Stanley Weintraub's book, *A Stillness Heard Round the World,* E. P. Dutton, New York, 1985, pp. 291–310.

2. *Note Book,* June 1952; Jacque Devine, "World War I Yeomanette Will Be Special Guest"; letter to Dessez, 30 September 1960, Dessez papers, Navy Archives.

3. *Newport Daily News,* 16 October 1918, p. 10, 11 November 1918, p. 1, 11 April 1919, Naval History Collection; "History of the First Naval District," file ZPN-1, Record Group 45, National Archives.

4. Hewitt, *Women Marines in World War I,* p. 33; Dessez, *The First Enlisted Women,* p. 56; papers of Pearl C. Oagley and Olive May Miller, Personal Collections nos. 788 and 981, boxes 3A24 and 2A27, respectively, USMC Historical Center; type-script by Katie W. Clagett, Daniels papers.

5. Vol. 1, pp. 78 and 109, box 1; letter from former Yeoman (F) Elizabeth Cromelin Godwin, entry under "G" in box 4, Dessez papers, Navy Archives.

6. Typescript by Kate W. Clagett, Daniels papers.

7. Lettie Gavin, "Women Marines in WWI," *Over There!*, Winter 1988, p. 4; papers of Pearl C. Oagley, PC no. 788; papers of Alma Roth Bishop, membership no. 110269, WIMSA Registry; Hewitt, *Women Marines in World War I*, p. 33; "Tomb of the Unknown Soldier," http://www.qmfound.com/tomb_of_the_unknown_soldier.htm.

8. Memo from Navy Department, 3 January 1919, file 0514-695, Record Group 72; letter from Great Lakes Commanding Officer to Bureau of Navigation, 19 April 1919, file 52.718, Record Group 52; Bureau of Navigation letter, 4 December 1924, file 9878-3532, Record Group 24, National Archives; papers of Dorothy Walton Wright, membership no. 257183, WIMSA Registry.

9. Letter from Commandant Fifth Naval District to Chief of Naval Operations, 25 January 1919, file 28550, document 28550-787, Record Group 80, National Archives.

10. Memo from Chief of Bureau of Construction and Repair to heads of department, 11 February 1919, Record Group 19; message from Secretary of the Navy to all naval districts, 15 March 1919, Record Group 52; Bureau of Navigation message, 9 July 1919, subject file 9878, file 1159, folder 1401-1454, entry 89, Record Group 24, National Archives.

11. Letter from Rose Volkman, 14 January 1960, vol. 7, Dessez papers, Navy Archives.

12. Navy Department Circular Letter from Secretary of the Navy, 3 July 1919, Record Group 52, National Archives.

13. Memo from USMC Adjutant and Inspector's Office, 15 July 1919, folder 1500-95, "Reserve Marine Corps, May 1917–April 1921," Record Group 127, National Archives.

14. Letter to Chiefs of Bureaus, Boards and Offices from Secretary of the Navy, 13 June 1919, file 28550-1083:2; responses, file 28550-1083:3, Record Group 80; letter from Maj. John A. LeJeune to Miss Smith, Navy Department librarian, 14 October 1920, Record Group 127, National Archives.

15. Mary Price Carey interview.

16. Letter to Commandant Fifth Naval District from Secretary of the Navy, 12 December 1920, referencing Secretary of the Navy letters of 21 October 1919, and 11 December 1920, file 1120, documents 2887, 2892 et al., Record Group 24, National Archives; box 1, p. 110, Dessez papers, Navy Archives.

17. Letter from Dessez to Mrs. Earl W. Graeff, 6 June 1953, box 4 under "G," Dessez papers, Navy Archives.

18. Bureau of Navigation memorandum, 3 October 1925 (corrected to 1932), subject file 1911-27, folder NC-1, Naval Personnel Losses, Record Group 45; letter from

Maj. John A. LeJeune to Miss Smith of the Navy Department Library, 14 October 1920, file 1535-55, Record Group 127, National Archives.

19. Letter from Surgeon General to all naval hospitals, 3 February 1919, file General Correspondence, 1912-1925, Record Group 52, National Archives.

20. Circular letter from Bureau of Navigation to all Naval Districts and Navy Yards, 3 July 1919, file 1159-1425; telegram from Commandant Fifth Naval District to Bureau of Navigation, 29 July 1919, and reply, 7 August 1919, files 1120-1671 and 1120-1692; letter from Commanding Officer, Naval Hospital, Charleston, to Bureau of Medicine and Surgery, 29 July 1919, forwarded to Secretary of Navy, and reply, 20 August 1919, Record Group 24, National Archives; Nina Livermore Rhodes, "Women Who Were in War Service Tell Their Experiences," *Virginian Pilot*, 1 September 1921; papers of Margaret Mullaney, membership no. 281338, WIMSA Registry.

21. Circular letter to all naval hospitals from Bureau of Medicine and Surgery, 4 April 1919, file 129733(41), Record Group 52, National Archives.

Chapter 8. Women Are Veterans, Too

1. Typescript by Kate W. Clagett, Daniels papers; "Marine Girls Form Semper Fidelis Club," *Leatherneck*, 25 July 1919, p. 1.

2. *Note Book*, March 1944 and June 1958; Mary Ann Longacre interview.

3. *Note Book*, September 1939, March 1944 and 1981, June 1982; obituary of Mary Sheehan Dwyer, *North Adams Transcript*, North Adams, Mass., March 1978, copy supplied to authors by Dwyer's daughter, 26 April 1995; Mary Price Carey interview.

4. Letter from Bureau of Navigation to Commandant of the Washington Navy Yard, 5 January 1923, file 2175-116, General Correspondence, Record Group 24, National Archives; list compiled by Defense Advisory Committee on Women in the Service (DACOWITS), June 1998, copy given to authors by Capt. Barbara Brehm; papers of Ida Hunt DeLozier, membership no. 355098, WIMSA Registry; *Note Book*, 30 June 1960.

5. Letter to Secretary of the Navy from Secretary of Commerce, 28 April 1921, file 3104-237, General Correspondence, 1913-25, Record Group 24, National Archives.

6. *Note Book*, December 1931; Hancock, *Lady in the Navy*, pp. 64-65.

7. *Note Book*, March 1940.

8. O'Neill interview.

9. U.S. House of Representatives, *Hearings Before the Committee on Ways and Means*, 68th Congress, 1st session, 3-5 March 1924, pp. 1-3; O'Neill interview.

10. The nineteen states granting bonuses were Pennsylvania, New York, Massachusetts, Rhode Island, Maine, New Jersey, New Hampshire, Illinois, Iowa, Kansas, Michigan, Minnesota, Missouri, South Dakota, Ohio, Oregon, Vermont, Washington, and Wisconsin. Letter from Secretary of the Navy to Adjutant General, State of Minnesota, 3 November 1919, file 9875-305, General Correspondence 1913-1925, Record Group 24, National Archives; *Marine Corps Gazette,* May 1936, p. 45.

11. Raymond Moley, Jr., *The American Legion Story,* p. 20.

12. Navy Surgeon General's Reports of 1920, p. 25, and 1922, p. 10.

13. Letter dated 7 April 1923, received by T. Roosevelt Jr, April 16, file 57509-10, "General Correspondence 1813-1925," Record Group 24, National Archives.

14. Correspondence July and August 1923, documents 510 and 501.1, file 28553, Secretary of the Navy General Correspondence 1916-1926, Record Group 80; correspondence, July-November 1924, documents 129733(74) and 129733(104), file General Correspondence, 1912-1925, Record Group 52, National Archives.

15. *Note Book,* April 1930; June 1934; March 1935; June 1935; September 1935; June 1937.

16. Records of Veterans Affairs Committees, "Guide to the Records of The U.S. House of Representatives."

> Petitions for the constructions of hospitals and domiciliary facilities for veterans appear in the records of every Congress. Typical of these resolutions are a concurrent resolution from the State Legislature of Indiana requesting appropriations for a hospital in that state and a resolution passed by the State Senate of Michigan asking that a hospital be constructed in Wayne County. Some ten years later, organizations in Michigan were still petitioning for a hospital to be built in Wayne County, near Detroit, to enable Michigan veterans to be hospitalized in their home state. Depression era legislation intended to balance the budget through various economies including reductions in the pensions and other benefits.

From National Archives web site: www.nara.gov/nara/legislative/house. Despite many veterans' petitions, year after year, begging no cuts, the Economy Act of 20 March 1933, cut benefits; *Note Book,* 30 June 1935.

17. *Note Book,* June 1960.

18. *Note Book,* December 1954; Minutes of Executive Board meeting, National Yeomen F, 30 September 1972, box 704 E10, WIMSA collection.

19. *Note Book,* September 1981.

20. Public Laws 102-585, 103-452, 104-62, and 105-114.

21. Ebbert and Hall, *Crossed Currents: Navy Women in a Century of Change,* pp. 340-43; *Seattle Post-Intelligencer,* 24 September 1998.

22. Harold Wieand, "The History of the Development of the Naval Reserve, 1889-1941," Ph.D. diss., copy in Navy Department Library, Washington, D.C.

Chapter 9. Keeping in Touch

1. Seventeen-page history of Betsy Ross Post No.1 (later USS *Jacob Jones* Post No. 2) prepared by Helen O'Neill in February 1926, later brought up to 1981 by O'Neill, copy given to authors by O'Neill; also found in O'Neill papers, Navy Archives.

2. *Note Book,* November 1928, September 1929.

3. *Note Book,* September 1937; typescript noted in note 1 above.

4. *Note Book,* December 1969 and December 1967; telephone conversation with Dr. Harold Langley, former curator for naval history at the Smithsonian Institution, by Jean Ebbert, 25 July 1999.

5. *Note Book,* June 1960.

6. *Note Book,* September 1935, December 1935, June 1937.

7. *Note Book,* June 1963, September 1980, July 1981; Pauline Greaves Collection, Southern Oregon Historical Society; Mary Ann Longacre interview.

8. Helen O'Neill interview; seventeen-page typewritten history of USS *Jacob Jones* Post, prepared by Helen O'Neill; two-page history of NYF prepared in 1981 by O'Neill, copy given to authors. Between 1972 and 1982 the U.S. Navy's curators lost track of the portrait. One curator described it as "lost, probably tossed away." Upon reading about the "lost" portrait in *Navy Times,* Seaman Michelle Hughes, recently graduated from recruit training in Orlando, reported that the portrait was still there. Jean Ebbert, "Case of the Missing Yeomen F Portrait," *Navy Times,* 16 November 1981, and "Lost Portrait Rediscovered," February 1982.

9. *Note Book,* June and December, 1969.

10. *Note Book,* June 1950, December 1964, June 1965, March 1967, September 1980.

11. *Note Book,* March 1935, December 1937, September 1938.

12. *Note Book,* September 1968, March 1983.

13. *Note Book,* September 1943.

14. *Note Book,* June 1952; minutes of NYF Executive Board meeting December 1969, file 704.E7, WIMSA.

15. *Note Book,* June 1963, December 1965.

16. *Note Book,* March 1981.

17. *Note Book,* December 1959, March 1981.

18. From historical material submitted to authors by Shirley Mahoney of the Cathedral staff; *Note Book,* December 1967, June 1961 et al.; minutes, meeting of NYF Executive Board, 15 June 1969, file 704.E7, WIMSA.

19. The authors are privileged to have talked with O'Neill on several occasions and received papers and a photo from her during the 1980s. According to the *Note Book,* December 1957, in 1940 NYF member Sally Wolfe donated her manuscript

about women veterans of World War I and a copy of the NYF Congressional Charter to the World Center for Women's Archives, now defunct.

20. Letter from Dessez to Esther B. Jeffries, 8 December 1956, Dessez papers, vol. 1, Navy Archives.

21. Letter from Dessez to Rose Volkman, 5 February 1960, box 7, Dessez papers, Navy Archives.

22. Letter from Dessez to Beulah Bobo, 10 July 1961, box 7, Dessez papers, Navy Archives.

23. Questionnaires completed by Ruth B. Lounsbury, Julie Le Prince; letter from Dessez to Edith Strohmeyer, 21 March 1960, box 7, Dessez papers, Navy Archives.

24. Copies of responses from naval districts found under "O" (for "official records"); letter from Dessez to Lila Woodbury, 22 May 1961, box 7; letter from Dessez to Sara Dolan, 15 January 1954, box 1, Dessez papers, Navy Archives.

25. Dust jacket of first edition of *The First Enlisted Women;* correspondence between Dessez and Daisy Chapdeline, Christmas 1961; Kate de Gaffenried Fish, 7 August 1955; Margaret Kennedy, 18 August 18, 1955; and Mrs. George Bailey, October 9, 1958, box 7, Dessez papers, Navy Archives.

26. Memo dated 27 May 1963, from Chief, Manuscript Division, Library of Congress, photocopy supplied to authors by John Earl Haynes following telephone conversation on 18 November 1999.

27. Box 7, Dessez papers, Navy Archives; *Note Book,* December 1954, 1974, June 1955.

28. *Note Book,* March 1980; supplement to the issue of December 1985.

29. *Note Book,* September 1979.

30. *Note Book,* September 1979, June 1980, September 1982, August 1984, December 1985.

31. Letter, 20 March 1986, from Gertrude Howalt to Marjorie Cormack, Past Commander of the NYF (copy sent to authors by Mr. Harvey Howalt); *Note Book,* supplement to December 1985 issue.

32. *Leatherneck,* March 1987, p. 27; *WMA: The First 25 Years, 1960–1985,* pp. 1–2, Olga E. Bullock Collection, no. 321, WIMSA; *'Nouncements,* April 1975, pp. 6–7, October 1976, pp. 2–3 (some copies found at WIMSA Archives, others donated to authors by WMA members).

33. *'Nouncements,* October 1974, p. 2, April 1975, pp. 6–7, October 1976, pp. 2–3, February 1979, p. 2; *WMA: The First 25 Years,* p. 15.

34. *'Nouncements,* Special Issue No. 4, 1986.

35. *'Nouncements,* Special Issue No. 4, 1986; Summer 1988 pre-convention issue, p. SI-11; Winter 1993, p. 16; papers of Maybelle Musser Hall, membership no. 37854, WIMSA Registry.

36. Lt. Cdr. (Ret.) Dana Nielson, USN (Ret.), WIMSA Registry office, in response to query by Jean Ebbert, 16 November 1999.

Epilogue

1. Joy Bright Hancock, *Lady in the Navy*, pp. 31–45, 49–56, 64, 116, 235–239, 264–266; Hancock interviews; "Recollections of Captain Joy Bright Hancock, U.S. Navy (Ret.), oral history," U.S. Naval Institute, Annapolis, Md., 1971.

2. *Note Book*, March 1981, January 1945, January 1946; *The Skyscraper*, Naval Air Station, New York, 24 April 1944, p. 1; box 6, Dessez papers, Navy Archives.

3. *Note Book*, December 1957, June 1961; box 7, Dessez papers, Navy Archives.

4. *Note Book*, December 1985, Helen O'Neill interview.

5. *Note Book*, December 1985.

6. *Note Book*, December 1985; papers of Helen O'Neill, Navy Archives.

7. Hewitt, *Women Marines in World War I*, pp. 42–45.

8. William Bartley, "1st female sailors still 'shipmates,'" *Bridgeport Post*, 20 May 1978, copy in papers of Helen O'Neill, Navy Archives; DePass interview; "We honor the past in the person of our namesake, Edith Macias Vann . . ."; *WMA: The First 25 Years*, copy, papers of Olga E. Bullock, Collection no. 321, WIMSA.

9. Guy Anselmo, "A Woman's Place Is in the Ranks," Part 2, *Leatherneck*, March 1987, pp. 28–29,

10. *Note Book*, June 1941.

11. Box 2, Dessez papers, Navy Archives; *Note Book*, March 1946.

12. *Note Book*, April 1944.

13. *Note Book*, June 1977.

14. USS *Roberts*, FFG 58 web site: www.spear.navy.mil/ships/ffg58/namesake/htm.

15. *Note Book*, December 1982.

16. Robert Hanyok, "Still Desperately Seeking 'Miss Agnes,'" *Cryptolog*, Fall, 1997.

17. Box 2, Dessez papers, Navy Archives.

18. Box 4, Dessez papers, Navy Archives; Dessez, *The First Enlisted Women*, p. 79.

19. "Miss LeHand, Ex-Secretary to President, Dies in Hospital," *Washington Post*, 1 August 1944, pp. 1, 4, and "Marguerite Alice LeHand Dies; Roosevelt's Secretary 22 years," *New York Herald*, 1 August 1944, box 4, Dessez papers, Navy Archives.

20. Obituary of Dorothy Frooks, *New York Times*, 19 April 1997, p. 48.

21. *Note Book*, April 1984.

22. Papers of Violet Van Wagner Lopez, membership no. 82030, WIMSA Registry; *Note Book*, 1980 and December 1967; *'Nouncements*, April 1987 (a long article reprinted with permission from an AT&T newsletter).

23. Rogers, *Ginger, My Story*, p. 153.

24. *Note Book*, December 1969; Lillian Petersen Budd, *Full Moons: Indian Legends of the Seasons* (Chicago: Rand McNally, 1971).

25. Taylor Caldwell, *On Growing Up Tough: An Irreverent Memoir* (Old Greenwich, Conn.: Devin-Adair, 1971), pp. 143–144; *Ceremony of the Innocent* (Garden City, N.Y.: Doubleday, 1976), back jacket; papers of Janet Miriam Caldwell, membership no. 371903, WIMSA Registry.

26. Patricia Mathews, "Search for Former Navy Women Occupies Time of Ex-Yeoman-F," *Albuquerque News*, 7 November 1974.

27. Martha Chamberlain, "Lifetime Project of Sarasota Artist Tells 1000 Years of American History," *Bradenton (Fla.) Herald*, 28 December 1975, p. C-1, copy in papers of Mabelle Linnea Holmes, membership no. 507102, WIMSA Registry; *Note Book*, December 1980 and December 1981.

28. *Note Book*, December 1980.

29. *Note Book*, March 1980, December 1979.

30. Marjory Stoneman Douglas, *The Everglades: River of Grass; Time*, 25 May 1998, p. 33.

31. Margaria Fichtner, "Florida's Heroine," *Miami Herald*, 15 May 1998, pp. 1A, 8A.

32. Marjory Stoneman Douglas, *Voice of the River*, pp. 218–33.

BIBLIOGRAPHY

Archives

Library of Congress, Washington, D.C. Josephus S. Daniels Collection. "Correspondence, Secretary of the Navy, 1913–1921."

National Archives, Washington, D.C. Record Groups 19, 24, 38, 45, 52, 72, 80, and 127.

Naval War College Library, Newport, R.I. Naval History Collection. "Changes in Uniform Regulations No. 15."

————. Naval Station newspaper, 1917, 1918.

————. Newport newspapers, 1917–1919.

Navy Operational Archives, Washington, D.C. Papers of Eunice Dessez.

————. Papers of Helen O'Neill.

Smithsonian Institution, Museum of American History, Division of Naval History. *The Note Book.* Quarterly newsletter published by the National Yeomen F from 1926 through 1985.

Southern Oregon Historical Society, Jacksonville, Ore. Pauline Greaves Collection.

Stanford University Archives, Palo Alto, Calif. *1891–1920 Alumni Directory and Ten Year Book.*

————. *The Stanford Illustrated Review.* January 1919.

U.S. Marine Corps Historical Center, Washington, D.C. Selected personal collections.

Virginia State Archive, Richmond, Va., newspaper collection.

Women in Military Service for America Foundation, Arlington, Va. Selected papers and collections.

Books and Other Publications

Butler, Mrs. Henry F. *I Was a Yeoman (F).* Naval Historical Foundation Publication. Series 2, no. 7. Washington, D.C.: Naval Historical Foundation, 1967.

Crosby, Alfred W. *Epidemic and Peace.* Westport, Conn.: Greenwood Press, 1976.

Daniels, Josephus S. *The Cabinet Diaries of Josephus Daniels, 1913–1921.* Edited by E. David Cronon. Lincoln: University of Nebraska Press, 1963.

Dessez, Eunice. *The First Enlisted Women, 1917–1918.* Philadelphia: Dorrance & Co., 1955.

Douglas, Marjory Stoneman. *The Everglades: River of Grass.* Rev. ed. Sarasota, Fla.: Pineapple Press, 1988; originally published by Rinehart, 1974.

———. *Voice of the River.* Englewood, Fla.: Pineapple Press, 1987.

Ebbert, Jean, and Marie-Beth Hall. *Crossed Currents: Navy Women in a Century of Change.* 3rd ed. Washington, D.C.: Brassey's, 1999.

Foner, Jack D. *Blacks and the Military in American History.* New York: Praeger, 1974.

Gavin, Lettie. *American Women in World War I.* Niwot: University of Colorado Press, 1997.

Hancock, Joy Bright, Capt., USN (Ret.). *Lady in the Navy.* Annapolis, Md.: Naval Institute Press, 1972.

Hewitt, Linda L., Capt., USMCR. *Women Marines in World War I.* Washington, D.C.: History and Museums Division, Headquarters, U.S. Marine Corps, 1974.

Kolata, Gina. *Flu: The Story of the Great Influenza Pandemic of 1918 and the Search for the Virus That Caused It.* New York: Farrar Straus Giroux, 1999.

Lemons, J. Stanley. *The Woman Citizen: Social Feminism in the 1920s.* Urbana: University of Illinois Press, 1973.

McClellan, Edwin N., Maj., USMCR. *The United States Marine Corps in the World War.* Washington, D.C.: Headquarters, U.S. Marine Corps, 1920.

Miller, Kelly. *History of the World War for Human Rights.* Washington, D.C.: Austin Jenkins Co., 1919.

Moley, Raymond, Jr. *The American Legion Story.* New York: Duell, Sloan & Pearce, 1966.

Navy Department (Washington, D.C.). *Annual Report of the Surgeon General,* 1918, 1919, and 1920.

———. *Changes in Uniform Regulations, United States Navy.* No. 2, 1913.

———. *Report of the Secretary of the Navy,* 1918.

———. *Uniform Regulations of the United States Navy,* 1913.

———. *U.S. Naval Administration in World War II: 14th Naval District.* Vol. 1, 1947.

Rankin, Robert. *Uniforms of the Sea Service.* Annapolis, Md.: Naval Institute Press, 1963.

Rogers, Ginger. *Ginger: My Story.* New York: HarperCollins, 1991.

Schneider, Dorothy, and Carl Schneider. *Into the Breach: American Women Overseas in World War I.* New York: E. P. Dutton, 1988.

Scott, Emmett J. *The American Negro in the World War.* New York: Arno Press, 1969.

Tilley, John A. *A History of Women in the Coast Guard.* Washington, D.C.: Office of the Commandant, U.S. Coast Guard, 1996.

Warburton, Eileen. *In Living Memory.* Newport, R.I.: Newport Savings & Loan Association/Island Trust Company, 1988.

Weintraub, Stanley. *A Stillness Heard Round the World.* New York: E. P. Dutton, 1985.

Wilson, S. R. "The Womanly Art of Lighthouse Keeping." G-APA/83, USCG Historian's Office, Washington, D.C.

Newspapers and Other Periodicals

The AFIP Letter, vol. 155, no. 2, April 1977. Washington, D.C.: Armed Forces Institute of Pathology.

Ambrose, Joan. "21st Anniversary." *Leatherneck,* October 1965.

" . . . And to the Sugar'n Spice Too." *American Legion Magazine,* November 1977.

Banker, Grace. "I Was A 'Hello Girl,'" *Yankee,* March 1974.

Brown, Josie. "A Winding Sheet and a Wooden Box: A Navy Nurse Recalls the Great Influenza Epidemic of 1918." *U.S. Navy Medicine,* May–June 1986.

"Fair Marine Tells of Flight in Hydroplane." *Leatherneck,* January 1919.

Gavin, Lettie. "Women Marines in WWI." *Over There!* (Winter 1988).

Gillette, Jean. "Uncle Sam's First Women Recruits." *The Retired Officer Magazine,* July 1991.

Gladwell, Malcolm. "The Dead Zone." *The New Yorker,* 27 September 1989.

Godson, Susan. "Womanpower in World War I." U.S. Naval Institute *Proceedings,* December 1984.

Guthrie, Lou MacPherson, "I Was a Yeomanette." U.S. Naval Institute *Proceedings,* December 1984.

Keene, R. R. "Skirt Marines." *Leatherneck,* August 1993.

"Marine Girls Form Semper Fidelis Club." *Leatherneck,* July 1918.

Melhorn, Kent C. R., Adm., USN (Ret.). "As I Recall: Medical Duty with the Marines." U.S. Naval Institute *Proceedings,* December 1983.

Meriwether, Scott. "The Many-Sided Naval Reserve: Plumber's Helpers, Naval Architects, College Professors and a Corps of Able Women." *Sea Power,* March 1918.

The Note Book (quarterly publication of the National Yeomen F organization), 1926–1986.

"The Passing of the Marine Girls." *Leatherneck,* August 1919.

Stacey, John A. "What Happened to This Man's Navy?" *Military Images,* July–August 1989.

U.S. Naval Training Station series. *The Newport Recruit.* Naval War College Historical Collection, Naval War College Library, Newport, R.I., April 1917; May 1918; December 1918, April 1919.

"Well Known Scenario Writer Gives Talent to Marine Corps." *Leatherneck,* December 1918.

"Will Navy Commission Women?" *Army and Navy Journal,* 8 June 1918.

Interviews, Letters, Conversations

Bolhouse, Gladys Carr. Interview by Jean Ebbert. Telephone conversation, 18 August 1995.

Carey, Mary Price. Interview by Jean Ebbert. Fairfax, Va., 1 August 1995.

Coxhead, Helene Johnson. Interview by Jean Ebbert. Arlington, Va., 4 August 1995.

Danhakl, Anna. Interview by Jean Ebbert. Bethesda, Md., 9 August 1995.

DePass, Ruth Byer. Interview by Lt. Melanie Schwartz, USNR. Gulfport, Miss., 16 October 1995.

Grumbles, Dollie Purvis, Phyllis Kelly Peterson, and Marjorie Slocum. Interview by Jean Ebbert. U.S. Naval Home, Gulfport, Miss., 6 April 1983.

Hanyok, Robert. Interview by Jean Ebbert. 20 May 2001.

Heterick, Robert. Son of former Yeoman (F) Elizabeth Bacon Heterick. Interview by Marie-Beth Hall. Telephone conversation, 2 October 1995.

———. Letter to Marie-Beth Hall, 15 October 1995.

Howalt, Gertrude French, and Walter Howalt. Letters and papers, November 1986–January 1987.

Humphrey, Ardelle. Interview by Jean Ebbert. Gaithersburg, Md., 4 May 1983.

———. Letter to Jean Ebbert, 12 July 1983.

Ineson, Lee. Interview by Jean Ebbert. Cambridgeport, Vt., 20 September 1983.

Langeley, Harold. Interview by Jean Ebbert. Telephone conversation, 25 July 1999.

Longacre, Mary Ann. Daughter of former Yeoman (F) Kate Greene Keene. Interview by Marie-Beth Hall. Baton Rouge, La., 31 July 1995.

Milliken, Elizabeth Dwyer, daughter of Yeoman (F) Mary Elizabeth Sheehan Dwyer. Letter to Jean Ebbert, 26 April 1995.

O'Neill, Lt. Col. Helen, USMCR (Ret.). Interviews by Jean Ebbert. McLean, Va., 13 May 1982, 10 August 1984.

Richardson, Ruth Fisher. Interview by Jean Ebbert. Callao, Va., 30 January 1996.

Ruby, Estelle Richardson. Interview by Jean Ebbert. Washington, D.C., 12 July 1982.

Saul, Helen Douglas. Interview by Marie-Beth Hall. Gladwyne, Pa., 22 September 1995.

Schaffer, Grace. Interview by Lt. Melanie Schwartz, USNR. Gulfport, Miss., 16 October 1995.

Strobel, Catherine Alta, and Jerman McAusland. Interview by Jean Ebbert. Telephone conversation, 25 June 1998.

Tilghman, Virginia Kennerly. Interview by Jean Ebbert. Alexandria, Va., 4 May 1996.

INDEX

Absent Without Official Leave (AWOL), 68, 81

Adjusted Compensation Act of 1924, 101–3

administrative policies for navy women, 57–64; assignments, 58–59; marriage and dependents, 59–60; pregnancy, 60; survivors, 61; transfers and promotions, 61–64

American Legion: formation of, 98; supports benefits for women veterans, 97, 102, 112; announcement of plan to build domiciles, 106–7; membership of women, 98–99, 115, 116; women in leadership roles, 99, 123, 129, 134; memorial to Loretta Walsh, first enlisted woman, 117–18

American Red Cross: uniform cape, 35; contributes equipment and supplies, 53; verifies emergencies, 64; Motor Corps, former yeoman (F) serves in, 136

Arlington National Cemetery: Yeomen (F) buried at, 13, 100, 125, 140; yeoman (F) escorts Unknown Soldier to, 89; National Yeomen F and, 117; Women's Memorial, 130, 144

Armistice: signing of, 15; changes after news of, 34, 44; return to United States after, 53; celebration of, 82, 86–87, 105

Army Nurse Corps, 11

AWOL, 68, 81

Baker twins, Genevieve and Dorothy, 33, 51. *See also* Coast Guard, women serving in

Barnett, George C., 13, 68; praises women reservists, 97

base hospitals in Europe, 53

Battalion, the: pride in uniform, 35, 72; drill practice, 72; at victory parades, 88–89

benefits: burial rights, 100; civil service preference, 92, 100; insurance; 61, 100, 103; survivor, 61. *See also* bonuses; medical care for women reservists

Benson, William S., 46

black women in navy, 10–13, 100

bond sales: women parade for, 70, 87, 88; during influenza epidemic, 79

bonuses: upon entering civil service, 92; adjusted compensation, 102; state, 100, 103

British women serving as yeomen (F), 11, 125. *See also* Women's Royal Naval Service (WRENS)

Bureau of Construction & Repairs, 50, 91

Bureau of Medicine and Surgery: identifies desired yeomen (F), 8; navy women at, 43, 49, 60; military women's health care, 60, 73–75; and influenza epidemic, 75–85; postwar policy on care, 95–96, 104

Bureau of Navigation: recruitment of women, 3, 6, 8; uniforms, 32; urges women to buy War Risk Insurance, 61; and transfers, 61–62; policy on leave, 65; policy on dismissals, 66; women's release from active duty, 90–91, 95

Bureau of Supplies & Accounts, 7, 31, 42, 133

Bureau of Yards and Docks, 84

Bureau of War Risk Insurance, 61, 96, 104

Butler, Helen, 10, 122; on influenza, 73

Burleson, Lucy and Sydney, 42

Cable and Postal Censor's Office, duty at, 32

ABOUT THE AUTHORS

JEAN EBBERT holds B.A. and M.A. degrees from the State University of New York at Albany, which named her a Distinguished Alumna in 1984. In 1952 she was commissioned an ensign in the U.S. Naval Reserve. After two years of active duty and augmentation to the regular navy, she resigned as a lieutenant (j.g.) and married a retired captain and Naval Academy graduate. Ebbert has worked as a writer and editor for many years, including thirteen years as an information officer for the U.S. Naval Academy, four years as a featured columnist for *Navy Times*, and three years as a regular contributor to "One Woman's Voice," a nationally syndicated newspaper column. The Naval Institute Press published her first two books. She began working with Marie-Beth Hall in 1978, when she joined the Energy Information Administration, a job she held until 1989. Ebbert is a plankowner of the Women Officers' Professional Association and is currently at work on her memoirs.

MARIE-BETH HALL, daughter of a Naval Academy graduate and wife of a retired navy captain, holds a B.A. in history from Radcliffe College. She has also studied at the University of California at Berkeley and the University of Rhode Island. She became interested in history while studying at Harvard under naval historian Robert Albion. From 1978 to 1990 she was a writer and analytic editor with the Energy Information Administration (EIA), and since 1990 she has been an editor, researcher, and writer in the Office of Economic Policy at the Federal Energy Regulatory Commission. Many of the major EIA studies she and Ebbert edited are used by members of Congress, industry analysts, and academicians. Her first book with Jean Ebbert, *Crossed Currents: Navy Women from WWI to Tailhook*, was published by Brassey's in 1993 to wide acclaim. Along with her work as a writer and editor, Hall is also a nationally certified U.S. swimming official and a National Collegiate Athletic Association (NCAA) swimming referee.